always up to date

The law changes, but Nolo is always on top of it! We offer several
ways to make sure you and your Nolo products are always up to date:

1 **Nolo's Legal Updater**
We'll send you an email whenever a new edition of your book
is published! Sign up at **www.nolo.com/legalupdater**.

2 **Updates @ Nolo.com**
Check **www.nolo.com/update** to find recent changes
in the law that affect the current edition of your book.

3 **Nolo Customer Service**
To make sure that this edition of the book is the most
recent one, call us at **800-728-3555** and ask one of
our friendly customer service representatives.
Or find out at **www.nolo.com**.

please note

We believe accurate and current legal information should help you solve
many of your own legal problems on a cost-efficient basis. But this text
is not a substitute for personalized advice from a knowledgeable lawyer.
If you want the help of a trained professional, consult an attorney
licensed to practice in your state.

1st edition

Special Needs Trust

Protect Your Child's Financial Future

by Attorney Stephen Elias

FIRST EDITION	MAY 2005
Editor	MARY RANDOLPH
Cover Design	TONI IHARA
Cover Photo	KIRAN SINGH
Book Design	SUSAN PUTNEY
Index	BAYSIDE INDEXING SERVICE
Proofreading	ROBERT WELLS
Printing	CONSOLIDATED PRINTERS, INC.

Elias, Stephen.
    Special needs trusts : protect your child's financial future / by Steve Elias.-- 1st ed.
      p. cm.
   ISBN 1-4133-0145-2 (alk. paper)
    1. Children with disabilities--Legal status, laws, etc.--United States. 2. Estate
planning--United States. 3. Trusts and trustees--United States. 4. People with
disabilities--Finance, Personal. I. Title.

KF480.Z9E435 2004
332.024'016'087--dc22

                                    2004065414

Quantity sales: For information on bulk purchases or corporate premium sales, please contact the Special Sales Department. For academic sales or textbook adoptions, ask for Academic Sales. Call 800-955-4775 or write to Nolo, 950 Parker Street, Berkeley, CA 94710.

Acknowledgments

My acknowledgments start with Marcia Stewart, Nolo's fine acquisitions editor and friend who patiently spent several years coaxing me to take on this book.

I'll be eternally grateful to my sister-in-law Lois Persson Elias, an Exceptional Parent who taught me by example to appreciate the special qualities of special people. Lois wrote the magnificent beneficiary information letter included in the book and made many important comments and contributions to the manuscript.

Many thanks to Nolo author and friend Denis Clifford, San Jose, California estate planning attorney Liza Weiman Hanks, and Alan Kemp of The Arc of Indiana, all of whom provided helpful suggestions.

I can't mention Lois without acknowledging my nephew, Jason. Jason was born with Down syndrome. Jason's gentleness, sensitivity, and good cheer make him a role model for us all. In addition to his other unique qualities, Jason is a fine poet who unflaggingly adds much grace to family gatherings.

I'm grateful to Leslie Park, Chairman of the Board, and Roslyn Brilliant, Executive Director, of Life Services for the Handicapped, Inc., a New York-based pooled trust, for reviewing and commenting on my manuscript, and meeting with me in New York to help me better understand pooled trusts.

I'm thankful for the talented and dedicated staff at Nolo who keep Nolo afloat, make the book beautiful, ship it to destinations far and wide, and let the folks out there know that they shouldn't spend one more minute without putting in their order. I'm especially grateful to Susan Putney for her fine production work and to Clark Miller for his enthusiastic approach to getting the word out.

Special thanks to Stan Jacobsen, a Nolo stalwart and wise man who managed to place in my hands via snail mail a major portion of the research materials I used to write this book. All along Stan has had an infectious enthusiasm for special needs trusts that easily carried me over the rough spots encountered by all Nolo authors when their spirits flag in the face of a lot of serious work to be done. Thanks, Stan.

As luck would have it, I ended up with the best editor in the world, for none could be better. So many accolades have been tossed Mary Randolph's way by grateful Nolo authors that it's difficult to be original in my praise. But no one can feel a greater appreciation than I for Mary's willingness to take on this book in the midst of her busy and complex schedule. Needless to say, Mary deserves much credit for all that is good in the book, and the readers are as fortunate as I that she was up to the task.

And finally, I will always be grateful to Jake Warner for his friendship, for pioneering self-help law, and for creating the wonderful work space and place the world knows as Nolo.

About the Author

Born and raised in California, Stephen Elias attended the University of California at Berkeley and Hastings College of the Law, from which he received his law degree in 1969. He spent seven years doing legal aid work in California and New York and three years as the public defender of Vermont's Northeast Kingdom.

In 1980, Steve joined Nolo Press. Since then he has played an integral role in Nolo's mission to provide lawyer-free access to the law. In his long Nolo career as author, Senior Legal Editor, Associate Publisher and General Counsel, Steve:

- wrote *Legal Research: How to Find & Understand the Law,* which opened up the law library to people without formal legal training.
- helped create WillMaker, the first legal software designed exclusively for the average computer user
- coauthored *How to File for Chapter 7 Bankruptcy,* which helps people file bankruptcy without a lawyer
- worked with author and patent lawyer David Pressman to produce *Patent it Yourself,* the bestselling book that has given hundreds of thousands of small inventors direct access to the patent office, and
- led the successful defense to an attempt by the Texas State Bar to ban Nolo books and software from that state.

Now, with this book, Steve provides a way for people who can't afford a lawyer to leave property to loved ones who have a disability, without affecting important government benefits.

Steve lives with his wife Catherine Elias-Jermany in a small northern California town, where he continues to write for Nolo as well as practice law. In addition to being a member in good standing of the California State Bar, Steve is a member of the National Academy of Elder Law Attorneys and the California State Bar Section on Probate and Trusts.

Dedication

To Bob and Lois Elias, who have always been there for me.

In Memoriam

For Stephanie Harolde, who meant so much to me for so many years. I miss her.

Table of Contents

Chapter 3

How Trust Funds Can (and Cannot) Be Used

Chapter 4

Getting Money Into a Special Needs Trust

Chapter 5

The Trustee's Job

Chapter 6

Choosing a Trustee

Chapter 7

Joining a Pooled Trust

Chapter 8

Creating Your Special Needs Trust

Chapter 9

Adding the Special Needs Trust to a Will or Living Trust

Chapter 10

Where to Get More Help

Glossary

Appendix A

Pooled Trusts

Appendix B

Letter to Trustee/Trustee's Duties

Appendix C

Sample Beneficiary Information Letter

Appendix D

How to Use the CD-ROM

Index

Introduction

If you have been providing care for a child or other loved one with special needs, you've no doubt thought about what will happen when you're no longer able to give that care. Of course, you can leave property to your loved one, but—as you are probably aware—doing so without some careful planning will almost certainly jeopardize his or her ability to receive benefits under the Supplemental Security Income (SSI) and Medicaid programs. Unless you make the right legal arrangements, benefits simply won't be available until the inheritance is used up.

How a Special Needs Trust Can Help Your Family

To avoid unintentionally sabotaging a loved one's eligibility for benefits, you can leave an inheritance in what's called a "special needs" trust. You create this kind of trust by adding certain language (provided in this book) to your will or revocable living trust. The special needs trust takes effect after your death. Because the inheritance is held in the special needs trust, your loved one can keep receiving benefits.

Money you leave to a special needs trust is managed by the person you name as "trustee." Your loved one (the trust's "beneficiary") can request—but not demand—that the trustee use trust funds for special needs. Because your loved one has no legal control over trust funds, the funds will not be considered a "resource" for purposes of SSI and Medicaid eligibility. A special needs trust could hold millions of dollars and still not affect your loved one's right to SSI and Medicaid benefits.

The trustee is required to manage the trust property for the sole benefit of your loved one. The trustee can spend trust property on behalf of your loved one, as long as the payments don't jeopardize eligibility for government benefits. Basically, that means trust funds can be spent for anything except food, clothing, and shelter. (And in certain situations, it's okay for the trustee to spend trust money for those purposes.)

What This Book Can Do

This book takes you, step-by-step, through the process of drafting a special needs trust, including:

- choosing a trustee
- drafting the trust that's right for your situation, and
- adding the special needs trust to your will or living trust document.

The book also contains a detailed letter that you can give to the person you choose to serve as trustee, explaining the responsibilities that go with this very important role.

If you don't want to set up your own special needs trust, you'll want to investigate "pooled trusts." These trusts are run by nonprofit organizations and are available in roughly half the states. (Chapter 7 explains how they work and the pros and cons of choosing this option.)

Will You Need a Lawyer?

This book contains complete instructions for preparing a trust document yourself and adding it to a will or living trust made with other Nolo estate planning resources. It explains each clause and helps you make the few choices involved in this surprisingly simple process. Whether or not you actually draft your own documents, educating yourself with this book can only help you make informed choices along the way.

If you have a will or living trust created by an estate planning lawyer, your lawyer may be of great help in steering you in the right direction for your personal situation. Also talk to a lawyer if, while using this book, you ever feel adrift. Getting a few questions answered can keep you on the right track.

You should, however, be prepared for the lawyer to take a dim view of this book and what it offers. Many lawyers who specialize in this work are of the opinion that only specialists should draft special needs trusts. This may well be true for certain kinds of special needs trusts, as mentioned below, but not necessarily for the straightforward trusts covered in this book. Once you've learned about trusts from this book and the other resources it lists, you'll be in a good position to judge their opinions for yourself.

Other Experts

You may also find it helpful to work with an accountant or financial planner. Financial advisers can answer questions about how much money you should leave to the trust to accomplish a certain result, or how to assess your overall net worth to plan for other loved ones as well as the disabled beneficiary.

Chapter 10 provides some tips on finding knowledgeable lawyers and other experts.

What This Book Cannot Do

This book shows you how to set up a "third-party" special needs trust that takes effect upon your death. A third-party trust is one that's funded with your money, not the beneficiary's. There are other kinds of special needs trusts that this book doesn't cover.

You'll need to see a lawyer if you want to:

Fund a special needs trust with the beneficiary's own property. If you want to put the beneficiary's own money—for example, a large settlement from a personal injury lawsuit—in a special needs trust, this book is not for you. Trusts that contain the beneficiary's money are called "self-settled" special needs trusts. Self-settled trusts are subject to different rules than third-party trusts and require more state-specific information than this book can provide. (In this book, the term "special needs trust" refers only to third-party trusts unless stated otherwise.)

Have your special needs trust to go into effect now, while you are alive. Most people don't need to create a trust for their assets while they're alive—they simply spend whatever they wish on things for their disabled loved one. But if for some reason you want a special needs trust to take effect before your death, it can be done, with the help of a lawyer. Chapter 10 discusses how to shop for the right kind of lawyer.

Add a special needs trust to a non-Nolo will or living trust. Nolo publishes excellent books and software for creating your own will or living trust. If you use them to create your will or trust, you can use this book to create a special needs trust and add it to your will or trust (Specific directions are in Chapter 9.) If you obtain a will or trust from some other source—a lawyer, for example—we cannot provide instructions on integrating this book's special needs trust language. You'll need to consult a lawyer.

SSI AND MEDICAID RULES ARE SUBJECT TO CHANGE. This book is based on current SSI and Medicaid rules. It is your responsibility while you are alive-and your trustee's responsibility after you are gone—to keep up to date on changes. Chapter 10 explains how.

Icons Used in This Book

 CAUTION: A potential problem you should consider carefully.

 TIP: A bit of practical advice.

 EXPERT: Time to consult a lawyer or other expert.

 RESOURCE: Sources of more information about the topic discussed in the text.

Chapter One

Providing for a Disabled Loved One With a Special Needs Trust

Millions of us love and care for someone who lives with a disability—a son with Down syndrome, a daughter with cystic fibrosis, a niece with severe autism, a grandchild with schizophrenia, a spouse with emphysema. Such a disability usually means your loved one will require long-term support and medical assistance under the Supplemental Security Income (SSI) program and Medicaid programs.

This chapter introduces the special needs trust—a way to leave property to a loved one with special needs without jeopardizing those crucial SSI and (especially) Medicaid benefits.

Protecting a Disabled Person's Own Money

This book helps you leave money to a disabled loved one in what's called a "third-party" special needs trust. It does not discuss how to create a special needs trust for property your loved one already owns—for example, an insurance settlement.

Trusts for the beneficiary's own property are called "self-settled trusts," and they are subject to specific federal and state rules designed to keep applicants from sheltering their property in order to meet program eligibility requirements. They are also subject to "payback" rules that require that the state be reimbursed for medical expenses after the trust beneficiary dies.

Why It's Usually a Bad Idea to Leave Money Directly to a Disabled Loved One

Special needs trusts are used primarily as a means of preserving a loved one's access to government-subsidized health care. The special needs trust is a well-accepted estate planning technique that is logical—even essential—given this country's health care system. If our country adopted a universal health care system, the special needs trust wouldn't be necessary, and you could leave property directly to a disabled loved one without risking the loss of that person's access to health care.

Health Care for People With Disabilities

There are really three health care systems in America: the private system, Medicare, and Medicaid. These three systems share doctors, hospitals, and other medical resources, but each provides access to these resources in radically different ways.

The private health care system is most frequently available as an employment-related benefit. Great, perhaps, for working people, but usually a nonstarter for those with disabilities.

Medicare, a government-run health care system, pays for most medical services (but not long-term care) required by disabled people who are eligible for Social Security disability benefits because of their own work history or that of an eligible parent. A person need not be poor to get Medicare benefits, but many disabled people, regardless of their income and resources, fail to meet the work-related eligibility requirements.

Medicaid is left to pay for virtually all the health care delivered to people who don't have private insurance or qualify for Medicare. To get Medicaid, in most states you must be poor enough to qualify for SSI—an income-support program designed exclusively for people with limited income and few resources.

Many people who don't qualify for Medicaid are left with serious financial burdens from health care costs. For example, if parents leave money to an adult disabled child, the gift, if large enough, will disqualify the child from SSI and so from Medicaid until the money is used up. This is where the special needs trust comes in. It allows a person with special needs to enjoy the benefits of property received from others without losing SSI and Medicaid.

Medicaid Eligibility Rules

Within limits set by federal law, each state can determine who is eligible for its Medicaid program. In most states, someone who is eligible for SSI is also automatically eligible for Medicaid. (Some states, by the way, give Medicaid a different name: Medi-Cal in California, MassHealth in Massachusetts.)

In 11 states, however, eligibility for Medicaid is determined separately from eligibility for SSI. In these states, the income and resource limits for Medicaid are either roughly the same as for SSI or somewhat lower. So someone could be eligible for SSI but not for Medicaid. These states are listed below. They're called "209 states" after a section of the Social Security Act that allows states to determine Medicaid eligibility separately.

This book assumes that someone who is ineligible for SSI because of excess income or resources is also ineligible for Medicaid. However, in most states, a person with excess income or resources can become eligible for Medicaid by spending down the resources or excess income.

Medicaid and SSI Eligibility: State Differences		
Eligibility for SSI and Medicaid determined separately ("209 states")		**Eligibility for SSI same as eligibility for Medicaid ("SSI states")**
• Connecticut	• New Hampshire	All other states
• Hawaii	• North Dakota	
• Illinois	• Ohio	
• Indiana	• Oklahoma	
• Minnesota	• Virginia	
• Missouri		
For details, visit www.cms.hhs.gov/medicaid/consumer.asp and click on the link to your state.		

How Inherited Money Can Make Medicaid Unavailable

Inheriting money seems like a good thing. But for someone who relies on SSI and Medicaid, receiving an inheritance can have a disastrous side effect: losing support and, perhaps more important, health care.

That's because the SSI and Medicaid programs are available only to people who have low incomes and few resources. To qualify, a person's monthly income usually must be no more than about $600 to $800 (it varies from state to state), and the person must own less than $2,000 worth of liquid assets (bank accounts, securities, and the like) and many other types of property. Someone whose property is worth more than the limit is not eligible for benefits. However, the value of the person's home, car, personal effects, and household furnishings usually are not counted.

EXAMPLE: John's daughter Yolanda was born with cerebral palsy and will likely need lifetime medical benefits under the Medicaid program. John wants to provide for Yolanda but has been cautioned that leaving her property might disqualify her for Medicaid and support under SSI.

John is right to be concerned. An inheritance that would cause Yolanda to exceed the SSI resource limit would probably also make her ineligible for Medicaid. (Most states operate under this rule, as discussed above.) Yolanda would likely see the property she inherits quickly evaporate in a blizzard of medical bills and living expenses until she once again became eligible for those programs.

A disabled person who comes into money must spend it—or at least enough of it so that what's left doesn't exceed the resource limit—before reapplying for SSI and Medicaid benefits. The money doesn't have to be spent on support or medical care.

How a Special Needs Trust Can Help

How, then, can you make sure that your loved one receives the full benefit of an inheritance without losing eligibility for Medicaid and SSI? The answer is a special needs trust.

If you leave money in a properly drafted trust, the beneficiary never has a legal claim to it, meaning it won't be counted as the beneficiary's resource and so won't interfere with eligibility for benefits. And the funds can be used for your loved one's benefit for any good or service except food or shelter. (Under current rules, the trust can even provide food or shelter without causing the beneficiary to lose Medicaid coverage or most of his or her SSI grant.)

EXAMPLE: Janine, 45, an only child, has had schizophrenia since childhood. She is able to function under heavy medication, but she cannot work and depends on SSI for her income and Medicaid for treatment. Janine's sole surviving parent, Helen, wants to leave Janine her property, which consists of a house and liquid assets worth $75,000.

Helen creates a special needs trust for the sole benefit of Janine. When Helen dies, her property will go directly to the special needs trust rather than to Janine herself. The trustee will use the trust funds to supplement what Janine receives from SSI and Medicare. Because Janine does not control the trust money, it is not counted as a resource by SSI.

Do you need a lot of money to set up a trust? No, though you may decide that a trust isn't worth the trouble if you don't expect to leave a lot of money to the beneficiary. But if you have even $5,000 or $10,000, it may be well worth creating a trust, because that money can be stretched over a long period of time. If your trustee has even $100 a month over five years to spend, it could make life for your loved one a little easier.

Who Can Benefit From a Special Needs Trust

A third-party special needs trust can benefit anyone 65 or older, and anyone of any age who has a disability that qualifies him or her for SSI and Medicaid benefits. If you think your loved one may at some time need SSI or Medicaid, consider creating a special needs trust to take that possibility into account.

You most likely already have a gut feeling about whether or not your loved one qualifies—or will qualify—for SSI and Medicaid benefits. If you are providing for all of your loved one's needs now, the issue will most likely arise when the need for government benefits arise—presumably, after your own death.

The federal programs that provide assistance to disabled adults focus almost exclusively on whether someone has the ability to be gainfully employed. In other words, employability defines whether or not someone is disabled—at least for the purpose of qualifying for federal benefits.

For SSI purposes, disability is determined under a complex set of criteria fashioned by the Social Security Administration. Some conditions are considered to be automatically disabling—Down syndrome, for example. Others (an amputation, for example) require that a number of factors be taken into account, including age, work experience, and the type of function affected by the medical condition.

Chapter 2 discusses disability in more detail, and also discusses some other situations in which you may want to set up a special needs trust for a loved one.

Who Can Set Up a Special Needs Trust

Most literature on special needs trusts speaks to a parent or grandparent leaving property to a disabled child or grandchild. However, third-party special needs trusts can work for individuals of any age and relationship. You don't have to be the beneficiary's parent or any other relative to set up a trust.

Older couples sometimes set up special needs trusts for the survivor, to take effect when one spouse or partner dies.

EXAMPLE 1: Gavin and Dennis, both 70, have been domestic partners for the past 20 years. Dennis has been diagnosed with Alzheimer's disease and will need Medicaid in the near future. In his will, Gavin leaves $75,000 to a special needs trust to be used for Dennis's benefit. When Gavin dies, Dennis will be able to keep his SSI and Medicaid benefits and have those benefits supplemented from the money Gavin left to the special needs trust.

EXAMPLE 2: Rolf and Juanita are both in their 60s and about to be married. Rolf suffers from severe rheumatoid arthritis and has been receiving SSI and Medicaid for ten years. Juanita has a stock portfolio worth $50,000 in her name alone. She wants to leave the stock to Rolf but doesn't want him to lose his SSI or Medicaid. In her will, Juanita creates a special needs trust for the benefit of Rolf and leaves the stock to the trust. When Juanita dies, her will goes into effect, and the inheritance is available to enhance Rolf's quality of life.

You can even set up a special needs trust for someone to whom you're not related at all.

EXAMPLE: Agnes, age 75, leads a simple life in the house she grew up in. She puts in volunteer time at the local Boys and Girls Club and The Arc (an organization dedicated to the developmentally disabled). Unbeknown to the community, Agnes is worth several million dollars because of property she inherited from her father and mother. She gives handsome annual donations to the groups she works with, but has never given much thought to how to leave her property.

When Agnes learns about special needs trusts, she decides to create special needs trusts for 12 disabled children she has grown close to in her volunteer work. At her death, each trust will receive an equal share of her property. If, during her life, she meets other children who she wants to include, she can amend her trust to add them. She can also change her mind, revoke the trust, and leave her property in a different way.

Alternatives to a Special Needs Trust

Special needs trusts aren't the right solution for every family. Trusts do cost time and money to administer, and the trustee may be called on to make difficult decisions about investing and spending trust assets.

Leaving Money to a Friend or Relative

Rather than rely on a special needs trust, you may be inclined to leave some money to a friend or relative who agrees to watch out for your loved one's needs after your death.

If you don't expect to leave much property to your loved one, this approach may be preferable to setting up a trust that will last only a year or two before the money has been spent. You could attach a letter to your will or living trust explaining what you are doing and request that the money be spent in a way that doesn't interfere with your loved one's SSI and Medicaid benefits.

Unfortunately, this informal approach has several potentially major downsides. The fact is, money that legally belongs to one person will not necessarily end up benefiting someone else, no matter how honorable the intent at the outset.

Because the person to whom you leave the property will own it outright, it would be subject to that person's creditors in a lawsuit or bankruptcy. The property may pass to that person's heirs if he or she suffers an untimely death, or it may go to a spouse in the event of a divorce. Also, the laws that govern someone who is an actual trustee (described in Chapter 5) don't apply in an informal relationship. In other words, if the person spends the money for a new car instead of your disabled loved one's needs, there is nothing that anyone will be able to do about it.

Leaving Money Directly to Your Loved One

As a general rule, it may be better to leave property to your loved one outright if he or she is unlikely to qualify for SSI and Medicaid and can be trusted to manage the funds in his or her own behalf.

Using a Pooled Trust

If you don't want to set up your own special needs trust, you may be able to join a "pooled trust." Roughly half the states have nonprofit organizations that operate such trusts, in which gifts to many disabled beneficiaries are combined so that they can be efficiently and professionally managed. The trustee invests and spends funds for the beneficiaries without affecting their eligibility for SSI and Medicaid. If you sign up for one of these pooled trusts, you can leave the trust details to them. Chapter 7 discusses pooled trusts in detail.

How the Trust Works—Nuts and Bolts

A special needs trust is an arrangement under which a person (called the "grantor" or "settlor") places property in the hands of a manager (the "trustee"). The trustee is legally obligated to follow the terms of the trust document to use the property for the benefit of the disabled person identified in the trust document (the "beneficiary").

EXAMPLE: Albion (the grantor) creates a special needs trust for the benefit of his disabled daughter Chloe (the beneficiary). He leaves property under the management of his sister Rosie (the trustee).

All special needs trusts are defined by two basic characteristics:

- The trust document gives the trustee absolute control over when and how the trust property is spent, as long as it's spent for the sole benefit of the beneficiary, and

- The trust document expressly states that the grantor intends for the property in the trust to supplement, but not replace, the basic benefits and services provided by SSI and Medicaid.

By including these two provisions in the trust document, you ensure that SSI and Medicaid won't treat the property in the trust as a resource of the beneficiary.

Of course, the typical special needs trust contains a lot more verbiage as well, dealing with various events that may arise. For instance, what happens if the beneficiary recovers and is no longer concerned about SSI and Medicaid eligibility? Or if the beneficiary dies, leaving a lot of property in the trust? These and other issues can be resolved by including basic statements of intent in your trust document. (Chapter 8 takes you step by step through all the major issues of creating a special needs trust and offers plain-English provisions to address each of them. No rocket science here.)

When the Trust Takes Effect

The special needs trust you create with this book will take effect at your death. To accomplish that, you add language to your will or revocable living trust, directing that the trust be created when you die, and that certain property you want to benefit your disabled loved one be transferred into it. (Chapter 9 explains how to do this.)

This approach gives you maximum flexibility in what you do with your own property during your life. Also, by postponing the creation of the trust until your death, you'll have time to decide whether the trust is necessary and to take into account any changes in the SSI and Medicaid programs that occur before your death.

EXAMPLE: Barbara's daughter Kristin suffers from schizophrenia. Barbara, at age 55, drafts a will that includes language for a special needs trust for Kristin, to take effect at her death. Twenty years later, both Barbara and Kristin are still alive.

During the intervening years, an effective treatment has been developed for Kristin's condition, and Kristin is completely capable of self-support without SSI or Medicaid. So Barbara changes her will to leave Kristin her inheritance outright instead of tying it up in a special needs trust.

Revocable Living Trusts: The Basics

Revocable living trusts have become a common estate planning tool. They are an easy and private way to legally pass property without the delay and expense of a probate court proceeding. In the trust document (which is basically like a will) you appoint a "successor trustee" to take over at your death and distribute trust property to people named to inherit it.

Who Can Give Property to a Special Needs Trust

Anyone can contribute property to a third-party special needs trust. Although these trusts are most often created by parents for their children, you don't need any family relationship to create or give money to a trust for someone. And there is no limit to the number of trusts that may be created for a particular beneficiary.

EXAMPLE: Jennifer Roxford's cousin Harvey wants to leave her some money. Instead of leaving the property directly to Jennifer, he creates a special needs trust for her in his will, names Jennifer's mother Helen as trustee (after getting her permission), and leaves $20,000 to Jennifer to be placed in the trust.

Jennifer's close friend Ruth also wants to give Jennifer some money—both as a gesture of friendship and because she is making gifts as part of a plan to get her estate under the estate tax threshold. Ruth creates a special needs trust, names Jennifer's mother Helen as trustee, and transfers an $11,000 CD into Helen's name "as trustee of the Jennifer Roxford Special Needs Trust created 1/24/20xx."

Jennifer's aunt Frieda wants to leave Jennifer $15,000 in her will. As part of her will she creates a special needs trust and leaves the property to Jennifer to be placed in the trust.

What Types of Property Can Be Held in the Trust

Virtually any type of property can be left in a special needs trust, including real estate, stocks, collections, a business, patents, or jewelry. But because the primary purpose of a special needs trust is to supplement government benefits, typically the trustee is given the authority to sell tangible items (cars or jewelry, for example) to raise cash. Whether or not the trustee sells property will depend on:

- the significance of the items to the beneficiary, and
- the likelihood that the assets will appreciate in value—if they won't, it's better to convert them to cash that can be invested elsewhere.

For instance, a home or an heirloom ring might be important to the beneficiary, and the trustee probably wouldn't sell them. A valuable coin collection might be likely to go up in value, warranting keeping it in the trust as long as possible. On the other hand, jewelry that is of little interest to a beneficiary might as well be sold, with the proceeds invested in an asset that will produce income. Clearly, in order to make this type of decision, the trustee will need a good understanding of the beneficiary's personal needs. (Chapter 5 helps you create a written statement communicating these needs to the trustee.)

How Assets Get to the Trust

Commonly, a parent, grandparent, or other relative leaves property to a special needs trust by:

- leaving it through a will or revocable living trust directly to the special needs trust
- naming the special needs trust as a beneficiary on a designation form that controls what happens to a deposit or brokerage account, retirement plan, or stocks and bonds, or
- giving it to an existing third-party special needs trust.

More about this in Chapter 4.

How Trust Assets Can Be Used

The sole purpose of a special needs trust is to provide money for expenses that SSI and Medicaid don't pay for. Those expenses are the beneficiary's "special needs." An SSI grant is intended to provide only food and shelter. That's it. So expenditures for anything else are supplementary and don't affect the beneficiary's eligibility for a full SSI payment.

Generally, trust funds are used for services (hiring a personal attendant, for example) or experiences (travel, for example) rather than to buy items of property. That's because a beneficiary who owns too much valuable property will go over the resource limit and become ineligible for SSI and Medicaid. A trustee who used trust funds for a vacation home wouldn't be doing your loved one a favor—it would result in termination of public benefits. That's directly contrary to the express terms of the trust, so such a purchase is not authorized.

That's the relatively easy part. It's not so easy when the trustee wants to use trust funds for items classified as food and shelter. In some cases, buying these items with trust money is perfectly fine. For example, the SSI program does not pretend to provide adequate assistance for special dietary needs. So if a beneficiary needs unusually pricey food or nutritional supplements, this extra cost can often be met from the special needs trust without affecting the SSI grant.

Shelter is a special case. Special needs trusts commonly allow a trustee to pay for rent or any other basic need that the trustee deems necessary for the beneficiary's health and welfare under the circumstances if it isn't already being met by SSI or Medicaid, and if it doesn't make the beneficiary ineligible for those benefits altogether.

EXAMPLE: Eva, a 34-year-old woman with cystic fibrosis, lives in a studio apartment in a "low-rent" part of San Francisco, where she still must pay $800 a month. Eva's SSI grant—her sole source of income—is $700 a month. Obviously, Eva needs some help with her rent. Under SSI rules, the trust can pay the entire $800 rent, and Eva will lose only about $210 from her grant.

Whether or not to use trust property for food and shelter is entirely up to the trustee. So in the example above, Eva couldn't force the trustee of her special needs trust to cough up the rent money. If the beneficiary did have that kind of power over the trustee, all the funds in the trust would be considered available resources for SSI and Medicaid eligibility purposes. So, although a special needs trust may give the trustee authority to make supplementary rent payments, the trust also prohibits such payments if they would interrupt the beneficiary's eligibility for SSI and Medicaid.

Chapter 3 explains the ins and outs of paying for shelter and associated services such as utilities. It also provides a long list of items that are considered supplementary to the SSI and Medicaid programs.

The Trustee's Role

It's almost a cliché that the operative word in the phrase special needs trust is "trust." The person you choose to serve as trustee will manage and spend, without court supervision, the property you leave for the beneficiary.

Obviously, you want to pick someone you have complete faith in. In addition to being responsive and sensitive to the beneficiary's personal needs, the trustee has the absolutely crucial job of investing and spending trust assets.

You also need someone who will keep up on the law. The trustee is supposed to use trust funds only for goods and services that supplement—but don't disqualify the beneficiary for—benefits provided by SSI and Medicaid. For this the trustee needs a good working knowledge of how to spend trust money without affecting eligibility. As explained just above, this can be easy when the goods and services are obviously supplemental but more problematic where housing costs are involved. The trustee will learn about the rules from the SSI program administrators and their regulations, or from a qualified professional resource. (Chapter 10 has more on resources.)

In addition to dealing with the SSI and Medicaid programs, the trustee has a legal duty to invest the trust assets prudently. The trustee must obey state laws that set out rules for trustees as well as the terms of the trust document itself.

The trustee must also spend judiciously to make the trust's funds last as long as possible. This can be one of the hardest aspects of the trustee role, especially when the beneficiary's desires conflict with the trustee's duty to conserve trust funds.

EXAMPLE: Adrian, a 28-year-old with quadriplegia, rents a cheap apartment in a downscale Cleveland neighborhood. He receives SSI and Medicaid and is the beneficiary of a special needs trust containing roughly $200,000 left by his father. Adrian wants to live in a better neighborhood and asks the trustee to buy him a house that's for sale. If the trustee buys the house, almost all of the trust property will be used up. Should the trustee comply with Adrian's wishes, or refuse so the trust funds will last longer? Because Adrian has no authority to direct the trustee's disbursements, he'll have to abide by the trustee's choice.

So how should Adrian's trustee go about making this decision? The purpose of the trust is to supplement the SSI and Medicaid benefits Adrian receives—food, shelter, and basic medical services. Obviously, buying the house would conflict with that purpose, by depleting the trust of the funds necessary for that lifetime supplementation. The trustee's job is to fulfill the purpose of the trust, not just to please the beneficiary.

Unlike Adrian, some beneficiaries cannot coherently express their wishes because of their particular disability—for example, severe autism can have this effect. In such cases, trustees must rely on their own knowledge of the beneficiary's needs and desires, or on information provided in the trust document or by the beneficiary's family in a written needs statement (explained in Chapter 5).

The trustee will also be responsible for accounting for the trust income and disbursements and filing annual tax returns for the trust. Unless the trustee has tax and accounting expertise, this is something that should be handled by an outside expert and paid for with trust funds.

Fortunately, the special needs trust in this book provides that the trustee can be paid a reasonable amount from trust assets for doing all this work. Also, because the trustee's role can be demanding, you may want to name cotrustees to share the load. And if the property in the trust has a sufficient value—roughly $250,000 to $500,000 or more—you may want to turn over the financial management of the assets to a corporate trustee.

Whomever your choice as trustee, the trust will be managed under a law called the Prudent Investor Act, which in essence requires the use of common sense under all the circumstances. If necessary, however, the trust document authorizes the trustee to get expert help—and to pay a reasonable amount for it with trust funds.

Chapter 5 helps you get a grasp on these and other trustee issues so you'll know what's in store for the trustee you name. A sample letter to the trustee, which outlines the information your trustee will need to competently manage the trust, is included on the CD-ROM that comes with this book.

Pooled Trusts

As noted earlier, in many areas of the country it is possible to join up with an existing special needs trust that is managed for a number of disabled people by a nonprofit organization. Called a pooled trust, this option may be just the ticket if you are leaving a relatively modest sum or can't come up with a good candidate for trustee. Chapter 7 discusses pooled trusts in detail.

Terminating the Trust

The trust ends when it's no longer needed—commonly, at the beneficiary's death. There are four reasons to end a special needs trust:

- Trust funds are depleted.
- The beneficiary no longer needs government benefits.
- The beneficiary is no longer eligible for government benefits.
- The beneficiary dies.

The first reason to terminate a trust is simply because the funds run out. This may happen if the trust wasn't adequately funded to begin with, or if the beneficiary lives much longer than originally anticipated. The trustee doesn't have to spend the last dime; when funds dwindle to a low level, it may no longer make sense to keep the trust going, given the cost of expenses such as record keeping and expert advice.

EXAMPLE: Eden, age 60, is the beneficiary of a special needs trust that went into effect when she was 20. Eden has outlived her original life expectancy by 20 years. The trust was originally funded with the proceeds of a $200,000 life insurance policy, but over the next 40 years the funds were slowly depleted. Now, only $3,000 is left in the trust, and the trustee can no longer justify keeping the trust in effect, given the expenses of administration.

The second reason to terminate a trust is if it appears that the beneficiary either doesn't need or doesn't qualify for SSI or Medicaid. This may happen because eligibility rules change or because the beneficiary's condition improves.

EXAMPLE: Robert, who suffers from chronic schizophrenia, is the beneficiary of a special needs trust established when he was 28. Now Robert is 55 and, thanks to a new class of antipsychotic drugs, no longer has symptoms of his illness as long as he takes his pills. Because Robert is now able and willing to work, he no longer needs to rely on SSI and Medicaid.

The third reason to terminate the trust would be because a change in program rules made the beneficiary ineligible for SSI, Medicaid, or similar programs if the trust continues in effect.

EXAMPLE: Clara is the beneficiary of a special needs trust created when she was 21. At that time, the laws allowed a special needs trust to pay a beneficiary's rent without disqualifying the beneficiary for SSI. Fifteen years later, the SSI rules have changed to treat any rent payments from an outside source as a disqualifying factor, and to consider any trust that allows the trustee to make such payments as a disqualifying resource. Because Clara absolutely needs her Medicaid and SSI benefits, the trustee must avoid their cessation by terminating the trust.

In any of these three situations, after all taxes and debts legally owed by the trust have been paid, the trust document directs the trustee to distribute as much of the property to the beneficiary as possible without interfering with his or her eligibility for benefits. If the beneficiary has a legal guardian or conservator, or a person who has been designated to receive benefits on his or her behalf (representative payee), the trustee distributes the property to that person.

EXAMPLE: The trustee of Emma's special needs trust decides to terminate the trust because federal law changes will make Emma ineligible for benefits if the trust stays in existence, and Emma really needs the benefits. There's about $10,000 in the trust.

The trustee distributes $1,999 to Emma, which keeps her under the $2,000 resource limit (she doesn't have any other nonexempt assets) so she can continue to receive SSI and Medicaid. The trustee gives the rest of the money to Emma's sister, who is named as the remainder beneficiary in the trust document.

If the beneficiary won't lose any needed benefits as a result, the trustee gives all of the trust funds to the beneficiary.

EXAMPLE: Eli no longer needs government benefits, so the trustee of his special needs trusts ends the trust and gives all of the funds directly to Eli.

The last reason to terminate the trust is when the beneficiary dies. In this case, the trustee is directed to distribute any remaining trust funds to the person you named, in the special needs trust, to inherit them. This person is called the "remainder beneficiary" of the trust. (Chapter 5 discusses remainder beneficiaries.)

Making a Special Needs Trust: Checklist
❏ Decide whether or not you really want to create a special needs trust.
• Will you be leaving enough money to make administering a trust worthwhile?
• Is there someone who's willing and able to serve as trustee?
• Will your loved one need SSI and Medicaid after your death?
• Would a pooled trust serve your needs better?
❏ Choose a trustee.
• Not necessary if you're joining pooled trust
❏ Educate the trustee.
• Prepare and give to the trustee a Beneficiary Information letter.
• Give the trustee the Trustee's Duties information in this book.
❏ Create the special needs trust language.
❏ Decide how much property to leave to the trust.
❏ Add the special needs language to your will or revocable living trust.
❏ If you use a living trust, transfer property to the trust.

Chapter Two

Who Can Benefit From a Special Needs Trust

Special needs trusts are designed to supplement support and medical assistance that people receive under the Supplementary Security Income (SSI) and Medicaid programs. If you want to leave money to a loved one who receives these benefits, creating a special needs trust as part of your estate plan is probably a smart move. The trust will ensure that your loved one can keep SSI and Medicaid benefits while receiving financial help from the money you leave in the trust.

There are a few other situations in which you might want to set up a special needs trust as well. This chapter discusses them.

Someone With a Permanent Disability

Special needs trusts are most commonly used for people who likely will need government assistance from the SSI and Medicaid programs their entire lives because of a permanent disabling condition.

To qualify for SSI and Medicaid, a person must have a low income, few resources, and a condition that:

- likely will last at least 12 months or end in death, and

- prevents the person from engaging in substantial employment.

Only United States citizens automatically qualify for SSI benefits. Noncitizens can qualify for SSI if they are legally in the country and meet some additional qualifications.

Low-income people 65 or older are also eligible for SSI. When someone applies for SSI or Medicaid benefits, the Social Security Administration makes a determination, under criteria it's developed, as to whether or not the person is disabled. (Chapter 10 lists references to these rules and other sources of law regarding SSI and Medicaid rules that affect special needs trusts.)

People with blindness, developmental disabilities, Down syndrome, organic brain damage, chronic mental illness, physical paralysis (paraplegia), or congenital disabling afflictions such as cerebral palsy or cystic fibrosis have been the most common beneficiaries of special needs trusts. But there are many other physical and mental conditions that meet the Social Security Administration's definition of disability and that are likely to last a lifetime. Some of them are listed below.

Conditions That Can Cause Disability: A Partial List

agoraphobia	hemophilia	organic brain syndrome (OBS)
Alzheimer's disease	HIV	Parkinson's disease
amputations	Huntington's chorea	phenylketonuria (PKU)
bipolar disorder	kidney malfunction	severe autistic disorder
cancer (many types)	leukemia	sickle cell anemia
congenital heart disease	lupus	spina bifida
diabetes mellitus (type 2)	multiple chemical sensitivity	Tay-Sachs disease
emphysema	multiple sclerosis	thalassemia
fetal alcohol syndrome	muscular dystrophy	traumatic spine damage
fragile X syndrome	obsessive-compulsive disorder	Turners syndrome

Someone Who May Get Better

Many disabling conditions are not permanent. For example, many combat veterans suffer from conditions such as post-traumatic stress disorder, which has a combination of mental, emotional, and physical symptoms that make it impossible to work for years, but not always for a lifetime. You may want to create a special needs trust for someone even if the disability probably isn't permanent.

How the Definition of "Disabled" Is Changing

Many factors make it hard to predict whether someone who's disabled now is likely to remain that way and will always need to rely on SSI and Medicaid.

Changes in the workplace. For SSI eligibility purposes, someone who can't work is disabled. So as the workplace changes, so does the definition of disabled. For instance, when most people worked on farms, someone with a severe learning disorder might not have been considered disabled, because formal learning wasn't necessary to heft a pitchfork, milk cows, plant corn, or do housework. In 21st-century high-tech America, however, a pronounced difficulty in learning makes it difficult to find a job. On the other hand, technological advances have made it possible for people with paraplegia or severe visual impairment to perform a large range of productive work.

New treatments for old disabilities. Modern medical techniques involving gene therapy, stem cells, and neurotransmitters (molecules that facilitate nerve impulse transmissions) offer the possibility of cures for a broad range of conditions that currently are incurable. Parkinson's and Alzheimer's disease are two devastating conditions that may be amenable to treatment in ten or 20 years. Similarly, techniques to regenerate damaged or severed nerve cells may someday offer relief to people who cannot move their limbs because of a spinal injury. Mentally disabling conditions also are reaping the benefits of modern medical technology. The pharmaceutical industry, whatever else its sins, has given us drugs that let people with a large range of formerly incapacitating mental conditions engage in productive activity.

Technological advances. There have been profound changes in technologies available to ameliorate physically disabling conditions. For example, hearing aides or surgery largely eliminate the disability of deafness for many Americans. More change is on the way in such fields as robotics and nanotechnology. For example, research is underway to help people whose arms or legs have been amputated to regain near-full functionality with the help of "intelligent" prostheses and to develop a computerized interface that helps blind people experience visual feedback from the environment.

Planning With Recovery in Mind

The SSI and Medicaid programs have not, by and large, taken medical and technological advances into account when determining disability. A condition that prevented employment in 1950 is often assumed to do so today. However, this could change at any time. Your loved one may not always be eligible for SSI and Medicaid, either because disabilities are defined differently or because he or she enjoys a dramatic recovery

There's no way to know, now, whether your loved one's disability will improve with time, either naturally or through medical and technological intervention. But even so, you can create a special needs trust without worrying that you will needlessly tie up your loved one's inheritance. The trust document takes into account the possibility that the trust, for whatever reason, may not always be necessary, and gives the trustee power to terminate the trust under certain conditions. For example, the trust allows the trustee to end the trust if at some point the beneficiary no longer needs or qualifies for SSI and Medicaid.

EXAMPLE: Jeanne leaves $100,000 in her will to a special needs trust for the benefit of her daughter Cassie, who is ten and has been diagnosed with childhood schizophrenia. Jeanne names Joanne, Cassie's aunt, as trustee. The trust gives the trustee complete discretion as to how the funds may be spent for Cassie's benefit, provided that disbursements do not disqualify Cassie for SSI and Medicaid.

The trust document also states that if someday Cassie does not need or does not qualify for SSI or Medicaid, the trustee may terminate the trust and distribute the remaining trust money to Cassie outright.

Twenty years later, when Jeanne dies, the trust goes into effect. By that time, Cassie, now 30, has "grown out of" her illness and is no longer considered disabled for purposes of SSI and Medicaid. The trustee terminates the trust and distributes the property to Cassie outright.

Another option, if you think that a disability is likely to get better, is to leave the funds to your loved one outright, with the expectation that a "self-settled" special needs trust will be created if needed. (A self-settled trust is one funded with the beneficiary's own money—unlike the trust you make with this book, which is funded with someone else's money.) Remember, though, that this kind of trust is more expensive to set up than the special needs trust covered in this book. Your loved one will need an attorney's help to make sure that the trust complies with the rules of your state.

Someone Who May Need a Special Needs Trust Later

Some people who aren't disabled now may need assistance from SSI or Medicaid at some point because of a condition that is likely to get worse, making it impossible for the person to be self-sufficient.

In this situation, creating a special needs trust involves some guesswork. But if you think it's more likely than not that a loved one will need government assistance for a significant length of time, it makes sense to set up a special needs trust. There's really no risk. The trust in this book includes a clause that allows the trustee to end the trust if it's not needed by a certain age. And if the trust is needed, the trustee can use trust funds to pay for all kinds of useful things, such as tuition, travel, tools, cultural events, and companion services. (See Chapter 3.) And because the trustee has complete control over how funds are used, you don't need to worry about the beneficiary spending it in ways you wouldn't approve of.

In fact, people who may not be able to wisely manage an inheritance are good candidates for a special needs trust, even if they ultimately won't need SSI. Such trusts are often called "spendthrift" trusts when used to keep assets out of the hands of a beneficiary (and of his or her creditors) and in the firm control of a wise trustee. For example, someone with mild developmental disabilities, mild autism, attention deficit disorder, or bipolar syndrome might benefit from a trust that prevents reckless spending of inherited money.

Ultimately, only you can decide whether it makes sense to provide for long-term management of a loved one's inheritance—which a special needs trust provides—or to leave the inheritance directly to your loved one. If you do decide to use a special needs trust, the beneficiary is sure to receive much the same benefit from the inheritance as would be the case with an outright gift, even though a small portion of the trust assets will be spent on administrative fees over the years.

Someone Who Is Eligible for Medicare or SSDI

A loved one who receives Medicare or Social Security Disability Insurance (SSDI) may not need a special needs trust, because these programs are not concerned with an applicant's resources. There's no need to keep an inheritance in trust; your loved one can own it outright without losing SSDI or Medicare benefits.

If, however, the SSDI payment is low, SSI may be a valuable way to supplement your loved one's income. And Medicaid may be necessary to provide benefits not included in the Medicare program—for instance, prescriptions or long-term nursing home care.

In other words, if your loved one is likely to need expensive prescription drugs—for example, for AIDS—you will probably want to create a special needs trust even though he or she is eligible for Medicare. The same is true if the person is suffering from a degenerative mental illness that almost certainly will require long-term care in a nursing facility. However, if you don't expect either expensive prescription drugs or long-term nursing care, you may prefer to not tie up the person's inheritance in a special needs trust. Instead, you can leave the property directly to your loved one, who can continue to receive Medicare and SSDI.

EXAMPLE: Julia was born with cystic fibrosis. Her parents have worked for many years in jobs covered by Social Security, to they qualify for Social Security benefits should they become disabled or reach retirement age. Because of her parents' work history, Julia also qualifies for Social Security Disability Insurance benefits and Medicare.

Sources of Support and Medical Care for Disabled People		
	Who Qualifies	**Benefits**
SSI	People with limited income and few resources. If a noncitizen, must meet certain criteria.	Monthly cash payments (amount depends on living arrangement, marital status, and disability)
Medicaid	People who don't qualify for Medicare and do qualify for SSI.	Most medical services, including long-term nursing home care and pharmaceuticals
SSDI	People who have paid enough Social Security taxes, without regard to resources or income. People who become disabled before age 22, if their parents qualify for either SSDI or Social Security retirement benefits.	Monthly cash payments
Medicare	People who are eligible for Social Security disability benefits because of their work history or that of an eligible parent.	Most medical services, but not long-term care or complete prescription coverage. Some prescription costs will be covered beginning in 2006.
For more information, see www.ssa.gov.		

 MEDICAID GOES BY DIFFERENT NAMES IN DIFFERENT STATES.
Medicaid is a combined federal and state program, and is known by a different name in some states. For example, in California it's called Medi-Cal, and in Massachusetts MassHealth.

How Trust Funds Can (and Cannot) Be Used

This chapter has but one purpose: to explain how a special needs trust can provide your disabled loved one with a large variety of goods and services while at the same time preserving his or her SSI and Medicaid benefits.

SSI Income and Resource Limits: An Overview

You're using a special needs trust so you can leave your loved one money without jeopardizing SSI and Medicaid benefits. That means the person you choose to serve as trustee will need to know the rules about how trust money can be used. Otherwise, your loved one's benefits could be cut or even lost altogether. Much of the information in this chapter is summarized in a letter you can give to your trustee (see Chapter 5 and the CD-ROM that comes with the book).

Here's a quick summary:

- Monthly SSI payments can be reduced if the trustee gives the beneficiary cash or pays for the beneficiary's food or shelter.

- SSI benefits can be lost for any month in which the beneficiary receives too much cash or owns too much in the way of "countable" assets. And a beneficiary who no longer qualifies for SSI won't qualify for Medicaid, either.

⚠️ SSI AND MEDICAID RULES CAN CHANGE AT ANY TIME. Keeping up with applicable rules will be your responsibility during your life and your trustee's after your death. See Chapter 10 for information about how to keep up to date.

Resource Limits

Anyone who owns more than $2,000 worth of countable resources is not eligible for SSI. (The limit for a couple is $3,000.) Countable resources are cash or any asset that could readily be converted to cash, or real estate that isn't the person's primary residence.

Countable Resources: Examples
• Bank accounts
• Stocks and bonds
• Real estate (other than home)

Your loved one will not have to live in dire poverty to qualify for SSI. That's because many kinds of assets are not counted toward the $2,000 limit. Some examples are listed below.

Noncountable Resources: Examples
• Beneficiary's home (house and land, condo)
• Necessary car or van
• Furnishings and personal effects
• Burial and life insurance with a face value of up to $1,500

How does the SSI program know what and how much a recipient owns? Generally, the bureaucracy relies on the recipient's own required reports and in information from the IRS, state motor vehicles department, and banks. If for some reason an investigation is begun, the recipient's financial affairs will be examined more closely.

Income Limits

An SSI recipient can receive only a certain amount of income in a given month. Federal regulations divide income into three categories: earned, unearned, and in-kind. Each kind is treated differently.

Earned income comes from a job (including wages earned in a sheltered workshop) or a business. If the beneficiary earns more than $65 a month, his or her SSI payment is reduced. If earnings are too high, the SSI grant (and as a result, Medicaid benefits) can be lost altogether.

Unearned income is cash (or assets that can be easily converted into cash) from gifts, donations, prizes, interest from bank accounts, dividends, and similar sources. If the trustee gives the beneficiary money from the trust, that's unearned income. If you left money directly to your loved one, that would be unearned income in the month is was received; whatever was left the next month would be treated as a resource of your loved one.

The first $20 of unearned income each month has no effect on a beneficiary's SSI grant. After that, the grant is reduced, dollar-for-dollar, up to the amount of the unearned income.

EXAMPLE: Sadie, who receives SSI, receives a $200 check as a birthday gift. Her SSI grant is reduced by $180 that month.

Gifts of items that aren't countable resources aren't considered unearned income.

EXAMPLE: The trustee of Maya's special needs trust buys her a big TV. Because the TV is a noncountable home furnishing, it doesn't count as income. Maya's SSI grant is not reduced by the gift.

Income in kind consists of food or shelter, including payments for such shelter costs as mortgage and utilities. Gifts of other items are not in-kind income (though they may count as a resource).

Income in kind reduces an SSI grant up to the lesser of:

- the value of the gift, or
- one-third of the maximum federal portion of the SSI grant plus $20. For 2005, the maximum reduction is $213.

How these rules will affect your trustee's management of the trust funds is discussed in more detail in the rest of the chapter.

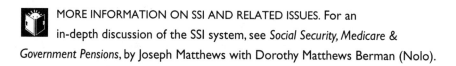 MORE INFORMATION ON SSI AND RELATED ISSUES. For an in-depth discussion of the SSI system, see *Social Security, Medicare & Government Pensions*, by Joseph Matthews with Dorothy Matthews Berman (Nolo).

Assets in the Special Needs Trust

Assets held in a properly drafted special needs trust are not considered resources of the beneficiary because the beneficiary has no control over them. So they are not subject to the $2,000 resource limit. Theoretically, a special needs trust could hold houses, cars, jewelry, stocks, and commercial properties of enormous value, and yet the trust beneficiary would still qualify for SSI.

EXAMPLE: A vacation cabin that Estelle's family has owned for years is held in the name of Estelle's special needs trust. Although the cabin is worth far more than $2,000, it isn't considered a resource that Estelle can draw on, and so it doesn't affect her eligibility for SSI.

What Trust Funds Can Pay For

The trustee of the special needs trust can pay for anything on behalf of your loved one, as long as it does not violate the SSI limits on income and resources outlined above.

It's common for the trustee to pay for services provided to the beneficiary—for example, travel, education, or medical services not provided by Medicaid.

The trustee can also buy the beneficiary noncountable assets without worrying about how much they're worth. That means the beneficiary can own a substantial amount of property without losing eligibility for SSI and Medicaid.

EXAMPLE: Pauline, the trustee of Meg's special needs trust, buys her a special van that Meg, who can't drive an ordinary car, can use. Because the van is a non-countable asset under SSI rules, Meg still qualifies for SSI even though the van is worth much more than $2,000.

Here are some of the main noncountable resources:

One Home of Any Value

Owning a home won't disqualify your loved one from receiving SSI. This provision of the law is extremely important to many people, of course. It means you can leave your loved one a home without worrying that to do so would jeopardize SSI eligibility. It might, however, be better to leave the home in the special needs trust so the trustee can make important decisions about the home—such as selling it someday if your loved one doesn't need it anymore. Also, if your loved one owns the house outright, trust expenditures on maintenance will be counted as in-kind income. But if the trust owns the home, the trust can spend whatever is necessary to maintain the home without affecting the beneficiary's SSI grant.

On the other hand, if the trust owns the home and the beneficiary doesn't pay market rent, SSI might treat the free lodging as in-kind support and maintenance, which would result in a monthly dollar-for-dollar grant reduction up to $213. Whether this would happen depends on whether SSI considers your loved one, as beneficiary of the special needs trust, to have an "equitable" ownership interest in the house. There is still some dispute about this point throughout the country.

One Motor Vehicle

The beneficiary can own one motor vehicle, regardless of value, without affecting SSI eligibility.

EXAMPLE: Conor, the beneficiary of a special needs trust, urges the trustee to buy him a second car. If the trustee spent $10,000 on a second car, Conor's resources would go over the $2,000 resource limit and make him ineligible for SSI. Such a purchase is forbidden by the terms of the trust in this book, because the trustee is required to avoid disbursements that would make Conor ineligible for SSI and Medicaid.

Home Furnishings and Personal Effects

These categories are extremely broad and have no limiting definition. Pretty much anything that can fit in your loved one's home is covered.

EXAMPLE: Bob, a trustee of a special needs trust for his niece Sandra, buys her a $1,200 computer. The computer is not counted as a resource because it's considered a household furnishing. Owning it doesn't affect Sandra's SSI eligibility.

Property Essential to Self-Support

This category encompasses property that is used for work, either as an employee or running a trade or business. There are limits on the value of these items depending on the rate of return they provide and other variables.

More information about this category is available in the guidelines relied on by workers at the Social Security and local district offices. These guidelines, called the *Program Operations Manual Systems* or POMS, are available online at http://policy.ssa.gov/poms.nsf/aboutpoms.

Things Necessary for an Approved Plan of Self-Support

Under a program known as Plan for Achieving Self-Support (PASS), an SSI recipient can submit a plan for self-support to an SSI field office. If the office's PASS expert approves the plan, assets used to fulfill it—for example, tools or business assets—will not be counted as resources.

Under PASS, people set their own work goals and use their own money (often their Social Security Disability Insurance, or SSDI, benefits) to finance them. They are then reimbursed by SSI. They also decide what goods and services they need to reach their goals.

Burial and Life Insurance Policies

Life insurance policies that together have a face value of $1,500 or less aren't counted toward the $2,000 SSI resource limit. Often the face value is the same as the amount that will be paid upon the beneficiary's death, but sometimes a greater amount is payable because dividends have been added to the policy. Burial insurance policies up to $1,500 are also generally not countable resources.

Some Things Special Needs Trusts Can Pay For

out-of-pocket medical and dental expenses	home improvements
medical equipment not provided by Medicaid	computer or electronic equipment
eyeglasses	cable television
exercise equipment	telephones, televisions, and radios
annual independent checkups	cameras
transportation	trips and vacations
motor vehicle	visits to friends
vehicle maintenance	entertainment
vehicle insurance premiums	home furnishings
life insurance premiums	newspaper and magazine subscriptions
physical rehabilitation services	athletic training or competitions
essential dietary needs	personal care attendant or escort
materials for hobbies	vocational rehabilitation or habilitation
tickets for recreational or cultural events	professional services
musical instruments	tuition and expenses connected with education
cosmetics	costs of attending or participating in meetings, conferences, seminars, or training sessions
membership in book, health, record, video, or other clubs	

Gifts of Cash

There is little point in giving an SSI beneficiary cash from a special needs trust. That's because if a beneficiary receives cash or its equivalent (countable resources that can be readily converted to cash, such as a bank CD or shares of stock), the SSI grant will be reduced, dollar-for-dollar, in the month the income is received. (A small exception to this rule is that the first $20 of a gift received in a given month is not counted.) SSI recipients must make regular reports to the Social Security Administration about income they receive.

EXAMPLE: Peter is the trustee of Erica's special needs trust. For Erica's birthday every year, Peter writes her a check from the trust for $100. Erica then goes shopping with the money. Erica must report the receipt of this cash and, as a result, $80 is deducted from her SSI grant.

The trustee can, however, give the beneficiary noncash items that aren't countable resources. These items are not income.

EXAMPLE: Peter stops writing Erica checks and instead starts taking her shopping for her birthday. He lets her pick out $100 worth of birthday gifts and pays for them with trust funds. The gifts—things for her apartment and personal items such as clothing and jewelry—qualify as "personal effects and household furnishings" (discussed above), and Erica's SSI grant stays intact.

If the income is high enough to reduce the SSI grant to zero, the recipient will also lose Medicaid eligibility for that month, in many states.

EXAMPLE: When Erica turns 21, Peter writes her a trust check for $1,000. Because Erica's monthly SSI grant is only $680, Erica will lose her SSI eligibility for that month as well as her Medicaid benefits. Erica's grant will also be reduced by $320 the following month. She will regain her SSI and Medicaid benefits the month after that, provided that the balance of the $1,000 ($320) doesn't send her over the $2,000 resource limit.

The trust in this book, like virtually all special needs trusts, prohibits the trustee from making disbursements like this one, which would make the beneficiary ineligible for SSI and Medicaid. The trustee is also directed to conserve trust assets so they'll be available to the beneficiary for as long as possible. So the trustee should avoid making disbursements that reduce the size of the SSI grant unless there is a very good reason to do so.

To avoid wasting trust funds or interfering with SSI eligibility, trustees almost always make disbursements to a third party on the beneficiary's behalf, not directly to the beneficiary.

EXAMPLE: Jonas, age 35, receives SSI and Medicaid because the brain injury he suffered in a car accident as a teenager left him unable to work. Ten years ago, his mother left $50,000 in her will to a special needs trust set up for Jonas's benefit. The trust's value is now down to $30,000.

The trustee, Jonas's sister Peggy, would like to give Jonas $300 a month in spending money. But she knows that this would result in a dollar-for-dollar reduction of Jonas's SSI grant and so would be a waste of trust money. In addition, it would deplete the trust assets in about eight years. So Peggy doesn't give cash to Jonas, but instead uses trust funds to pay for goods and services he wants. That way, the trust disbursements don't affect his SSI grant.

Payments for Food or Shelter

If the trustee pays for a recipient's food or shelter, the amount paid is considered income to the beneficiary. Specifically, it's called in-kind income or in-kind support and maintenance (ISM). The SSI program treats ISM differently from other types of income.

If the ISM can be assigned a specific value, that amount is deducted from the SSI grant—up to a limit. The amount of the deduction is currently capped at $213. That's one-third of the maximum federal portion of the SSI grant ($579 in 2005) plus $20.

EXAMPLE: Leo, who receives an SSI grant because of his Down syndrome, loves to eat out. Each month Leo's restaurant tab averages $120. If the cost of the meals is picked up by a special needs trust or other outside source, Leo's SSI grant will be reduced by $120.

If Leo had fancier tastes and, courtesy of his special needs trust, spent $500 a month eating out, his grant would also be reduced, but only by $213.

These rules mean that if necessary, a special needs trust can provide your loved one with food or shelter—and still leave him or her with the lion's share of the SSI grant as well as continued eligibility for Medicaid benefits.

EXAMPLE: Maureen has a developmental disability that prevents her from working. She lives with four other people in a group home owned by the parents of one of the tenants and operated by a live-in housemother. Maureen's SSI grant pays for her share of the arrangement, but there is nothing left over. Before Maureen's grandmother died, she created a special needs trust for her and named Maureen's mother Shirley as trustee.

Shirley takes Maureen on several short vacations each year, spending a few nights in a hotel each time. Shirley uses trust funds to pay for Maureen's expenses. SSI counts Maureen's share of hotel and restaurant (shelter and food) expenses—about $300 for each trip—as in-kind income to Maureen. Under the ISM rules, Maureen loses only $213 (the maximum deduction) from her monthly SSI check.

The question of ISM comes up most often with shelter, because the SSI grant is so inadequate when it comes to paying rent in the private housing market. Trust payments for rent or mortgage payments on a house owned by the beneficiary are considered ISM, so they trigger a reduction of the SSI grant. Still, if a beneficiary's shelter needs can be met only through rental assistance from the special needs trust, a $213 reduction in the monthly SSI grant is probably an acceptable price to pay.

EXAMPLE: Sonya, the beneficiary of a special needs trust, receives SSI and Medicaid. When Sonya's group home closes, she is forced to seek shelter at private market rents. She finds a suitable apartment for $1,000/month—considerably more than her $680 SSI grant. The trustee of Sonya's special needs trust decides to pay for all of Sonya's rent and utilities, a total of $1,300 a month.

Trust payments for rent and utilities are ISM, so Sonya's SSI grant will be reduced. The federal portion of the grant is $579, so Sonya will lose only $213 of her grant (1/3 of $579 plus $20) and will continue to be eligible for Medicaid. In other words, Sonya's trust can provide $1,300 in ISM on Sonya's behalf but cost her only a $213 reduction in her monthly SSI grant.

As mentioned earlier, if a special needs trust owns a house or has enough assets to buy one outright, the beneficiary may be able to live in the house rent-free without affecting his or her SSI grant. (See "Resource Limits," above.)

However, if the trust pays other expenses associated with shelter—such as electricity, heat, or water—the amounts are considered ISM, and the grant is reduced dollar-for-dollar up to the $213/month maximum deduction. If the trust were making mortgage payments on the house, those payments would also be considered ISM and would result in an SSI reduction, up to $213/month.

EXAMPLE: Kathy, who uses a wheelchair because of a childhood accident, receives a $639 monthly SSI grant ($579 federal, $60 state) and Medicaid. Kathy is also the beneficiary of a special needs trust created by her mother in her will. Kathy lives in the family home, which is now held in the special needs trust, rent-free. Kathy's SSI grant is not affected by the market value of the shelter because her local SSA office does not count the value of the shelter as in-kind income.

The trust pays for the utilities, which average about $180 a month. Because this amount is considered ISM, Kathy would lose $180/month from her SSI grant.

Computing the Maximum Deduction for ISM

The maximum federal SSI grant increases every year, as the cost of living increases. In 2005, it is $579. One third of this amount is $193; add $20 to get the maximum deduction of $213/month.

For more information on federal and state SSI benefits, visit the Social Security Administration's website at www.ssa.gov.

How can a trustee know when it makes sense for the trust to pay for one of the core items—food or shelter—and take a hit on the SSI grant? Payments from a special needs trust for food or shelter make the most sense when the payment exceeds the maximum reduction—again, $213 in 2005. Payments of smaller amounts should be made from the SSI grant, because payments from the trust would result in a dollar-for-dollar reduction in the grant and waste trust money.

When to Use Trust Funds—And When Not To
If payment for food or shelter is:
• less than $213 (maximum reduction in SSI grant in 2005)...... use the SSI grant
• more than $213 (maximum reduction in SSI grant in 2005), and a necessary expenditure.................... use special needs trust funds

Government Benefits

Food stamps, low-income housing assistance, state-funded cash benefits, and other noncash government benefits don't count as income in kind for purposes of computing an SSI grant.

Gifts of Food or Shelter From Other Sources

When someone gives food or shelter directly to a beneficiary, often there is no way to place a precise dollar value on the gift. In that case, its value is presumed to be one-third of the maximum federal SSI grant, even though its actual value might be much lower. This is called the "presumed maximum value," or PMV.

EXAMPLE: Mohammed, an SSI recipient, lives with his family and receives his food and shelter for free. Because there is no way to put a specific dollar value on this income in kind, SSI simply presumes the value is one-third of the federal SSI grant ($193). So each month Mohammed receives $487 ($193 less than his $680 grant).

Technically, this isn't the trustee's concern. The trustee is responsible only for reporting trust activity; the beneficiary should report other income or income in kind separately in the month it is received. But there are two things the trustee will need to know:

- The maximum reduction to the grant is $213 (in 2005) regardless of the combined value of income in kind received through the trust and from outside resources.

- If the trustee is responsible for making the reports to SSI (for example, if the beneficiary has cognitive impairments and there is no guardian or conservator), then these outside gifts should be reported along with any income in kind provided by the trust.

What the Trustee Cannot Pay For: Countable Assets

If the trustee buys the beneficiary things that are counted as the beneficiary's resources, there is a danger that the $2,000 resource limit will be exceeded, making the beneficiary ineligible for SSI and so for Medicaid. So the trustee must be careful.

The value of property is measured by how much it could be sold for, not what it originally cost.

EXAMPLE 1: Pete receives SSI and Medicaid and is the beneficiary of a special needs trust. He already owns a car that he uses for everyday transportation (not a countable resource). If the trustee spends $5,000 on a motorcycle, which Pete could sell for $4,100, Pete will lose his SSI and Medicaid eligibility. That's because the motorcycle is a countable resource, so its value puts Pete over the $2,000 resource limit.

EXAMPLE 2: Sam also owns a car and a motorcycle. But his cycle would bring only $1,500 if he sold it, so by itself it wouldn't make him ineligible for benefits. But if he owned $500 or more of other nonexempt assets—a savings account, for example—he would lose his SSI and Medicaid eligibility, at least temporarily, because the value of his assets would be more than $2,000.

Chapter Four

Getting Money Into a Special Needs Trust

This chapter takes a closer look at actually getting money into the special needs trust you create for your loved one. In lawyers' language, this is called getting the trust "funded." You also need to decide just what kinds of assets to leave in trust for your loved one; this chapter discusses that issue, too.

What Assets to Put Into a Special Needs Trust

You can hold virtually any type of property in a special needs trust. This includes real estate, collectibles, deposit accounts, stocks, bonds, heirlooms, furniture, jewelry, intellectual property (patents, copyrights, trademarks), businesses, cars, tools, hobby collections, wheelchairs, and just about anything else you can think of.

But a trustee usually has little use for assets that gather dust in an attic or safe deposit box. The trustee needs cash to invest and spend. The primary function of a special needs trust, after all, is to meet needs that aren't covered by SSI and Medicaid. And the trustee does that largely by paying for goods and services that enhance the beneficiary's quality of life.

To raise cash, most trustees sell tangible trust assets and keep the proceeds in liquid assets such as deposit accounts, certificates of deposit, stocks, or other types of property that can easily be converted to cash.

EXAMPLE: Fred was born with a genetic condition known as fragile X syndrome. Among other things, Fred has profound mental deficiencies, qualifying him for SSI and Medicaid. In her will, Fred's mother Jolene leaves all of her property to a special needs trust to be established for Fred's benefit and names her brother Carl as trustee. Jolene leaves a broad array of items, including clothing, furniture, appliances, a boat, a vacation cabin, and the house where Fred grew up and still lives. She leaves almost no liquid assets.

Although Fred can use some of what Jolene left, most of it is not essential to his well-being and has no particular sentimental value to him. What Fred does need is services from various health and disability professionals, which he won't get unless the trust can pay for them. To fulfill his duties as trustee, Carl keeps the house and furniture that Fred can use, but sells everything else to raise cash for Fred's special needs.

Sometimes the beneficiary wants to use tangible property owned by the trust. In that case, there is no point in selling these items. On the other hand, if the trust owns jewelry, for example, it will probably make sense to sell it and invest the proceeds in a way that will produce income.

EXAMPLE: Violet is the trustee of a special needs trust created for her nephew Sam by Sam's mother, Peg. Peg funded the trust with jewelry valued at $14,000, a coin collection worth $5,000, family heirlooms valued at $25,000, and a house in which Sam lives rent-free. The trust document gives Violet the power to sell any property in the trust to further the purpose of the trust.

After checking with Sam, Violet sells the jewelry, coin collection, and heirlooms and invests the $44,000 in an index mutual fund. Sam continues living in the house.

How Much Money Will Your Loved One Need?

If your loved one is the only person you want to provide for after your death, then you'll probably want to put your entire estate into your special needs trust and hope it lasts as long as your loved one needs help. Many people, however, want to leave money not just to a disabled loved one, but to other family members or charities as well. Or you may have the good fortune to have more money than you think your loved one will need. In either case, you'll need to decide how much to leave to the special needs trust and how much to others.

The answer depends on:

- **Your family.** Do you want to divvy your property up evenly or leave a larger share to the special needs trust, on the theory that your other loved ones can take care of themselves? There are no easy answers, but talking with family members may help you reach a conclusion you feel right about

- **Your life insurance.** Many parents of disabled children take out life insurance. This approach lets you leave a sizable sum to the special needs trust under the life insurance policy and still provide for your other family members out of your other property. Types of life insurance are discussed later in this chapter.

- **Your loved one's life expectancy.** Grim as it is, you'll have to take your loved one's life expectancy into account when deciding how much property to leave to the special needs trust. Needless to say, if your loved one's life expectancy is low, then the trust will need less money than if it were long.

- **Your loved one's needs.** Although it involves some guesswork, you need to think about what you want the trust funds to supply for your loved one, and how much money that will take.

So, how should you juggle all of these factors so that you come out with the right funding for your special needs trust? The short answer is, you shouldn't—unless you are a professional in the area of financial management. It's almost impossible to come up with meaningful numbers without the right calculators, and expertise, at your finger tips.

The organization that is most deeply involved with special needs trusts—The Arc—refers its members to the MetLife insurance company for serious number-crunching. Why MetLife? It has a special division, known as MetDESK (Division of Estate Planning for Special Kids), that was created just to help parents in this situation. You can also get help from certified financial planners. (See Chapter 10 for more about them.)

 CONTACTING METLIFE'S SPECIAL NEEDS DIVISION. Call 877-MetDESK (638-3375) or visit the company's website, www.metlife.com/desk.

How to Leave Money to a Special Needs Trust

You'll probably use your will or living trust to leave money or other property to your loved one's special needs trust. There are, however, other ways to make sure property goes to the trust at your death. You may want to use more than one method.

Wills

The best-known estate planning document is the will, or "last will and testament." It's simple to create, and you can use it to set up a special needs trust to take effect at your death. You also specify, in the will, which property you want held in the trust.

EXAMPLE: In her will, Phyllis leaves her valuable art collection to her elder daughter, Katie, and her house to her other daughter, Ruth. She wants to leave her vacation cabin to her son Mickey, but he qualifies for SSI because of a long-term disability, and Phyllis knows that if he inherits valuable property, he will no longer be eligible for SSI and Medicaid. (See Chapter 3.)

So instead of leaving the cabin directly to Mickey, Phyllis uses her will to create a special needs trust and direct that the cabin be held in trust at her death. The part of the will that creates the trust sets out Mickey's rights to benefit from the property.

Will Basics

You can leave almost any kind of property in your will—bank accounts, houses, businesses, personal property of any description, or intellectual property (patents, copyrights, trademarks), to name a few examples.

Contrary to popular belief, there is no need to use magic words or legal jargon in a will. In fact, the more simple and straightforward the language, the better. (Take the will of the French philosopher Rabelais: "I have nothing, I owe a great deal, the rest I leave to the poor.")

A will must, however, be signed in front of at least two witnesses who also sign it, stating that the person making the will appears to be of sound mind. Witnessing is intended to provide protection against forgery, or duress on the part of greedy relatives.

You can prepare a will at any time during your life and change it whenever you wish, provided any changes are signed and witnessed just like the original was. Once you die, the person handling your estate—called an executor, personal representative, or administrator, depending on the circumstances—distributes your property to persons and entities you named in the will to inherit it. These recipients are your will beneficiaries.

What You Can't Leave Through Your Will

You cannot leave an asset through your will if you have already arranged for it to pass under another estate planning document—such as a beneficiary designation form, a revocable living trust, or a joint tenancy deed. In that case, your will won't have any effect on it. (The one exception is in Washington, which has a "superwill" statute allowing a will to override a previous beneficiary designation.)

Jointly owned property. Certain forms of ownership give all co-owners the "right of survivorship." This means that when one owner dies, the surviving co-owner owns the entire property. Forms of ownership that have the right of survivorship include joint tenancy, tenancy by the entirety, and community property with right of survivorship. If you're not sure how you own property with someone else, check the deed or other title document.

Property held in a trust. If you've transferred title to assets to yourself (or someone else) as trustee of a trust, your will has no effect on the asset.

Property for which you've named a beneficiary in a binding document. If you've made an arrangement with an institution that holds an asset—for example, a bank that holds your money—to give your money to a certain beneficiary at your death, then that agreement is legally binding. Your will has no effect on what happens to the property at your death.

EXAMPLE 1: On a beneficiary designation form provided by her bank, Flora names her son Angelo as the pay-on-death beneficiary of her savings account. Her will contradicts this and directs that the same account pass to her daughter Rosa.

Who gets the money in the account? Angelo, because Flora's will has no effect on property for which she names a beneficiary. (See "Beneficiary Designations," below, for more on these forms.)

EXAMPLE 2: Harvey makes a will leaving all his property in equal shares to his nine children. In addition to household furnishings and personal effects (worth a total of about $15,000), Harvey owns a house in joint tenancy with his second wife, Clara. At Harvey's death, Clara will own the house. Harvey's children will split the household furnishings and personal effects in equal shares.

Revocable Living Trusts

Because many wills must go through the probate process—which can be both costly and time-consuming—other estate planning devices have become very popular. One of these is what's known as the revocable living trust.

Like a will, a living trust can be used to create a special needs trust that will become effective at your death. The trust document lists the trust property that should pass to the trust rather than directly to the beneficiary.

EXAMPLE: Adam creates a revocable living trust and transfers title to his main asset, his house, into the trust. As part of the living trust document, Adam creates a special needs trust for the benefit of his son Porter, who has spina bifida. Adam also directs in the revocable living trust document that, upon his death, his house be held in the special needs trust.

A simple living trust works much like a will does to distribute property after your death. But a trust offers one big advantage over a will: trust property does not need to go through probate court proceedings.

Here is how the most common kind of revocable living trust works. You, the "grantor," draft a trust instrument in which you name yourself as "trustee" of the trust and as its initial beneficiary. You transfer any property you want to pass after your death into the trust. Because you are both trustee and beneficiary while you are alive, you have absolute control over the property in the trust. And because the trust is revocable, you can change your mind and take some or all of the property out of the trust at any point.

In the trust document, you direct what is to happen to the trust property after your death. When you die, the person you named in the trust document as "successor trustee" takes over as trustee after you die and distributes the trust property as you instructed.

No one will supervise your successor trustee. The executor you name in your will, on the other hand, will probably be accountable to a probate court. But in both positions you want someone (perhaps the same someone) you trust completely.

A living trust controls only property that's legally held in the trust. As long as your property is formally held in trust, your will has no effect on it.

EXAMPLE 1: After creating a living trust and transferring title to his house to his name as trustee of the trust, Adam makes a will in which he leaves his house directly to Porter. The house will not pass to Porter under the will because it has already been disposed of in Adam's revocable living trust.

EXAMPLE 2: Joyce creates a living trust but forgets to transfer title to her house to her name as trustee of the trust. At her death, the house will pass under her will—not under her trust document, as she had intended.

Property that isn't held in your revocable living trust, or that hasn't been legally passed some other way, will pass under the terms of your will. It is precisely for this reason that most people with a living trust also make a will—to handle any property that hasn't been transferred to the living trust or left through some other means.

EXAMPLE: Julian creates a revocable living trust for his house, business, and investments. He then transfers title to these assets to the trust. He names two of his three children to each take one-third of the property. He leaves the remaining third to a special needs trust for his other child, who has cerebral palsy. Julian also creates a will that leaves any property subject to the will (that is, not held in his trust or left some other way) to the successor trustee of the trust, to be distributed under the terms of the trust document.

After he makes his will and living trust, Julian inherits $200,000 from his sister. He never gets around to adding the money to his revocable living trust. So after his death, the money passes, under Julian's will, to the successor trustee of his trust. The trustee distributes it under the terms of the trust just like the rest of the trust property.

Beneficiary Designations

These days, an increasing amount of property passes not by will or trust but under the terms of beneficiary designations that apply to specific items of property. For example, it's very common for people to name beneficiaries for bank and brokerage accounts, retirement plan money (IRAs, Keoghs, 401(k) plans), securities, and certificates of deposit. The owner of the funds simply uses a form provided by the fund or securities manager to designate who gets the property upon his or her death. Doing so ensures that the named beneficiary—a special needs trust, if you choose—will receive the property without probate.

EXAMPLE: Justine wants to leave everything she owns to her only surviving relative, her younger brother Leonard. When she sets up her IRA, she names Leonard as the person to get the funds at her death. Similarly, Justine names Leonard as the pay-on-death beneficiary for her bank CD, using a form provided by the bank. And she can pass her stocks to Leonard by submitting a "transfer on death" beneficiary form to her broker.

Once she's taken these steps, Leonard will inherit the funds in the IRA, the CD, and the stocks without the need for probate court proceedings.

It all seems simple enough. But if you want property to go to a special needs trust in this way, you may run into problems. That's because until your death the trust will exist only on paper, and not hold any property. Some brokers and banks insist that only the trustee of an existing trust can be named as a beneficiary.

EXAMPLE: Suppose that Leonard has severe brain damage from a childhood accident, and Justine's will creates a special needs trust for him that will take effect after her death. She asks her broker to arrange for her to change the beneficiary on her account from Leonard to the special needs trust. The broker refuses to name the trust as a beneficiary (the trustee, not the trust, legally owns the property). And there is no trustee to name because the trust won't exist until after Justine's death.

There are a couple of ways to get around this problem.

- **Create a revocable living trust now.** You could create a revocable living trust and name the trustee as the pay-on-death beneficiary. Because a trust—even though it's not the special needs trust itself—now exists, the broker will name the trustee as a beneficiary. After your death, your successor trustee will become trustee and qualify to receive the funds. The revocable living trust document would also direct the successor trustee—now the acting trustee—to place the proceeds into a special needs trust.

- **Create the special needs trust now.** You could also go ahead and create the special needs trust while you're alive. Once the special needs trust exists, its trustee would qualify as beneficiary. You could name yourself as the first trustee, and name as successor trustee the person you want to manage the special needs trust after your death. That person would become the trustee at your death and would receive the funds to be placed in the special needs trust. (The trust in this book, however, is designed to take effect only at your death.)

⚠️ MANY TAX-DEFERRED RETIREMENT ACCOUNTS REQUIRE ANNUAL DISTRIBUTIONS TO NAMED BENEFICIARIES AFTER THE ACCOUNT OWNER DIES. An SSI recipient may become ineligible for benefits if he or she, rather than a special needs trust, is named to receive the distributions.

Life Insurance

For many people, buying a life insurance policy is the only way to raise enough money to fund a special needs trust that will help the beneficiary over many years or decades. They might find it impossible to save $100,000 or more during their life out of their paychecks—but they could probably afford a small monthly payment for a $100,000 term life insurance policy.

EXAMPLE: Frank and Jane, a married couple, buy a $100,000 term life insurance policy that will pay out when the surviving spouse dies, as long as they keep the policy in force by paying the premiums. Their cost is very low, roughly $25 a month. When it becomes clear to them that their daughter Emily will need SSI and Medicaid for life because of a childhood accident, they decide to route the insurance proceeds to a special needs trust.

You can make sure that life insurance proceeds go to a special needs trust by creating a revocable living trust and naming the trust (the trustee, actually) as the policy beneficiary. The trust document directs that the policy proceeds go to the special needs trust that goes into effect at your death.

EXAMPLE: Frank and Jane create a revocable living trust. The trust document states that when the second spouse dies, all trust property will go into a special needs trust for their daughter Emily's benefit. They name a close family friend, Elmer, as successor trustee of both the revocable living trust and the special needs trust. They then name Elmer—in his capacity as successor trustee of their revocable living trust—as the beneficiary of their life insurance policy.

When Frank and Jane have both died, the special needs trust takes effect. Elmer, its trustee, receives the proceeds of the life insurance policy and uses the money for Emily's benefit.

There are many, many kinds of life insurance policies (or "products," as the companies call them) including term, universal life, whole life, and more. Term insurance is the simplest; if you die while the policy is in force, your beneficiary gets the proceeds. That's it. Other kinds of policy are part insurance and part investment; they build up equity you can borrow against or cash in. Annuities can give you a steady income throughout retirement.

 MORE INFORMATION ON LIFE INSURANCE OPTIONS. *Plan Your Estate*, by Denis Clifford and Cora Jordan (Nolo), discusses life insurance choices, including how to find the right kind of policy and a solid company.

At least one life insurance company, MetLife, has a separate division specifically to deal with planning for disabled loved ones. Its website is at www.metlife.com/desk.

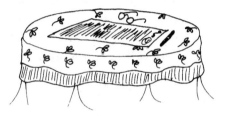

Adding the Beneficiary's Property to the Trust

Once the special needs trust you create is up and running after your death, your loved one may come into some property of his or her own—perhaps a personal injury settlement or an inheritance from a relative. At first thought, it might seem like a good idea to put that money straight into the existing special needs trust, to keep it from being counted as the beneficiary's resource and disqualifying him or her from getting SSI. Bad idea. In fact, adding the beneficiary's own property to the special needs trust would almost certainly make your loved one ineligible for SSI and Medicaid.

That's because if the beneficiary's own property is mixed with the property you left in the special needs trust, it could all be considered the beneficiary's resource. And the total amount would almost certainly exceed the resource limit (currently $2,000) that's imposed on SSI recipients. (Chapter 3 has more on resource and income limits.)

EXAMPLE: Bonnie, who receives SSI and Medicaid, is the beneficiary of a special needs trust created by her father in his will. This has worked out well for ten years. However, Bonnie unexpectedly (of course) wins $10,000 in the state lottery.

She deposits the money in her existing special needs trust—and only later learns that as a result, all of the money in the trust is now considered her resource because her lottery winnings and the original funds from her father were mixed together.

A better alternative than adding property to a third-party trust is to create a separate special needs trust, called a "self-settled" trust. That way, assets in the original trust will remain off-limits as a resource, and eligibility for SSI and Medicaid will not be affected.

 DON'T TRY THIS ON YOUR OWN. Self-settled trusts must meet several federal and state requirements that third-party trusts (the kind you make with this book) are not subject to. For example, self-settled trusts must provide for reimbursement of Medicaid costs from trust assets after the beneficiary's death. If you must decide what to do with funds owned by the beneficiary, see a lawyer. Chapter 10 can help you find and work with one.

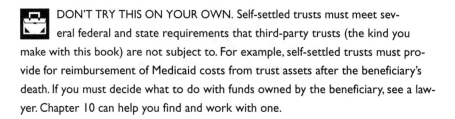

Chapter Five

The Trustee's Job

Choosing someone to manage your special needs trust is possibly your most important task when setting up the trust. After all, it makes no difference what a trust instrument says if the person left in charge doesn't honor its terms. But to make a good decision, you should know what the job entails. This chapter tells you. The next chapter takes you step-by-step through the process of choosing the right trustee.

Once you've chosen someone to act as trustee, you'll need to find out whether he or she is willing to serve. (See Chapter 6.) To help the person you choose make an informed decision, this book contains a letter that explains the job. You'll find it in Appendix B and on the CD-ROM that comes with this book.

Consider Signing Up for a Pooled Trust

If you don't know anyone you feel confident naming as trustee, you may want to consider joining a "pooled trust" instead of setting up your own special needs trust. If you use a pooled trust, you won't need to choose a trustee; the nonprofit organization that administers the trust will serve as trustee. Chapter 7 discusses pooled trusts.

The Trustee's Basic Duties

The trustee's most fundamental legal duty is to always act honestly and put the interests of the trust beneficiary first. This is commonly called the trustee's fiduciary duty.

EXAMPLE: Peter is the trustee of a special needs trust created for his younger brother Paul. Peter's older brother Simon needs money to fund a high-risk start-up company. Wanting to help Simon, Peter invests part of the trust money in Simon's company. Peter has violated his fiduciary duty to act only in Paul's best interests.

The trustee may, however, take actions that indirectly benefit other parties, as long as the sole purpose of the action itself is to help the beneficiary. For example, it's all right to use trust money to buy a home for a beneficiary even if a relative may also live in the home and so also benefit.

A trustee who acts in good faith won't be personally liable for losses caused by his or her actions. Without such a provision, the trustees could be held personally liable for acts that are judged to be unreasonably careless or, to use the legal term, negligent. Negligence is generally defined as the failure to take the proper care that a prudent person would take in similar circumstances.

For instance, if the beneficiary lost several months of SSI and Medicaid eligibility because the trustee forgot to prepare a report required by those programs, the trustee might be considered to have been negligent. The beneficiary, or the beneficiary's guardian, could sue the trustee. But unless the trustee acted in bad faith, he or she would not be liable.

The trustee could still be held accountable for acting in bad faith. Bad faith is when you know (or should know) that what you are doing or not doing will very likely harm the trust or the beneficiary's interests, and you do it anyway. For example, if the trustee makes an obviously unwise investment to help out a friend or other relative, that might be judged to be acting in bad faith.

The trustee must also:

- Avoid any activity that conflicts with the purpose of the trust, which is to supplement your loved one's SSI and Medicaid benefits for as long as possible.

- Respond to the beneficiary's personal needs for goods and services that aren't covered by SSI or Medicaid.

- Keep up with SSI and Medicaid income and resource rules so that the trustee's spending doesn't affect your loved one's eligibility for SSI and Medicaid. (See Chapter 3.)

- Invest and manage trust property following the terms of the trust and state law, in the beneficiary's best interests.

- Keep your disabled loved one and other interested persons (such as anyone who will inherit what's left of trust property upon the death of your loved one) up to date on trust activity.

- Keep accurate records, prepare reports that the SSI and Medicaid programs require, and file necessary federal and state tax returns.

- Go to court, if necessary and financially reasonable, to uphold the trust and require the SSI and Medicaid programs to comply with applicable law.

All of these responsibilities are discussed in this chapter. Remember, as you read, that the trustee is entitled to reasonable compensation from the trust assets.

SHARING THE BURDEN. As you can see, there is a lot on the trustee's plate. You don't have to choose one person to handle everything; these tasks can be shared by two or more cotrustees, handled by experts hired by an individual trustee as needed, or carried out by a trustee working for a pooled trust. The pros and cons of each approach are discussed in Chapter 6.

Working With a Guardian or Conservator

People with disabilities that interfere with their cognitive functioning—such as Down syndrome or organic brain damage—often need someone to help them make sound financial and personal decisions. The same is true of children under 18.

For many people, this assistance comes from an informal advocate—a friend or relative who is always there to help the disabled person cope with the world. But if the disability is severe, a court may need to appoint someone to make decisions on behalf of the beneficiary. This person is usually called a guardian or conservator.

If your loved one has a court-appointed guardian or informal advocate, the trustee of the special needs trust will have to work closely with that person. In essence, they must function as partners, each contributing to the business of meeting the needs of the disabled person. Frequent communications—in person or by telephone or email—are necessary to make sure the guardian and the trustee are on the same page.

EXAMPLE: Nicolas was diagnosed with severe autism when he was three years old. His father died when he was ten. His mother, Theresa, cared for Nicolas until he turned 18. At that time, she asked the probate court to appoint her as conservator, in charge of Nicolas's person and property. She also drafted a special needs trust in her will and left everything to this trust for Nicholas's sole benefit. Her will named her brother Zeke as trustee.

Shortly after Nicholas's 36th birthday, Theresa died. As part of the probate process, Theresa's executor (the person named in her will to wind up her affairs) asked the court to appoint Nicolas's aunt, Katie, as his conservator. As conservator, Katie made all necessary financial and personal decisions for Nicholas while Zeke invested and spent trust assets as he saw fit. Katie couldn't require Zeke to make a disbursement, and Zeke couldn't second-guess any of Katie's decisions.

Katie and Zeke made it a point to talk at least once a month to discuss any issues that had arisen. Zeke relied on Katie to tell him about Nicholas's day-to-day needs because Katie was more attuned to them than Zeke. Similarly, Zeke, who was more comfortable with financial decisions than Katie was, frequently had good suggestions for Katie in that area.

Sometimes, however, the trustee is also the court-appointed guardian. In that case, the roles must be kept strictly separate. For instance, income received by a guardian for the benefit of your loved one must be kept in a separate account—it can't be placed in the trust. Similarly, records of trust activity must be kept separate from records kept as part of the guardianship.

Investing Trust Property

The trustee of your special needs trust must safeguard and invest the trust property, following the instructions in the trust document. This book's trust directs the trustee to act in accordance with the Prudent Investor Act, a law that has been adopted by most states. It makes significant demands on trustees, but also gives them a lot of flexibility in making investments.

THE TRUSTEE CAN GET HELP. Investment decisions can become complex. For that reason, many trustees hire financial advisers to help them come up with a sensible investment strategy that complies with the Prudent Investor Act. Chapter 10 explains how to find such people.

The Prudent Investor Act sets out four major rules for trustees:

- Balance risk against return.
- Diversify investments.
- Act in ways that will further the trust purposes.
- Evaluate the investment portfolio as a whole.

When you examine each of these principles, they seem nothing more than common sense. Basically, they tell the trustee to invest conservatively if the circumstances indicate caution, as is usually the case with a special needs trust. But if the purpose of the trust, the amount of funds available to invest, and the knowledge of the trustee combine to make a more aggressive strategy reasonable under the Act's guiding rules, then it's allowed.

The Old Rules for Investing

Many older state laws limited trustees to certain very low-risk, low-return investments. This gave trustees certainty, but didn't allow them to protect trust funds from being eroded by inflation or to diversify investments. Also, under the old rules, every investment decision could be scrutinized separately if challenged in court. Under the Prudent Investor Act, the trustee's performance as an investor is looked at in its entirety.

A trustee who acts sensibly and follows the Prudent Investor Act rules will not be liable for losses to the trust caused by a particular investment that goes bad. Instead, a court (if there were ever a lawsuit, which is unlikely) would look at the overall performance of the trust investments. Acting sensibly means having a reason for the investments you make that fairly balance the four rules set out above.

A fairly detailed explanation of the Prudent Investor Act is contained in the letter to your trustee set out in Appendix B and on the CD-ROM that comes with the book. Take a look at the investment portion of that letter so you'll have an understanding of what you're asking your trustee to do, and what will happen to trust assets after your death. Because the trust won't take effect until after your death, you won't be investing trust funds, and you don't need to absorb all the details of investment rules yourself.

Spending Trust Money for the Beneficiary

When spending trust property, the trustee will have to keep an eye on two sometimes conflicting goals:

- meeting the trust beneficiary's current special needs (remember, basically that means things other than food and shelter), and
- keeping enough property in the trust to provide for the beneficiary's needs for as long as possible.

Calculating an Annual Budget

How much money can the trustee spend to meet the beneficiary's special needs? At the simplest level, to compute an annual budget, the trustee could divide the value of the trust property by the number of years the beneficiary is expected to live. For example, if the beneficiary's life expectancy is 30 more years, and there is $100,000 in the trust, the trustee could spend about $3,300 each year.

This calculation, of course, doesn't take into account any income that the trust assets might earn. If you assume an average return of 6% a year on the $100,000, then the annual budget would be increased to account for the trust income.

You or your trustee can get help in making these calculations simply by searching for the phrase "investment calculators" on the Internet. But most trustees consult a financial planner or other adviser who's had experience with trust investing and with estimating how much a disabled beneficiary's needs are likely to cost.

FIGURING LIFE EXPECTANCY. Life expectancy tables are easily available on the Internet (search for "life expectancy tables"), but those figures may not apply to someone with a disability. If relevant figures aren't available, the trustee might ask the beneficiary's doctors for a ballpark figure.

Knowing the Beneficiary's Needs

For a special needs trust to benefit your loved one in the way you want it to, the trustee needs to understand and respond to the beneficiary's needs. This won't be a problem if the beneficiary can communicate them clearly. But if the beneficiary's disability impairs the ability to think or communicate, then the more background information the trustee has about the beneficiary, the better. It is up to you to make sure that the trustee will be adequately informed.

A good way to start is to write a "beneficiary information letter." This is a different from the trustee's duties letter mentioned above. This letter sets out your loved one's needs. Writing a beneficiary information letter is a good idea even if the trustee you pick is the person's parent, sibling, other close relative, or friend who already has a deep understanding of the beneficiary's likes, dislikes, proclivities, habits, needs, and desires. That's because your initial choice for trustee may die or become unable, because of circumstances you can't foresee, to serve. And if you use a corporate or professional trustee, or you opt for a pooled trust, the trustee will have only the information you provide. (Chapter 6 discusses professional trustees, and Chapter 7 explains pooled trusts.)

You can give the beneficiary information letter to your trustee, or attach it to your will or revocable living trust (the document you will use to create the special needs trust) so that it will be easily available to the trustee when the time comes.

The letter should cover, among other things, your loved one's family and medical history, education, employment, living situation, social life, routines, and religion. A sample beneficiary information letter is included in Appendix C and on the CD-ROM, to give you an idea of how to approach it.

What to Cover in Your Beneficiary Information Letter

Family history. The names of and contact information for relatives who have a good relationship with your loved one.

General medical history. How the disability came to be, how the person has coped, and what you expect in the future.

Current medical care. Your opinions about whether it is appropriate or could be improved. List doctors and other health care providers, including physical or occupational therapists.

Education. Specific courses and teachers that bear on your loved one's present abilities.

Employment history. Jobs or volunteer positions your loved one has held, if any, or his or her potential for employment.

Current living situation. What you think about the current situation and whether a different one might be better, especially if circumstances change. For instance, perhaps your loved one now lives alone, but you feel strongly that he or she would do better in a group home after you die. If you think the beneficiary needs day care or nursing home facilities, note this fact as well.

Social environment. Relationships with friends and acquaintances.

Day-to-day routines. Favorite foods, daily routines, and recreational likes and dislikes.

Religious proclivities. Religious history, any religious leaders with whom the beneficiary has a relationship, and religious activities.

Preferences for funeral arrangements. What you want to happen when your loved one dies. Do you want a first-class funeral? Burial or cremation? Organ donation? Because the trust may be paying for a funeral and the disposition of last remains—if there is money left in the trust—you'll also want to think about the trust's remainder beneficiaries. If the trustee spends $10,000 on a funeral, that's $10,000 the remainder beneficiaries won't inherit. It's up to you.

Other relevant information. Whatever you think a trustee would need to be fully responsive to your loved one's special needs.

Making the Hard Decisions

Clearly, a disagreeable but essential part of a trustee's job may be to refuse the beneficiary's requests for money when they would make it impossible to provide for the beneficiary's special needs later. This conflict is more likely to occur when the beneficiary's powers of persuasion are intact.

EXAMPLE: Johnny, a 28-year-old former athlete with paraplegia, wants to climb the famed El Capitan monolith in Yosemite National Park. The cost, including paying a highly skilled fellow climber and renting lots of special equipment, will exceed $50,000.

Johnny's special needs trust currently contains assets worth $150,000 and Matthew, the trustee, has computed a rough budget of $10,000 a year. Matthew balks at spending one-third of Johnny's trust fund—and five times the annual budget—on one event, especially because Johnny may live another 50 years and will undoubtedly have many special needs over that period of time. Matthew decides to deny Johnny's request. Unfortunately, his decision causes bad feelings between him and Johnny, and Matthew seriously considers turning his trustee marbles over to somebody else and going home.

People with cognitive disabilities are less likely to confront the trustee over such issues. The trustee's role is likely to be easier when the beneficiary has few or modest needs and can be expected to be content with whatever the trustee provides.

EXAMPLE: Aaron has moderate Down syndrome. He is reasonably self-sufficient, lives in a group home, and works in a sheltered workshop. He receives a partial SSI grant and Medicaid services and is the beneficiary of a special needs trust with funds valued at $200,000. Aaron loves Rolling Stones music and is always looking to add to his collection. He also enjoys visiting a nearby lake that features boat rides and likes to fly several times a year to visit his sister, who lives halfway across the country. The trustee can pay for these expenses for many years without exhausting the trust funds.

Nonetheless, even a beneficiary with a cognitive disability may express a need that the trustee disagrees with or that threatens the fiscal health of the trust.

EXAMPLE: Freddy, who has Asperger syndrome, is the beneficiary of a special needs trust with $150,000 worth of assets. An acquaintance wants Freddy to accompany him on a trip around the world and tells Freddy to ask his trustee for $25,000 to finance it. Freddy's trustee honestly doesn't think that Freddy will enjoy the trip and suspects the acquaintance of trying to take advantage of Freddie's resources. The trustee refuses Freddy's request.

However, sometimes a trustee must make a large expenditure, regardless of how severely it will deplete the trust funds. It's up to the trustee, who must decide based on the circumstances.

EXAMPLE: Valerie, a special needs trust beneficiary, needs a liver transplant. Medicaid may ultimately pick up the cost of the transplant through a local hospital, but Valerie wants to use the Houston Cancer Center, reputedly the best in the country. The extra cost is likely to bankrupt the trust. However, the difference in quality of treatment may be a life-or-death matter that makes Valerie's request a reasonable one.

The trustee is torn—but finally decides that Valerie's parents would want him to use the Houston clinic and let tomorrow take care of itself.

COMMUNICATION IS KEY. A disbursement decision that seems perfectly reasonable to the trustee may seem arbitrary or even punitive to the beneficiary. For instance, if the beneficiary asks the trustee to buy a stereo system, and the trustee goes low-end to stay within the annual budget, the beneficiary may feel frustrated. The greater the effort the trustee makes to explain disbursement decisions to the beneficiary, the more likely it is that relations will remain cordial.

Understanding the Remainder Beneficiary's Interests

The remainder beneficiary is the person you name to inherit the assets, if any, that are left in the special needs trust when the disabled beneficiary dies.

Although the remainder beneficiaries will naturally be interested in how the trust is administered, the trust document you prepare with this book makes it clear that the disabled beneficiary's interests always come first. The trustee must provide for the beneficiary's special needs, even if nothing will be left and even if a remainder beneficiary complains about it.

EXAMPLE: In their wills, Carlos and his wife Maria leave their property to each other and provide that when the second spouse dies, $25,000 will go to their son Ricardo and the rest to a special needs trust for their daughter Rocio, who has a developmental disability. Their wills also provide that Ricardo will receive any property left in the special needs trust at Rocio's death. The leftover property (if any) is the remainder, and Ricardo is the remainder beneficiary.

Carlos and Maria die together in a car accident, and their property (after the $25,000 gift to Ricardo) goes into the special needs trust. The trust property is worth about $250,000. The trustee can spend whatever is necessary to provide for Rocio's special needs, including a trip around the world or tuition at an expensive private college.

Ricardo is resentful and thinks the trustee doesn't need to spend so much on Rocio. The trustee, obeying the terms of the trust, pays no attention to Ricardo's frustrations and concentrates on Rocio's needs.

Managing a Remainder Beneficiary's Property

If, when the special needs trust beneficiary dies, there is money left in the trust, your trustee's job may not end quite yet. That's because if the remainder beneficiary is younger than 18, an adult must manage the property for his or her benefit. Under the terms of the trust document in this book, the trustee is given that job.

The special needs trust document makes the trustee the "custodian" of the remaining property, under a law called the Uniform Transfers to Minors Act (UTMA). The UTMA, which has been adopted in all but two states (Vermont and South Carolina), sets out the custodian's duties. Basically, the job is like that of a trustee—a custodian must prudently invest and spend the money on behalf of the minor beneficiary.

The custodianship ends when the beneficiary reaches a certain age, 21 in most states. This book's trust document directs that the custodianship end when the beneficiary turns 21 unless the state's law requires distribution at age 18. When the custodianship ends, the custodian simply gives any remaining property to the beneficiary.

EXAMPLE: Greta creates a special needs trust in her will for her daughter Frieda. Greta names her grandchildren Hans and Lena as remainder beneficiaries to inherit any funds left in the trust when Frieda dies. About a year after the trust is created (at Greta's death), Frieda dies. At that time, Hans is 23 and Lena is 18.

The trustee gives half of the remaining money to Hans and keeps the other half in a custodial bank account for the benefit of Lena. When Lena turns 21 (the age custodianships end in her state), the trustee gives her what's left in the account outright.

Preserving Eligibility for SSI and Medicaid

Preserving the beneficiary's eligibility for SSI and Medicaid is a crucial part of the trustee's job. That, after all, is the reason for creating the trust in the first place.

Understanding SSI and Medicaid Rules

When spending trust money, the trustee must comply with SSI and Medicaid income and resource rules so that the beneficiary's eligibility for SSI and Medicaid is not compromised. There's a summary of these rules just below and in the trustee's duties letter in Appendix B.

Medicaid and SSI Eligibility Rules: A Summary

- With some exceptions, someone who is eligible for SSI is automatically eligible for Medicaid.
- Someone who owns resources worth more than $2,000 (not counting a home, car, or furnishings), does not qualify for SSI.
- Assets in a special needs trust funded with assets other than the beneficiary's are not counted as a resource.
- If the beneficiary earns income, about half the amount earned is deducted from SSI payments. A beneficiary who earns too much loses SSI eligibility.
- After a $20 exemption, unearned income results in a dollar-for-dollar reduction of the SSI grant. Too much unearned income causes loss of SSI eligibility.
- If the beneficiary receives personal property that can be readily converted to cash, it counts as income in the month it's received and results in a dollar-for-dollar reduction of the SSI grant and possible loss of SSI eligibility for that month.
- If this property is kept, in later months it is counted as a resource.
- If trust funds are spent for food or shelter, the SSI grant is reduced, up to one-third of the federal portion of the grant plus $20. The beneficiary does not lose SSI eligibility (unless, because of other income, the SSI grant is less than the amount deducted).
- If the trustee makes payments to third parties on the beneficiary's behalf for anything other than food or shelter, the payments are not counted as income for purposes of SSI eligibility (unless the items purchased can easily be converted to cash).

The trustee must have a sound understanding of these rules and must keep up to date on any changes. Fortunately, these rules are fairly straightforward and shouldn't prevent a reasonably competent person from serving as trustee. The current rules are set out in plain English as part of the trustee's duties letter in the appendix.

Making Reports to SSI

To remain eligible for SSI and Medicaid, your loved one (or someone authorized to act on his or her behalf) must submit an annual report to the state agency administering the SSI program, as well as reporting monthly on any changes in income, resources, or living arrangements. If your loved one has a legal guardian or conservator, that person will probably do the reporting. Otherwise, the beneficiary (or your trustee, if necessary) will handle the job.

The trustee's job is to make sure that the beneficiary or guardian has accurate information about the trust activity—that is, a record of all disbursements on behalf of the beneficiary and all trust income received during the reporting period. If the trustee buys things and gives them to the beneficiary—that is, if they're not held in the trust—they must be reported monthly.

Disbursements made for property that is held in the trust don't, at least theoretically, need to be reported, because the beneficiary doesn't acquire income or resources as a result. But some SSI offices may take exception to this approach if the beneficiary actually has exclusive use and control over the property in question. The better practice is for the trustee to report all property acquired for the use of the beneficiary with an accompanying explanation that the trust owns the property.

EXAMPLE: Grace, the beneficiary of a special needs trust, wants a motorized wheelchair that has features that aren't available on the chairs that Medicaid will pay for. The trustee buys the chair in the name of the trust by making sure the receipt or bill of sale references the trust as the purchaser. The trustee also itemizes the chair as a trust asset in the trust records. Because the chair is held in trust in this manner, it probably doesn't need to be reported as an asset belonging to Grace. But the trustee decides that it's better to report the chair with an explanation that it's owned by the trust.

Terminating the Trust

Due to advances in medical technologies, people with disabilities who might have survived only until 25 or 30 in the early 20th century can now count on a fairly long life—to age 50 or beyond. For example, the average life expectancy for a child born with Down syndrome is now more than 55. This, of course, means that a special needs trust can last for decades. And, needless to say, massive—and completely unpredictable—changes in agency rules and medical treatments can occur over this period.

To take this uncertainty into account, the special needs trust you create with this book lets the trustee terminate the trust if changed circumstances warrant it.

If the Trust Would Interfere With Eligibility for Benefits

If the trust's continued existence would jeopardize the beneficiary's eligibility for SSI and Medicaid, the trustee has the authority to end the trust.

EXAMPLE: Roberto is the beneficiary of a special needs trust created by his aunt, Mary. Years after Mary dies, changes in SSI and Medicaid eligibility rules make Roberto ineligible for those programs because of the trust assets. To get around these changes in the eligibility rules, the trustee uses his authority under the trust document to terminate the trust and disburse the funds. The trust document directs the trustee to give as much of the trust funds to Roberto as possible without disqualifying him for SSI and Medicaid, and the rest to Arturo, the remainder beneficiary Mary named in the trust.

The trustee does this. Roberto continues receiving SSI and Medicaid, but no longer has the benefits of a special needs trust. Arturo might, for moral or ethical reasons, choose to use the money for Roberto's needs.

If the Trust Is No Longer Needed

A condition that is disabling today may not be disabling in the future. It may be cured or ameliorated by advances in medical technology, or workplace demands may change, allowing someone who cannot now work to enter the job market. Or the SSI and Medicaid programs might change in a way that makes a special needs trust unnecessary.

In light of these possibilities, the trust in this book lets the trustee terminate the trust if the trust isn't necessary to preserve the beneficiary's eligibility for government benefits.

EXAMPLE 1: Vivian uses her revocable living trust to create a special needs trust for her brother Charles, who has hemophilia. Five years after the trust goes into effect at Vivian's death, a cure for hemophilia is found, and Charles no longer needs Medicaid or the protection of the trust. Using the authority granted by the trust document, the trustee ends the trust and distributes the trust assets directly to Charles.

EXAMPLE 2: Joanna, a recipient of SSI and Medicaid, is the beneficiary of a special needs trust. Ten years after the trust takes effect, a national single-payer universal health care system is implemented, and the resource test for SSI is abolished. Because Joanna no longer has to worry about Medicaid or SSI eligibility, the trustee terminates the trust and gives the remaining money to Joanna outright.

Paying Taxes

The trustee must file a separate tax return for the trust every year. The special needs trust you create with this book is an irrevocable trust, meaning it can't be revoked after it takes effect at your death. After it takes effect, the trust must have its own tax ID number, which the trustee can get from the IRS by submitting a simple form (IRS Form SS-4).

Trust income (the money earned from investing trust assets) is taxed at a special trust rate, currently 38%. Because this rate is so much higher than the rate that applies to most individuals, most types of trusts direct the trustee to distribute trust income to the beneficiary rather than keep it in the trust. But in most special needs trusts, the trustee is directed to keep all income in the trust rather than give it directly to the trust beneficiary. That's because letting the beneficiary receive trust income might make him or her ineligible for SSI and Medicaid, defeating the purpose of the trust.

There is a way, however, to give the beneficiary the benefit of trust income but avoid the high trust tax rate. Under IRS rules, trust income that is spent on the beneficiary's behalf is taxed at his or her individual rate, not the trust rate. So if the trustee spends the income on the beneficiary's behalf—and keeps careful records showing that trust income, not assets, was spent—the IRS should tax the income at the beneficiary's lower rate. The trust records must clearly show that the source of the disbursements was the income (interest), not the principal, and that the income was spent for the benefit of the beneficiary, not the trust itself.

EXAMPLE: Joey is the trustee of a special needs trust for his sister Angela. The trust funds are invested in several funds managed by a big brokerage company, which sends Joey a monthly statement showing interest earned on the money. For the current year, the interest amounts to $5,000. In his trust accounting book, Joey records that disbursements for Angela's benefit were made out of this income, not the trust principal.

When the trust taxes are computed, any money spent from the income for Angela's benefit is taxed at Angela's rate. Income that is added to the trust and not disbursed is taxed at the higher trust rate. So is income spent on assets that remain in trust rather than given to the beneficiary outright.

Going to Court

It's very unlikely, but some person or government agency might attack the validity of your special needs trust or question the trustee's actions under its terms. For example, the SSI or Medicaid program might change its rules and try to force the trustee to contribute to the beneficiary's support even though that would deprive the beneficiary of SSI and Medicaid. If this happens, this book's trust authorizes the trustee to defend the trust in whatever forum is available, including court.

Going to court is expensive. It can easily cost $75,000—possibly much more—in attorney's fees. So if a special needs trust has just $75,000 worth of assets, the trustee's decision is easy: terminate the trust. On the other hand, if the trust were worth $500,000, it would probably be worth it to hire a lawyer and challenge the government decision.

If a lawsuit is ever necessary, the trustee will have to hire a lawyer to handle it. The trustee cannot represent the trust in court; only a lawyer can do that. (Chapter 10 discusses finding and working with lawyers.)

The Trustee's Duties Letter

Appendix B contains a long letter that you may want to adapt and send to the person you ask to serve as trustee of the special needs trust you're creating. It's intended to give the trustee an overview of the job and also to be a reference later on, when the trust actually takes effect. You may also find the letter a good source of information if you're interested in more detail about the trustee's responsibilities.

The letter is also on the CD-ROM that comes with this book, so it's easy to tailor it to your situation. Parts of it may not apply to you—for example, if you're appointing a single trustee, you'll want to delete the material on cotrustees.

Choosing a Trustee

Who should you put in charge of the property you're leaving to a disabled loved one in a special needs trust? It's a hugely important question.

Picking a reliable trustee is crucial because trusts operate pretty much on the honor system. It's true that the law imposes a duty on the trustee to honestly and faithfully carry out the trust's terms, but in most cases there is no court supervision. If a beneficiary (or someone acting on behalf of a beneficiary) sues the trustee, a court will examine the trustee's behavior and can remove a trustee who has failed to meet the standards set out by law. But because getting a trustee replaced usually involves an expensive and difficult lawsuit, it doesn't happen often.

After reading Chapter 5, you should have a good idea of what the trustee will be called on to do when managing and spending trust assets. This chapter helps you make the best choice given your individual circumstances.

An Overview of Your Options

You can name one trustee or several, an amateur or a professional. The trust in this book offers several options, one of which will probably work for you:

- an individual trustee—a relative or friend to handle the entire job, and one or more alternates in case your first choice is unavailable (the most common approach)
- a professional trustee, who will manage the trust for a fee, provided the value of the trust property is large enough, usually in the neighborhood of $250,000 to $500,000
- a combination of individuals and professional trustees who will serve as cotrustees, or
- a nonprofit organization that operates a pooled special needs trust.

The pros and cons of each approach are discussed below

Signing Up for a Pooled Trust

If you sign up with a pooled trust, you won't have to pick a trustee—all pooled trusts offer their own trustee services. A pooled or community trust is a special needs trust, run by a nonprofit organization, that has many beneficiaries. You contribute money, which is held in a separate account but pooled with other families' funds for investing. The trustee spends it on behalf of the beneficiaries according to the contributions. (Chapter 7 discusses pooled trusts in detail, and a selected list of pooled trusts is in Appendix A.)

The preferred way to use a pooled trust is to sign up while you are alive. This means you pay an initial fee, sign an agreement that creates an account for you with the pooled trust, and commit to paying an annual fee. You don't have to contribute money to the trust now. Rather, you can provide in your will or living trust that the trust be funded at your death. If you do it this way, your annual fees will be modest up until the trust becomes operational at your death. After that, the fees will be based on the amount of funds you contribute. Fees vary from one pooled trust to another.

Whether or not you fund the trust when you sign up or at your death, you'll have the security of knowing that your disabled loved one's inheritance will be managed by experienced people affiliated with a nonprofit organization intended to benefit the disabled.

Currently, about half the states have pooled trust programs. Most prefer to accept members only from their state. The reason for this restriction is that the trustee of the pooled trust doesn't want to take on the extra burden of keeping up to date on the laws in different states. Most pooled trusts are associated with The Arc (a national organization created to benefit people with developmental disabilities) or the National Alliance for the Mentally Ill (NAMI). Fortunately, their pooled trusts usually are also available to people with other physical and mental disabilities.

Instead of signing up while you are alive, you can direct the executor of your will or the successor trustee of your revocable living trust to hunt for a suitable pooled trust. If the executor or trustee can't find a suitable pooled trust, the inheritance can be routed to the special needs trust you created, as a backup, in your will or revocable living trust. (Chapter 9 tells you how to add language to your will or living trust to accomplish this goal.)

The Ideal Trustee

People who are leaving less than about $250,000 to $500,000 to a loved one's special needs trust commonly choose one or two family members or close friends to serve as trustees. If that's the way you are leaning, take a little time to see how well-suited the people you have in mind are for the trustee role. Ideally, you want trustees who are:

- willing to serve

- able to manage the trust for your loved one's sole benefit

- personally familiar with your loved one's needs

- of roughly the same generation as your loved one

- able to cope with government benefit eligibility rules, and

- able to conduct financial affairs in a consistent, organized, and responsible manner.

Willingness to Serve

The special needs trust you create with this book won't take effect until after your death. When you make your choice for trustee, it is key to make sure now the person you've chosen will be willing to serve then.

EXAMPLE: Loretta, 60 years old and recently widowed, prepares a will in which she creates a special needs trust for the benefit of her blind daughter, Luanne. Loretta names her brother Paul as executor of her will and Luanne's cousin Peter as trustee of the special needs trust. Because Peter and Loretta are very close, she assumes that Peter will agree to serve as trustee but doesn't get around to mentioning it to him.

When Loretta dies ten years later, Peter learns that he has been named as trustee. Surprised and overwhelmed by the idea of taking on this responsibility, Peter refuses the appointment.

You should also name an alternate to serve if, after your death, the person you named isn't willing or able to serve as trustee. (See "Naming Alternate Trustees," below.) If the alternate is also unavailable, your executor (if you create the special needs trust in your will) or successor trustee (if you create it in your living trust) has authority to choose someone else to serve as trustee.

How should you raise the subject with the person you think would make a good trustee? It's not enough just to ask, "Hey, will you serve as trustee of Johnny's special needs trust?" You must take the time to educate the person about what's involved in managing a special needs trust. Appendix B contains a sample "trustee's duties" letter you can give to the potential trustee; it will give your choice an informed basis for deciding whether or not to serve. (You can also find the letter on the CD-ROM that comes with this book.)

If your choice for trustee is concerned about handling the job, consider naming one or more cotrustees to share the responsibility. You can also reassure the prospective trustee that the trust in this book gives him or her authority to hire experts when they're needed. (See "Naming an Individual Trustee," below.)

ASK AGAIN LATER, TOO. The person you initially choose as trustee may not be called on to serve for years or even decades. For example, if you are 50 years old now and have a typical lifespan, the trust won't go into effect for 30 or 35 years. So even if your choice for trustee happily agrees to serve when you first ask, circumstances may change. Check in with your choice every few years so that if necessary, you can amend your will or revocable living trust to name a new trustee for the special needs trust.

No Conflicts of Interest

A special needs trust must be managed for the sole benefit of the beneficiary. This means that the trustee must not act in his or her own interests—or the interests of others—when making investment or spending decisions. Put another way, the trustee must avoid conflicts of interests. Ideally this means that the trustee should not have anything to gain from the trust, either while it is in operation or after it ends.

In real life, however, it is not uncommon to name the same person as both trustee and remainder beneficiary—the person who gets any trust property that is left when the beneficiary dies. This arrangement creates a direct conflict of interest, because every dollar of trust money spent on behalf of the disabled beneficiary is one dollar less that the trustee will receive at the disabled beneficiary's death.

EXAMPLE: Jonas names Ralph to be the trustee of the special needs trust Jonas is creating for his sister Clara. Jonas also provides that Ralph should receive any property left in the trust should Clara die before Ralph. Clara dies ten years after the trust goes into effect, leaving $50,000 in the trust. Under the terms of the trust, Ralph gets the money.

There is no absolute rule against naming the same person as trustee and a remainder beneficiary. An honest and honorable trustee will make decisions based solely on the beneficiary's needs. And if you don't expect the remainder beneficiary to inherit anything—for example, if the trust funds just won't last that long—it may not be a big issue for you.

It's best, though, to name different people to serve as trustee and remainder beneficiary. One path that works for some families is to name a favorite charity as the remainder beneficiary—perhaps a church, senior center, or disability organization such as The Arc.

Familiarity and Empathy With the Beneficiary

A special needs trust is intended to give the beneficiary goods and services that supplement the food and shelter paid for (at least in theory) by the SSI grant. So a special needs trust functions most smoothly if the trustee has a good working knowledge of the beneficiary's needs. This relationship requires good communication that is most likely to exist if the trustee has—or is able to develop—a close personal relationship with the beneficiary. A personal relationship is especially important if the beneficiary's ability to communicate is impaired.

EXAMPLE: Douglas has schizophrenia and lives in a group home. He is the beneficiary of a special needs trust managed by his bother Phil. Douglas has little awareness of the special needs trust or the benefits that it can provide.

Fortunately, Phil is familiar with Douglas's likes and dislikes and makes sure that his special needs are provided for within the limits of the trust funds. For instance, Phil knows that Douglas likes to play video games and so makes sure that he receives a steady supply, courtesy of the trust.

Even if the beneficiary can communicate effectively, familiarity—and empathy—between the trustee and the beneficiary are still important. A good relationship makes it easier for them to negotiate requests that the trustee may be reluctant to grant because they threaten to deplete trust assets. Also, the more familiar a trustee is with a disabled beneficiary, the less likely it is that the trustee's decisions will be based on bias or misconceptions about disabled people that are, unhappily, all too common.

EXAMPLE: Angela, the beneficiary of a special needs trust, became quadriplegic after an automobile accident when she was a girl. She graduated from regular high school thanks to support she received from her family and access accommodations offered by the school. Now Angela wants to attend college and major in communications so she can pursue a career in television broadcasting.

Tomas, the trustee of Angela's trust, is her distant cousin and has not spent much time around Angela or other people with disabilities. Tomas believes that given

Angela's physical condition she is chasing a pipe dream, and rejects her request for tuition and other expenses of college. Tomas thinks he is being reasonable. Angela believes he is making unwarranted assumptions about what she can accomplish.

See Chapter 5 for more on potential disagreements between the beneficiary and the trustee.

Closeness in Age to the Beneficiary

Special needs trusts can last for months, years, or decades. In many instances, their duration is very hard to predict. Today, many people with disabilities live much longer than their doctors or families originally expected. Such dramatic increases in lifespan are due both to medical advances and shifting attitudes towards the disabled. Institutionalization used to be the norm for people with many kinds of disabilities, but now they often live at home and are integrated into mainstream educational and social activities—and live a lot longer as a result.

When you're choosing a trustee, you should do your best to estimate your loved one's likely life span, despite the inherent uncertainty. You need to think about how long you can expect the trustee to be able to manage the trust.

It's best, of course, if your choice for trustee will be around as long as the beneficiary is alive. So if you are creating a special needs trust for your child, who may outlive you by decades, your choice for trustee should be someone closer to your child's age than to yours. On the other hand, if your loved one's disability makes a long life very unlikely, it's reasonable to choose a trustee who is closer to your age.

It's important to keep in mind that the special needs trust you create as part of your will or living trust will kick into action only at your death. If you're in your 40s or 50s, you likely have several decades to live, and it is wise to choose a trustee who is likely to live even longer.

 KEEP YOUR ESTATE PLANNING DOCUMENTS CURRENT. You can amend your will or revocable living trust—and the special needs trust contained in it—right up until your death. So, if you name the trustee when you are in your 40s, you might name someone your age now and, assuming you and the beneficiary live for a significant period of time, later revise the trust to name a new trustee closer to your loved one's age. This approach can be an excellent way to proceed, but it runs somewhat counter to human nature—which is to put the will or revocable living trust in a drawer and never look at it again, happy that you're done with all that stuff.

Willingness to Cope With Government Rules

Your trustee will need to become familiar with the rules that determine eligibility for SSI and Medicaid—and how the special needs trust can be used to supplement the beneficiary's needs without violating these rules. Fortunately, the rules aren't all that difficult to understand. And your trustee can hire an expert in government benefits (a lawyer or nonlawyers) to help out in this area, if necessary. (See Chapter 10.)

As long as the trustee obeys the SSI and Medicaid rules, the trust won't affect the beneficiary's eligibility for SSI and Medicaid. If the rules change, however, the trustee will need to adjust management of the trust accordingly. Some resources that will help the trustee keep up to date are listed in the trustee's duties letter out in Appendix B and on the CD-ROM.

Financial Knowledge and Competence

Using trust money to provide for the special needs of a disabled beneficiary is usually the fun part of being a trustee. Not so much fun is the business side of trust management: making reports, keeping records, filing tax returns, and making appropriate investment decisions. There are plenty of people who are quite comfortable with these tasks, but you may not know any among the group of people who you would naturally choose to be trustee.

EXAMPLE: Marian wants to create a special needs trust in her will for her daughter Jessica, who has cystic fibrosis. Marian's quandary is that there is no candidate for trustee able to handle all aspects of the job.

Jessica has a brother and sister who are close to her but who have problems managing money. Marian's older sister is comfortable with routine financial tasks but is too old to be a viable candidate for trustee. Jessica also has several cousins who might be able to handle the business tasks, but they aren't particularly close to Jessica.

Naming an Individual Trustee

If you have one specific person in mind as your choice for trustee, you'll want to consider all the issues discussed just above.

But remember that even if you don't find the ideal trustee, the person you name can always get help. A trustee who isn't savvy in business matters is authorized, by the trust document, to hire experts for financial advice. For instance, an accountant or tax service could help prepare the trust tax returns, while a financial planner could give advice on investment strategies.

The fact that the trustee gets help from experts doesn't mean that the trustee is off the hook for the various tasks. The trustee's ultimate responsibility for carrying out all the terms of the trust cannot be outsourced (delegated) to anyone else.

It may cost the trust more for your trustee to rely on experts than if you simply named a professional trustee in the first place (if the trust will have enough property to make this option feasible).

If you do stick with a relative or friend as your choice for trustee, you'll want that person to understand that he or she should do as much of the work as possible and use outside experts only when necessary. But just how much of the trust property will be spent on these experts will ultimately be up to the trustee—making the expense hard to predict. On the other hand, if you work with a professional or corporate trustee, you can negotiate a fee up front. (See "Hiring a Corporate or Professional Trustee," below.)

Requiring the Trustee to Consult Advisers

Some special needs trusts name people to serve as "advisers" to the trustee on various issues, such as investment strategies or compliance with SSI and Medicaid rules. These advisers have no legal authority over the trust, but the trustee is required to consult them.

This may sound like an ideal solution if your choice for trustee lacks expertise in certain areas. However, having to consult advisers—who may get pushy—may be the thing that drives your original trustee to resign. If you prefer this option, you'll need to consult an attorney about including it in your special needs trust.

Naming Cotrustees

If you don't have a candidate for trustee who can handle all aspects of the job, and you don't want the trustee to rely on experts you don't know, consider naming more than one trustee, to spread the work around.

For some families, naming cotrustees is a very good way to make sure the trust—and your loved one—will be well looked after.

EXAMPLE: Marla is ten and has Down syndrome. She has three siblings. Only her oldest sister, Beth, is willing to sign on as trustee for Marla's special needs trust. However, Marla's parents are hesitant to put Beth in charge of all the record keeping, investments, trust disbursements, and tax obligations.

The trust property will consist of $500,000 from a "last to survive" life insurance policy taken out by Marla's parents, so the trust will have enough money to pay a professional or corporate trustee to handle the business stuff. So Marla's parents name a corporate trustee and Beth as cotrustees.

But if you go this route, you've got a number of issues to consider. Will the trustees cooperate? Should each be able to act for the trust alone, or must all agree to every action? These issues and some others are discussed next.

Picking People Who Work Well Together

As you can probably imagine, naming cotrustees can cause difficulties. Record keeping, investment decisions, and tax reporting all become problematic unless there is excellent communication among the trustees.

Just finding people willing to work with each other and commit to trustee obligations over a period that might last decades can be difficult. Don't name more than one trustee unless you're confident that they can work together well, on issues that are both financial and emotional, over the long term.

Some Alternatives to Cotrustees

Pay a professional. If the trust contains enough money to pay the fairly hefty fees charged by professional and corporate trustees, this may be the preferable option. (See "Hiring a Corporate or Professional Trustee," below.)

Let one trustee name cotrustees. Why not let your original trustee name cotrustees if needed? This might seem sensible, but it can get messy. For example, it may be hard to get rid of a new trustee if the original one decides the arrangement isn't working. You'll need to see a lawyer if you want your trustee to have this authority.

Name alternates. If you are blessed with a number of good candidates for trustee, consider naming them as alternates rather than as cotrustees. That way, if one person becomes unable to shoulder the burden, the next person in line can take over. (See "Naming Alternate Trustees," below.)

May Cotrustees Act on Their Own?

Cotrustees—and the people, businesses, and institutions they deal with—need to know to whether each of them can act independently or whether they must sign off on everything jointly. For example, if you name two trustees, and one of them wants to write a check from the trust account to pay for a plane ticket for your loved one, must the other one sign the check, too?

In your trust document, you must state whether the trustees should act jointly or independently. Each way has its pros and cons. If you require that all trustees must agree before they can act on behalf of the trust, it may be tough to get any decisions made. There may be gridlock because the trustees disagree or simply because one or more of them is not available when decisions need to be made.

On the other hand, if you let each trustee act independently, you are increasing the chances that mistakes will be made that impair the beneficiary's eligibility for SSI and Medicaid. This is because the more people who have to understand and follow the benefit program eligibility rules, the more likely it is that a misunderstanding will occur.

EXAMPLE: Melissa creates a special needs trust for her daughter Penelope and names Penelope's two siblings as trustees. Each trustee has authority to act independently. Penelope's brother John takes his duties seriously, learns the income and resource rules for SSI eligibility, and is judicious in the disbursements he makes from the trust.

Penelope's sister Gwen, however, is very loving but has little sense of money or program rules. Gwen sees no harm in slipping Penelope cash as needed. When making her report to SSI, Penelope mentions the cash—which, because of its amount, makes her temporarily ineligible for SSI and Medicaid.

Assigning Specific Duties to Each Cotrustee

The trust document in this book does not spell out specific duties for each cotrustee. Instead, the trustees work out a division of labor on their own.

It's possible, however, to give each trustee specific responsibilities. For example, you could give one trustee financial responsibility (investment, spending, taxes, and so on), make another responsible for communicating the beneficiary's needs to the money person, and charge a third trustee with monitoring the other two and doing anything that falls between the cracks. See a lawyer if you want your trust document to be structured in this way.

Hiring a Corporate or Professional Trustee

If you don't want to put the special needs trust funds into the hands of a family member or friend, and a pooled trust doesn't seems like the right choice either, you have another option: You can hire an expert. Financial institutions such as banks, savings and loan institutions, and many brokerage houses have trust departments that will administer a trust for a fee. These are called corporate trustees.

Professional trustees—independent professionals who are in business for themselves—are also widely available. But for most people, professional trustees aren't really an option. Few will assume responsibility for a trust worth less than $250,000; many won't touch anything with less than $500,000 in assets.

If your trust does have enough property to interest a corporate or professional trustee, you may have to do a lot of shopping to find a trustee you are comfortable with. It's always more convenient for the trustee to be located close to where the beneficiary lives, although it's not required.

Talk to at least two or three people before you settle on someone. Here are some questions to ask during your search:

- How much experience does the trustee have in managing special needs trusts?

- Does the trustee have direct experience working with individuals with disabilities?

- Does the trustee have expertise in the Social Security Administration and state Medicaid rules and regulations, or access to this expertise?

- What is the trustee's investment experience?

- Is the trustee open to working with a family member or friend as cotrustee or adviser?

- What are the trustee and investment fees? Are these charged separately or bundled? Are there any hidden transaction or other fees? For example, in addition to a monthly fee measured by a percentage of the trust assets, is there a charge for each disbursement or for issuing reports of trust activity?

- Do the fees suddenly increase when a particular threshold is crossed? For example, do they charge one fee for ten or fewer disbursements and a higher fee for more than ten?

- Exactly what services are included? For example, is the trustee prepared to take care of all the functions discussed in Chapter 5 or will you have to make separate arrangements for one or more of them?

- How will the trustee keep current on the beneficiary's needs?

Some uncertainty is always involved in appointing a corporate or professional trustee. The special needs trust will not take effect until your death—and by that time, the trustee's fees may have gone way up. The minimum value of trusts that the trustee will accept may have risen as well.

EXAMPLE: In her will, Bonnie creates a special needs trust for her grandchild Stacey. The trust will be funded with the proceeds of a $300,000 life insurance policy. Bonnie names Stacey's mother Francine as trustee, but has great reservations about Francine's ability to manage the trust appropriately. So she shops around and finds a professional trustee, who is willing to serve as a cotrustee if the trust has at least $300,000 in assets. Based on that information, Bonnie names that professional trustee as cotrustee.

Bonnie lives for another 20 years without updating her will. When she dies, the professional trustee accepts only trusts worth at least $600,000. The result? Francine will be sole trustee, in complete charge of the trust.

To avoid this problem, it's wise to name one or more alternates to take over if the professional trustee doesn't work out. The next section discusses naming alternates.

Naming Alternate Trustees

Unfortunately, the people you choose as trustee may not be available to serve when the moment arrives. Things happen—people may become ill or die, move to another part of the country, or simply get too busy to serve because of their own responsibilities. Whatever the reason, it's important to name one or more trustees to step in as alternates if it's ever necessary.

EXAMPLE: Edward is creating a special needs trust for his domestic partner Sam, who has three siblings, Drew, Kai, and Chris. Any of them would do just fine as trustee. Edward decides to name Drew as trustee, Kai as alternate if Drew can't or won't serve, and Chris as second alternate, to serve if neither Drew nor Kai is available.

Even if you name an agency or institution, rather than an individual, as trustee, you'll still want to name an alternate. Companies do go out of business. And even though you expect to leave enough money in the trust to make it feasible to hire a corporate or professional trustee, there may not be enough when the trust goes into effect years from now. If a problem such as this does come up, you'll want someone to step in to carry out the terms of the trust.

If you name cotrustees, you've got built-in alternates. That's because the trust document in this book states that if one cotrustee becomes unavailable, the others take over the whole job. Or you can name an alternate for each cotrustee, if you wish.

As with regular trustees, it's important that you contact anyone you want to name as alternate and ask for permission. Otherwise, naming them may be in vain.

If you can't think of anyone you want to name as alternate trustee, you can simply leave out that part of the trust document. If your original choice is someday unavailable, the trust document gives the executor of your will, or the successor trustee of your revocable living trust, power to name a trustee to take over.

Chapter Seven

Joining a Pooled Trust

Instead of creating your own special needs trust and naming a trustee to handle it, you may be able to have your loved one's inheritance managed as part of a group trust. These pooled trusts, also known as a community or master trusts, are managed by nonprofit organizations dedicated to serving disabled people and their families.

Pooled trusts are a great alternative to doing your own special needs trust if you, like many people, can't come up with a logical choice for trustee or don't think the amount of money you plan to leave your loved one justifies a separate trust. Just sign up with a pooled trust, and you can let them handle the rest.

EXAMPLE: Mildred's daughter Cassie will need SSI and Medicaid for the rest of her life. Mildred wants to leave Cassie her property, consisting of a house and $50,000 cash, without jeopardizing Cassie's benefits. A special needs trust is perfect for this purpose, but Mildred can't think of anyone she can count on to assume the role of trustee. And without a trustee, a special needs trust won't work.

Mildred decides to join a pooled trust and have it act as trustee. Because most pooled trusts are run by people dedicated to serving an entire community of disabled persons, Mildred has faith that Cassie will be well taken care of and that her special needs will be met by the pooled trust as she continues to receive SSI and Medicaid benefits.

This chapter gives you a general description of what pooled trusts are and how they work. If you think a pooled trust might work for you, check Appendix A for one in your loved one's state (there's also a national special needs trust).

GET HELP FROM THE ARC. The Arc, a nonprofit organization dedicated to helping families with members who are cognitively impaired, has been a pioneer in the area of pooled trusts. For more information, visit www.thearc.org and download a useful publication called *Pooled Trust Programs for People with Disabilities: A Guide for Families.*

An Overview of Pooled Trusts

Pooled trusts are run by nonprofit organizations set up to expertly and efficiently administer a master special needs trust on behalf of individual beneficiaries with disabilities. Assets are combined and invested together; funds are spent on beneficiaries in proportion to their share of the total amount.

Like snowflakes, no two pooled trusts are exactly alike. Every one has its own fees, menu of available services, and contracts under which it operates. Some offer many options, complicated contracts, and complex fees schedules. Others offer a single agreement and an easy-to-understand fee schedule. Some are organized to provide complete care of beneficiaries while others stick to their knitting—which is to just manage the money in an appropriate manner.

But whatever their differences, all pooled trusts share some basic features that make them worth considering:

- The people managing the trust and its assets will be very knowledgeable about agency rules regarding income and resources and will be able to deal with any questions from the SSI or Medicaid programs.
- The trust directors usually are relatives of people with disabilities and are attuned to that community.
- Even if you don't have a lot of money to leave to your loved one, a pooled trust can give your loved one the benefits of a special needs trust.

If you find a pooled trust that looks like it might work for you, give it a call or visit its website. The information in this chapter should help you understand what you learn from the program itself.

As a general rule, if you plan on using a pooled trust, it is good to set up an account for your loved one during your life, even if you don't put any money in it. It gives you an opportunity to see how the program works and get to know the people who will be caring for your loved one after your death. In fact some pooled trusts insist on this approach so that they can become fully conversant with your loved one's background and needs and your experiences as a caregiver.

Most pooled trusts let you establish an account without funding it immediately. You will be required to pay a small annual renewal fee (in the $75 range) to keep the account active. Then, you can use your will, a living trust, or another estate planning tool such as life insurance to leave property to the account at your death.

EXAMPLE: Craig creates an account for his daughter Ashley with the ABC Pooled Trust. Although he doesn't have to, Craig transfers a $10,000 CD into Ashley's account to avoid paying renewal fees. He also plans to leave $25,000 to the account through his living trust and another $25,000 through a term life insurance policy payable at his death.

If you don't set up an account with a pooled trust during your life, you can direct your executor or successor trustee to join a pooled trust after your death, if one is available. However, this approach deprives you of control over which pooled trust to use (some states have several programs to choose among) and makes it more difficult for the pooled trust to arrange a smooth continuity from your care of the beneficiary to theirs. Also, some pooled trusts charge a higher enrollment fee for accounts set up after the beneficiary's parents have died.

EXAMPLE: Billie, a Tennessee resident, uses her will to create a special needs trust for her developmentally disabled granddaughter Kai. Billie names Kai's brother Thom to serve as trustee when Billie dies, but she's uneasy about whether Thom can do the job.

A few years later Billie learns that Tennessee has a pooled trust that would give Kai the same benefits as the special needs trust she created in her will. Billie visits the pooled trust's website and learns that the trust program offers all the services that, in Billie's opinion, Thom might be unable to handle.

Billie also finds that she can sign up in advance for the trust for a nominal fee and introduce the program's staff to Kai so a smooth transition will be possible. Billie creates an account with the pooled trust and changes her will to eliminate the separate special needs trust and leave Kai's inheritance directly to Kai's pooled trust account.

How Pooled Trusts Came About

Many pooled trusts were created in response to a 1994 change in the Social Security Act. The change authorized disabled persons to shelter their own money (from consideration as a resource by SSI and Medicaid) by placing it with a nonprofit organization for management. The new law also allowed the nonprofits to keep a portion of any funds remaining in the trust after the beneficiary's death—creating a lucrative fundraising opportunity. (Not all pooled trusts impose this requirement.) Existing organizations such as The Arc and the National Association for the Mentally Ill (NAMI), which in some states already operated pooled trusts, were well-placed to expand their trust operations.

Can You Use a Pooled Trust?

A pooled trust might not be an option for you. It all depends on where your loved one lives, what kind of disability he or she has, and the amount of funds you have available to place in the trust.

The Beneficiary's Residence

Pooled trusts currently exist in roughly half the states. (See Appendix A for a list of pooled trusts.) Most of them accept only beneficiaries who live in the state where the trust is established.

EXAMPLE: Ralph's mother Charlene wants to join a pooled trust on Ralph's behalf. Ralph lives in Vermont; his mother lives in California. Even though three are several pooled trusts in California, Charlene can't use them; it is the beneficiary's state of residence that counts. No pooled trust has been established in Vermont, so the only option for Charlene is to try to make arrangements with a pooled trust that is willing to operate across state lines.

If you don't find a pooled trust in your loved one's state, call one in an adjoining state. That program may be able to steer you in the right direction.

Also, at least one pooled trust—Life Services for the Handicapped, Inc., headquartered in New York City—is willing to accept a beneficiary from any state if the program determines that it and the prospective beneficiary are a good match. This trust is open to beneficiaries from different states because, unlike other pooled trusts, it accepts only funds from third parties. (For more on Life Services for the Handicapped, Inc., see "Extra Services," below.)

Why Most Pooled Trusts Stick Close to Home

Most pooled trusts accept only beneficiaries in their own states because these trusts are experts about the state laws that apply to self-settled trusts (trusts funded with the beneficiary's own property). (This book covers only third-party trusts, not self-settled trusts.) Because every state has its own Medicaid rules, rules governing self-settled trusts vary from state to state—and it's very difficult to keep up with them in all states. So most pooled trusts have become expert on the rules of their own state and prefer not to venture into uncharted territory.

Pooled Trusts: A Summary	
Advantages	**Disadvantages**
• If you don't know someone who is willing and competent to be trustee, a pooled trust program can provide one.	• If you change your mind after joining a pooled trust and withdraw, you may forfeit some or all of the enrollment fee you've already paid.
• Pooled trust staff or volunteers often have expertise and experience with people who have disabilities.	• Your agreement with the pooled trust program may give it the right to keep part of any assets that remain in a trust after the beneficiary dies—a result you may not want.
• You can get professional management for trusts that are too small (less than about $250,000) for most banks and trust companies.	
• Pooled trusts usually work closely with banks and trust companies and can tap their investment expertise.	• If the pooled trust requires that it be allowed to keep a portion of any remainder, an unethical program could refuse to disburse funds in an attempt to keep more money for itself.
• Experts manage the trust assets and make the required reports after the fund starts disbursing money.	
• You don't have to worry about what might happen if an individual trustee died or couldn't serve. With a pooled trust, there will always be a trustee.	• Unless you pay extra fees, the trust may operate in a remote and bureaucratic manner, far removed from your loved one's actual needs.
• Management fees are generally much lower than those of banks and trust companies.	• It's unlikely, but the pooled trust program could cease to operate. (Many program contracts address this possibility.)
• You don't have to draft and maintain your own special needs trust document; the program will provide one. It may have been reviewed by Medicaid and SSI to make sure it complies with their rules.	
• The program will probably be overseen by volunteers who likely include legal and financial experts, family members of people with disabilities, and disability advocates.	

Kind of Disability

Virtually all pooled trusts require their beneficiaries to be disabled under Social Security standards set for SSI and SSDI eligibility. They may also require that the beneficiary have the type of disability for which the pooled trust was created in the first place. For instance, pooled trusts set up by The Arc are intended primarily to help people with developmental disabilities. Some may not accept, for example, a polio survivor as a beneficiary.

The reason for this "discrimination" is not sinister. Most pooled trusts are dedicated to providing a broad range of services to people with a certain disability. Staff members trained to deal with autism, for example, may not be comfortable or familiar with the needs of the physically disabled or the blind.

On the other hand, most pooled trusts are willing to at least consider each applicant on a case-by-case basis—which means there is no harm in asking a particular program what its disability requirements are, if any.

This potential hitch in acceptance of your loved one by a pooled trust is another good reason to sign up while you are alive rather than leave this important step to your executor or successor trustee.

Kinds of Property

Most pooled trust programs accept only cash, which can be invested to earn more money for beneficiary. They don't want to be in charge of tangible items that actually cost money because they must be stored, insured, and maintained. So you probably don't want to use a pooled trust if you are leaving tangible property—for example, jewelry, heirlooms, vehicles, or collections—that you would want preserved in its tangible form. If you leave that type of property to the pooled trust, it will be sold for cash.

Some pooled trusts, however, accept a beneficiary's home as a trust asset. But because a home is not counted as a resource by SSI or Medicaid, regardless of its value, you could leave it directly to your loved one and leave the cash part of your loved one's inheritance to the pooled trust.

Amount of Property

All pooled trusts require a minimum level of funding. The "buy-in" amount for a pooled trust is surprisingly affordable, usually between $5,000 and $25,000. That's about 1% to 5% of the minimum amount many banks and trust companies require. A few pooled trusts require more—much more—than these amounts, but in turn offer a higher level of service. (See "Extra Services," below.)

Funding requirements change over time. If you fund the pooled trust while you are alive, you will be sure to meet the minimum funding requirement. If you plan to leave money to the pooled trust requirement, however, you risk having less in your estate than is necessary.

EXAMPLE: Trudy joins the ABC pooled trust for her daughter Emily. At that time, the buy-in is $15,000. Instead of depositing money in Emily's account then, Trudy decides to wait and fund the account with the proceeds of a $25,000 life insurance policy payable at her death.

When Trudy dies 15 years later, however, the buy-in amount has gone up to $50,000. Because Emily will not qualify for the pooled trust and will receive the $25,000 outright, she will lose SSI and Medicaid eligibility.

How Pooled Trusts Work

Most pooled trust programs have similar structures and work in similar ways.

How Pooled Trust Programs Are Organized

The typical pooled trust program is overseen by a board of directors. Directors are commonly volunteer nonprofit organization leaders, members of The Arc or similar organizations, parents and relatives of the disabled, and professional and business leaders. The board sets direction for the organization.

A trustee who is knowledgeable about the resource and income rules of the SSI and Medicaid programs is responsible for managing the trust. The trustee usually works with an independent bank trust department responsible for managing and investing the trust funds for the benefit of the trust beneficiaries.

Finally, many pooled trusts have a social services component dedicated to providing individualized services for each beneficiary of the trust.

Your Contract With the Trust

If you want to put assets into a pooled trust on behalf of a loved one, you sign an agreement authorizing the program or trustee to manage the account as part of the pooled trust.

Typically, the contract also:

- authorizes the program to provide typical special needs services—such as making disbursements appropriate to the beneficiary's needs on a timely basis.

- authorizes specific life services, and

- sets the fees, if any, for those services.

The agreement is discussed in more detail in "Joining a Pooled Trust," below.

Basic Trustee Services Under a Pooled Trust

A pooled trust program usually takes on all the responsibilities of a regular trustee (discussed in Chapter 5). The trustee and program staff hired by the program will:

- invest trust property
- handle requests for disbursements
- keep up to date on government rules regarding eligibility for SSI, Medicaid, and other benefits
- keep records for each beneficiary's account, including your loved one's
- report to various agencies that might be affected by disbursements, such as SSI and Medicaid
- prepare necessary reports for the beneficiary and other interested parties, and
- prepare tax returns.

Extra Services

For many people, it's enough that the pooled trust manages the trust fund and makes disbursements to meet the beneficiary's special needs. But some pooled trusts do much more.

Some beneficiaries, for example, can't make appropriate decisions for themselves and need somebody on the scene to act as a substitute parent. If a court has appointed a guardian or conservator, that person will do the job. (See Chapter 1.) But many adult beneficiaries have no court-appointed guardian.

In that situation, the pooled trust may furnish, for an additional fee, someone who will provide a wide range of services. This person might frequently visit the beneficiary, attend meetings with SSI and Medicaid officials about the beneficiary, and be the beneficiary's advocate in dealings with benefit agencies. This unofficial guardian might also:

- periodically evaluate the beneficiary's health and health care
- evaluate the suitability of living arrangements
- promote and improve social contacts and recreational opportunities
- monitor daytime activities by making random visits and obtaining feedback from the beneficiary

- assist the beneficiary with daily money management

- provide help and support in emergencies, and

- identify and find solutions for problems that affect the beneficiary's quality of life (for example, obtaining psychological help if the beneficiary seems depressed).

If you want these personal one-on-one services, which are often called "life services" or "care coordination," you'll need to meet with the appropriate program personnel to complete a plan and arrange for payment. But be careful. As with any social service program, the services delivered may be less than what were promised. If these services are a major reason you are choosing a pooled trust, ask for some references of people currently receiving the services and get their opinion. Also, use your common sense. The longer and more detailed a plan is, the less likely it is to be read, let alone followed.

As you would expect, highly personalized services cost extra. Each pooled trust offering these services sets its own fees. If there are several pooled trusts available to you, do some comparison shopping; the cost of the services you need will help you determine which trust is the best fit for you and your family. If only one pooled trust is available, you'll have to decide whether the services are worth the price.

Going the Extra Mile: Life Services for the Handicapped, Inc.

This program, based in New York City, accepts beneficiaries from any state as long as the beneficiary seems suitable for the program and funding comes from someone other than the beneficiary. Accounts must be funded with at least $100,000 or $3,000 annually.

After an initial assessment, you pay a one-time membership fee, currently $3,000. This finances a year-long process in which the program and your family (including the beneficiary) get to know each other and fashion a future care plan. A personal advocate, who the program assigns to the beneficiary and his or her family, facilitates this process. Once the planning process is complete and the beneficiary's account is funded, the program begins providing lifetime services.

This program is unique not only because it accepts beneficiaries from all states but also because it pays organizational and administrative costs from money donated through independent fundraising. For more information, visit www.disabledandalone.org or call 800-995-0066.

How Your Funds Are Managed

In a pooled trust, the funds you contribute stay in a separate "subaccount" for accounting purposes, but are combined with other trust funds for investment purposes. This, naturally, saves on administrative fees.

The nonprofit administrator keeps records of the amount of each beneficiary's subaccount and the amount spent for that person. These figures are reported to the SSI and Medicaid programs, to interested members of the beneficiary's family, and to the remainder beneficiaries.

How the Trustee Spends Trust Funds

Like the trustee of an individual special needs trust, the trustee of a typical pooled trust has complete discretion over spending—provided, of course, that disbursements don't make the beneficiary ineligible for SSI, Medicaid, or similar government benefits.

Some trusts require beneficiaries or their representatives to ask for disbursements in writing; other trusts are more informal. Family members have no control over how trust assets are spent, but are encouraged to give the trustee information that will help the trustee make good decisions

When you enroll your loved one in a pooled trust program, you'll probably be asked for lots of information about him or her and how you would like to see the trust funds used. Some programs gather this information in an interview. Others will give you a questionnaire to fill out, probably called something like a "Needs and Resource Assessment."

Typical Questions for the Family

Here is some of the information requested by a pooled trust that is geared towards beneficiaries with mental illness. An entirely different set of questions would be appropriate for a person with cerebral palsy or paraplegia.

- Contact information for you and the beneficiary
- SSI and Medicaid eligibility status
- SSDI, SSA, or Medicare eligibility status
- History of hospitalization over last five years
- Status of current medications, if any
- Cooperativeness in taking meds
- Mental health services received currently
- Contact information for psychiatrist and case manager
- History of conservatorship or guardianship
- Type of crisis beneficiary is most likely to experience
- History of suicide or violence ideation, if any
- History of substance abuse, if any
- History of unannounced departures, if any
- Does relative manage his/her own money?
- What expenses family currently pays for on relative's behalf
- Is family considering making a condo/house available for the beneficiary?
- Beneficiary's private insurance, if any
- Does family desire that relative receive living skills training, recreation, vacations, travel and/or quality of life enhancement out of trust resources? If so, prioritize
- What are your relative's interests and pastimes, and which does the family wish to support/promote via the trust?
- Anything else you think the social services staff or trustee should know.

If the pooled trust you choose is oriented toward a type of disability that is different than your loved one's, it will be up to you to provide the necessary information in an interview or in your own letter. (Chapter 5 discusses writing a "beneficiary information" letter; a sample is in Appendix C.)

The trust will also want to know whom to consult when questions come up about the beneficiary's needs and personal situation. Of course, the more completely you document your wishes and desires regarding care of your loved one, the less likely such consultations will be necessary. But because it's impossible to predict what may happen, the more people you can line up to be available for the trust to confer with, the better.

EXAMPLE: Phil's father joins a pooled trust to handle the inheritance he plans to leave Phil, who needs a wheelchair. Phil gives the trust program personnel lots of information about his needs as a wheelchair user.

After his father dies, Phil develops a severe mental illness and is unable to direct his own needs. The trust is uncertain about what type of treatment to obtain for Phil. Fortunately, Phil's father gave the trust a list of relatives he trusted to act in Phil's best interest. The trust finds a relative who is eager to help and becomes an important liaison between Phil and the pooled trust.

Fees

Generally, pooled trust programs charge much lower management fees than do the trust departments in banks and other financial institutions. Also, as discussed above, many pooled trusts offer life services; trust departments deal just with the money end of things.

Fee amounts, and when and how they are charged, vary from organization to organization. Some fees are due when you join the trust program. Others are paid out of the funds you leave the trust at your death.

Most programs have four types of fees:

- one-time nonrefundable enrollment or set-up fee
- annual renewal fee for unfunded accounts
- management (or "consulting") fee for funded accounts based on the amount of funds, and
- fees for specific life services.

An enrollment or set-up fee can run as little as $100 a year and as much as $3,000 a year, but most are between $500 and $1,000. Annual renewal fees for unfunded trusts are typically $75 to $100. And consulting or management fees tend to be based on the amount you have deposited in the account; they are often between 0.5% and 1.0% of the funds in the account.

Most pooled trusts charge an hourly or flat fee for specific services. These also vary among programs; there is really no typical amount.

Program fees are likely to increase from year to year, so you'll want to get a written statement of fees and payment schedules when you're investigating different pooled trust programs.

Pooled Trust Fees	
Type of Fee	**Typical Amount**
Enrollment	$500 to $1,000
Renewal fees for unfounded trusts	$75 to $100/year
Management	0.5% to 1.0% of the funds in the account
Specific services	Hourly rate or flat fee

Joining a Pooled Trust

If you find a pooled trust that you're really interested in, it's time to ask some detailed questions about how your loved one will be provided for.

Investigating Your Options

No government agency oversees pooled trusts to make sure they are managing assets wisely and honestly. In other words, they are unregulated. There is currently no certification or accreditation process for pooled trust programs.

As discussed above, pooled trusts vary considerably in terms of the services they offer. All offer trust management, investment services, and expertise in federal benefit resource and eligibility rules. The programs tend to differ in:

- the nature of the supplementary services offered (see "Extra Services," above)
- the relationship between the beneficiary and the trust manager
- fees, and
- what happens to money in the account when the beneficiary dies.

For this reason, it's very important to read the materials from any program you are considering and meet with a program representative to discuss the details of the program. Before you sign any papers, the program representative should carefully explain the process, including fees and the scope of services.

In the course of this process, you'll want to pay close attention to your feelings about the place you're dealing with and the people you encounter. For instance, if you get a polished presentation, you may be put off if you are more comfortable with "just plain folks"—or you may be impressed by the professionalism. If you are more confused than enlightened, it may be a sign to shop for a different program.

Here are some questions to ask before entrusting your loved one's inheritance to the program:

- Does the trust program have the financial or volunteer support of one or more well-known disability organizations?

- Does the board of directors include people with expertise or experience in disability, legal, and financial matters?

- Does the program use the services of a reputable bank, trust company, or other financial institution as a trustee or for account management?

- Does the trustee's investment strategy make sense to you?

- Does the program give you clear and comprehensive information about how the trust operates, including its fees and services, or do you feel confused?

- Are you satisfied that the program will always know about your loved one's special needs?

- Do program staffers answer your questions in easy-to-understand language?

- Are staff members knowledgeable about federal and state benefits, laws that affect planning, and the reporting requirements imposed by SSI and Medicaid after the trust is active?

- How happy are other families who use the pooled trust? Ask the program for evaluations it's received, and talk to other families directly if possible.

- Does the program's annual report make it clear that the program is operated in a businesslike manner? (If you're not comfortable deciphering the report, ask someone who is.)

- Is the trust financially self-sufficient, or does it depend on third-party funding that might decrease or, in the case of government funding, be withdrawn altogether? You want to be sure that the program could continue in the absence of those funds.

Signing the Agreement

Every pooled trust operates under a master trust document, which creates the special needs trust to which you'll be contributing. Master trusts contain provisions very similar to those of the special needs trust in this book, plus provisions unique to pooled trusts.

When you join the pooled trust, you sign what's called a "joinder" agreement and pay the one-time nonrefundable enrollment fee described above. The joinder agreement links your loved one to the master trust provisions, describes your duties as the person supplying the money (the grantor), explains what happens if you wish to withdraw the funds later, and specifies what will be done with any funds left in your loved one's account when it terminates. Some joinder agreements also let you describe your preferences for disbursements once the trust is funded and goes into effect.

After you die, the joinder agreement becomes irrevocable, which means any funds that have been put in the account will stay there. The trustee will manage and disburse them for your loved one's benefit under the terms of the trust.

Making an Appropriate Estate Plan to Fund the Trust

You may want to sign an agreement with a pooled trust during your lifetime but wait until your death to have money go into the trust. To make that happen, all you have to do is put some magic words in your will or living trust to route the property you are leaving your loved one to that pooled trust. Chapter 9 tells you how to do this.

There is, however, a risk that the trust won't in fact get funded.

EXAMPLE: Paula joins the Greater Springfield Community Trust on behalf of her sister Annabelle. She does this by signing a joinder agreement, paying a $500 set-up fee, and agreeing to pay an annual renewal fee of $75 until the trust is funded with at least $25,000. Paula's plan is to fund the trust through her will when she dies.

Paula makes the renewal payments while she is alive but dies broke. When the renewal payments stop and the trust is not funded, the account is closed.

If you don't want to sign up with a pooled trust now but would like the executor of your will or the successor trustee of your living trust to explore the possibility of using a pooled trust, you can provide for this in your will or living trust. As a backup measure, you should also establish your own special needs trust (in your will or living trust) to take the property if a suitable pooled trust isn't available when the time comes. (See Chapter 8.)

EXAMPLE: Joe uses his revocable living trust to set up a special needs trust for his niece Sophie. In his living trust document, Joe directs his successor trustee (her sister Catherine) to try to join the ABC Pooled Trust and to place Sophie's inheritance in it. If the ABC Pooled Trust doesn't work out, he directs Catherine to place Sophie's inheritance in the special needs trust established in the living trust document.

What Happens When the Trust Ends

Eventually, the pooled trust account for your loved one will no longer be necessary. The most likely scenario is that the account will end when your loved one dies. But it could also happen if Congress changes benefit laws, the pooled trust itself quits operating, or the trust runs out of money.

When the Beneficiary Dies

You may fully expect that all trust property will have been spent on your loved one by the time he or she dies. But your loved one may die sooner than expected, or if the trust account is quite large, some money may remain at the time of your loved one's death.

If there is money left, some or all of it will go to beneficiaries you name in the joinder agreement. Some of it may stay in the trust, usually to help it provide services that other trust beneficiaries might not be able to afford. This arrangement is required by many pooled trusts.

EXAMPLE: Joyce signs a joinder agreement with the XYZ Pooled Trust. The agreement provides that at her loved one's death, $300 of any money left in the trust account will be kept by the pooled trust. The rest will be paid to the beneficiaries Joyce names.

If the Pooled Trust Stops Operating

All corporations—profit and nonprofit—have the potential for eternal life, and most nonprofits have boards of directors who feel strongly about their organizations and want to keep them going if at all possible. But it's certainly possible that a particular pooled trust program will someday cease operations. There are many possible causes—financial difficulties, a failure of management, or lack of adequate membership, to name a few.

What happens to your money if the pooled trust goes out of business? Most if not all states require defunct nonprofits to distribute any remaining assets to another suitable nonprofit organization. The contract you sign with the pooled trust will probably address this question.

Chapter Eight

Creating Your Special Needs Trust

This chapter shows you how to create a valid special needs trust that you can add to your will or revocable living trust, so that it will take effect at your death.

So you can see what a finished product might look like, sample trust language is included at the end of this chapter. Your trust will undoubtedly look different because of the choices you make as you prepare it.

The language needed to create a special needs trust will probably add between ten and 15 pages to your will or living trust. That may seem like a lot of words (and it is), but the clauses aren't particularly complicated or hard to prepare.

GET HELP WITH OTHER KINDS OF SPECIAL NEEDS TRUSTS. If you want to create a trust that takes effect now (while you are living) or a trust funded with the beneficiary's own money (a "self-settled" trust) you'll need to hire a lawyer. See Chapter 10 for tips on finding one.

Drafting the Trust Document

Now you're ready to start. We'll go through the clauses (called "articles") in order, explaining what each one means and letting you know whether or not you need to make any choices or fill in any information.

Much of the trust document is what's called "boilerplate"—standard language that you must include but that you don't have to fuss with. All special needs trusts require certain language to ensure that the SSI or Medicaid programs won't count property held in the trust as a resource of the beneficiary.

In a few instances, you must choose among several alternative clauses. For example, when you name the trustee, you must pick from different phrases depending on whether you name one trustee or more than one. To help you make these choices, there's always a cross-reference to the part of the book that discusses the issue. If you need some help making the decision, just flip back and read more about your options.

The easiest way to assemble your special needs trust is to use the CD-ROM that comes with this book, which contains all the trust clauses. Just cut and paste the clauses you want into a finished product that's ready to add to your will or living trust. (Instructions for doing that are in Chapter 9).

⚠ DON'T CHANGE TRUST LANGUAGE. The trust in this chapter is designed to provide the maximum flexibility for the trustee and the minimum of extra obligations. But to keep the trust drafting process manageable, this book doesn't offer all potential options. If you want to add, delete, or change anything in this book's trust, you should consult an attorney. You need to be sure that your changes won't:

- interfere with the purpose of the trust
- create an inconsistency within the trust document, or
- change the numbering of the trust clauses (because of the extensive cross-referencing within the trust document).

Chapter 10 has some advice on how to go about finding a lawyer.

Article 1. Creation of the Trust

When property is held in a special needs trust such as the one in this chapter, the SSI and Medicaid programs shouldn't consider it a resource of the beneficiary. To pass legal muster, a special needs trust should be:

- operated for the sole benefit of the disabled beneficiary, and
- irrevocable (that is, it can't be changed) once it goes into effect at your death.

The first clause of your trust document makes sure the trust meets both these requirements. It also identifies both you (the "Grantor") and your disabled loved one (the "Beneficiary").

What you need to do: Fill in your name and the name of the beneficiary.

ARTICLE 1. Creation of Trust

[Your name] (Grantor) is creating this special needs trust for the sole benefit of _[name of beneficiary]_ (Beneficiary). At Grantor's death, this trust will become irrevocable.

Article 2. Purpose of Trust

Next, you state the central purpose of the trust: to provide for your loved one's special needs over and above the support and medical assistance provided by government programs. Should an agency or court be called on to interpret any part of this trust document, the purpose stated here will serve as the overarching guideline. It makes clear beyond any doubt that the trust property may never be considered available as a resource for the purpose of determining eligibility for SSI and Medicaid.

Option 1: If you wish, include here a brief description of the beneficiary's disability. This will inform anyone who reads the trust document about the nature of the beneficiary's disability and clarify why the trust is being created. However, describing a disability is not legally required. Here are some examples:

- The nature of the disability is: major mental illness.
- The nature of the disability is: Down syndrome.
- The nature of the disability is: cystic fibrosis.

Option 1

ARTICLE 2. Purpose of Trust

Beneficiary has a disability and will likely require government assistance after Grantor's death. The nature of the disability is:_____.

Grantor creates this special needs trust to enhance Beneficiary's quality of life while at the same time preserving Beneficiary's eligibility for government support and medical assistance programs, including SSI, Medicaid, or other similar programs. Grantor intends this Declaration of Trust to be interpreted in light of this purpose.

Option 2: If you don't want to describe the disability, simply omit the second sentence of the paragraph, as shown below.

Option 2

ARTICLE 2. Purpose of Trust

Beneficiary has a disability and will likely require government assistance after Grantor's death. Grantor creates this special needs trust to enhance Beneficiary's quality of life while at the same time preserving Beneficiary's eligibility for government support and medical assistance programs, including SSI, Medicaid, or other similar programs. Grantor intends this Declaration of Trust to be interpreted in light of this purpose.

Article 3. Defining Special Needs

This clause explains the types of goods and services you want the trustee to provide for your loved one.

The fact that something isn't mentioned in this list doesn't preclude your trustee from providing it, as long as it doesn't interfere with your loved one's eligibility for government assistance.

What you may want to do: Add items not included and delete ones that you're sure aren't necessary in your circumstances. Or you can just leave the clause as is.

ARTICLE 3. Examples of Special Needs

1. Grantor intends this trust to provide Beneficiary with goods and services to fulfill special needs, which are needs that are not provided for by the support and medical assistance Beneficiary receives from government programs.

2. Special needs include but are not limited to: out-of-pocket medical and dental expenses; medical equipment not provided by Medicaid; eyeglasses; exercise equipment; annual independent checkups; transportation; vehicle maintenance; vehicle insurance premiums; life insurance premiums; physical rehabilitation services; essential dietary needs; materials for hobbies; tickets for recreational or cultural events; musical instruments; cosmetics; home furnishings; home improvements; computer or electronic equipment; cable television; telephones; televisions; radios; cameras; trips; vacations; visits to friends; entertainment; membership in book, health, record, video, or other clubs; newspaper and magazine subscriptions; athletic training or competitions; personal care attendant or escort; vocational rehabilitation or habilitation; professional services; costs of attending or participating in meetings, conferences, seminars, or training sessions; and tuition and expenses connected with all types of technical degree programs and higher education.

Article 4. Identification of Trustees

Here, you state whom you want to serve as trustee of the trust after your death. (Chapters 5 and 6 explain the issues to consider when you're choosing a trustee.)

What you need to do: Once you've decided on your potential choices for the trustee position, choose one trustee (Option 1) or cotrustees (Option 2). Then fill in the names of the trustees and the alternates you've chosen. If you name cotrustees, you are also asked to specify how the trustees may act (independently or jointly) on behalf of the trust.

Option 1: One Trustee at a Time

Picking one person to serve as sole trustee is appropriate if you have a good candidate for trustee firmly in mind in light of the job description set out in Chapter 5. You should also name one or two alternates, called successor trustees, who will serve if your first choice cannot for some reason. They will serve in order—that is, if the first successor trustee were unavailable, the second one would be next in line.

If none of your choices are available, this option allows the executor of your will to name a trustee. If you don't have a will but do have a living trust, the successor trustee of your living trust may name a trustee for the special needs trust.

Option 1: One Trustee at a Time

ARTICLE 4. Trustee

1. The following persons or entities shall serve, in the order listed, as trustee of this special needs trust:

Trustee: _____

First Successor Trustee: _____

Second Successor Trustee: _____

2. If at Grantor's death no trustee named here is available to serve, Grantor's executor may name a trustee to manage this special needs trust. If there is no executor, the successor trustee of Grantor's revocable living trust, if any, may name a trustee to manage this special needs trust.

Option 2: Cotrustees

Use Option 2 if you want two or more trustees to serve together. You must declare whether the cotrustees must agree on all decisions or whether each cotrustee may act independently of the others. (See Chapter 6 for a discussion of the pros and cons of naming cotrustees and requiring them to act together or independently.)

EXAMPLE: When creating a special needs trust for her daughter Susan, Nora names Susan's brother Mick and sister Katie as cotrustees. Nora decides that because Mick and Katie are both very responsible and good at communicating with each other, she trusts them to act independently and make sure the trust purposes are properly carried out.

The trust document states that if one cotrustee becomes unavailable, the others take over the whole job. Or you can name an alternate (successor) for each cotrustee, if you wish. (See Section 2 of the cotrustee article, below.)

If none of your choices for cotrustee are available when needed, this option allows the executor of your will to name a trustee. If you don't have a will but do have a living trust, the successor trustee of your living trust may name a trustee for the special needs trust.

Option 2: Cotrustees

ARTICLE 4. Trustee

1. _____*[names of cotrustees]*_____ shall serve as cotrustees of this trust.

2. If any cotrustee named above is unavailable to serve, the other cotrustee(s) shall continue to serve. If no trustee named above is available to serve, *[names of alternate cotrustee(s)]* shall serve as trustee.

OR

2. If _____*[name of cotrustee]*_____ is unavailable to serve, __*[name of alternate cotrustee]*__ shall serve as a cotrustee instead. If *[name of cotrustee]* is unavailable to serve, _____*[name of cotrustee]*_____ shall serve as a cotrustee instead.

[Repeat as necessary]

3. The cotrustees shall act: ❑ jointly   ❑ independently.

4. The cotrustees shall cooperate with each other to carry out the trust purpose set out in Article 2, to prevent harmful and costly duplication of activities, and to avoid unnecessary delay in making disbursements to Beneficiary.

5. If no cotrustee or successor cotrustee named here is available to serve, Grantor's executor may name a trustee to manage this special needs trust. If there is no executor, the successor trustee of Grantor's revocable living trust, if any, may name a trustee to manage this special needs trust.

6. All references to trustee in this trust document include each cotrustee named in this Article.

Article 5. Powers of Successor Trustees

This article puts any successor trustee in the same position as the original trustee, once a successor trustee takes over. It lets the successor trustee show third parties—banks, for example—that he or she has power to act on behalf the trust.

What you need to do: Nothing. This is just boilerplate.

ARTICLE 5. Powers of Successor Trustees

All authority and powers, including discretionary powers, conferred upon a trustee or cotrustee shall pass to all successor trustees.

Article 6. Contributions to the Trust

This provision requires the trustee to keep the trust as a third-party trust—that is, one funded exclusively with property from someone other than the beneficiary. None of the beneficiary's own assets may be added to the trust.

It's fine, though, to accept property from other third-party sources. For example, once the trust is operational, a relative or friend may wish to throw some money the beneficiary's way. Because a gift made directly to the beneficiary might interfere with the beneficiary's eligibility for SSI and Medicaid, the friend or relative could instead put the money in the special needs trust.

THIS IS CRUCIAL. If the beneficiary comes into some money—for instance, wins the lottery or a lawsuit, or receives a gift or inheritance—those funds may **not** be put into this trust. If any of the beneficiary's property were added to the trust, all the trust assets might be considered the beneficiary's property—and the trust would no longer serve its purpose. Instead, a separate trust should be established for the beneficiary's own funds, with the help of a lawyer. (See Chapter 10 for tips on finding a lawyer.)

What you need to do: Nothing. This is just boilerplate.

ARTICLE 6. Contributions to the Trust

Trustee shall accept contributions to the trust only from third parties. No public assistance, Social Security benefits, or any other earned or unearned income received by Beneficiary shall be added to this trust for any reason.

Article 7. Use of Income and Principal

This article requires that income earned by trust assets be kept in the trust and not be distributed to the beneficiary. The reason is that income distributed to the beneficiary would be deducted dollar-for-dollar from the beneficiary's SSI grant and might interfere with the beneficiary's eligibility for SSI and Medicaid.

For bookkeeping purposes, the retained income must be used first when the trustee spends trust money for the beneficiary's benefit. This way, the income spent for the beneficiary can be taxed as the beneficiary's income (even though he or she doesn't actually get it). That's desirable because typically, the beneficiary's income tax rate is much lower than the trust income tax rate. (See Chapter 5 for more on the rules governing income earned by a special needs trust.)

What you need to do: Nothing.

ARTICLE 7. Use of Income and Principal

Income earned from trust property shall be retained in the trust to be used for trust purposes. When making disbursements for Beneficiary's benefit, Trustee shall keep adequate records to show that current and accumulated trust income is used first, and then trust principal.

Article 8. Trustee's Duty to Seek Government Benefits

This part of the trust document requires the trustee to secure all possible government benefits for the beneficiary. The greater the benefits, the longer the trust funds will last.

What you need to do: Nothing.

ARTICLE 8. Trustee's Duty to Seek Government Benefits

Trustee shall seek support and maintenance of Beneficiary from all available public resources, including but not limited to the Supplemental Security Income program (SSI), the Social Security Disability Insurance program (SSDI), the In-Home Support Services Program, Medicare, Medicaid, or similar or successor programs.

Article 9. Trustee's Discretion Over Disbursements

This provision is the heart and soul of your special needs trust. It gives the trustee unlimited discretion to make disbursements, as long as they:

- are consistent with the trust purpose described in Article 2,
- are made for the sole benefit of the beneficiary (though it's okay for others to benefit indirectly), and
- won't deprive the beneficiary of eligibility for SSI, Medicaid, or similar programs.

What you need to do: Nothing.

ARTICLE 9. Trustee's Discretion Over Disbursements

1. Trustee shall have complete discretion in how the trust property is used, provided that the property is used only for the purpose of helping the Beneficiary, providing Beneficiary with goods and services that supplement those provided by SSI, Medicaid, or similar programs, and never for a purpose that will impair Beneficiary's eligibility for those programs.

2. Trustee shall become and remain knowledgeable about the eligibility requirements for SSI and Medicaid, or similar programs, so that disbursements will not impair Beneficiary's eligibility for those programs. For example, under federal and state regulations in effect at the time Grantor executes this trust, Trustee may supplement Beneficiary's shelter cost without causing a loss of SSI and Medicaid eligibility, even though a portion of the SSI grant might be reduced. But if the laws change and supplementing rent would result in a loss of Medicaid eligibility, Trustee may not make a disbursement for that purpose.

3. Trustee's exercise of discretion under this Article may indirectly benefit another party, such as a relative, caretaker, or remainder beneficiary without violating this Article.

Article 10. Trustee's Duty to File Tax Returns and Make Reports

This article requires the trustee to:

- prepare and file all required trust tax returns
- assemble all information necessary to prepare reports required by government agencies as a condition of eligibility for SSI and Medicaid

- submit all information required by government agencies as a condition of eligibility for SSI and Medicaid or, alternatively, turn over the information to the beneficiary if he or she wants to submit it, and

- share basic information about trust activity with the beneficiary, a guardian or conservator if any, and other interested parties such as a person or entity who has been designated by a government agency to receive funds on the beneficiary's behalf (a representative payee).

The required information about trust activity includes:

- income and contributions (for example, money contributed by a relative) received by the trust,

- what trust income and assets were spent on, and

- the current amount of money in the trust.

This work must be done anyway to compute annual taxes and make reports required by SSI and Medicaid. This article requires that the people most interested in the trust be included in the information loop.

What you need to do: Nothing.

ARTICLE 10. Trustee's Duty to File Tax Returns and Make Reports

1. Trustee shall prepare and file all required trust tax returns.

2. Trustee shall provide to Beneficiary, or Beneficiary's legal guardian, conservator, representative payee, or agent, if any, all information necessary for the reports required by a government agency as a condition of the Beneficiary's continued eligibility for SSI, Medicaid, and other similar benefits.

3. Trustee shall annually provide Beneficiary, Beneficiary's legal guardian, conservator, representative payee, or agent, if any, and the remainder beneficiaries named in Article 12, with written information about trust activity, including an accounting of current trust assets, income earned by the trust, contributions from outside sources made to the trust, disbursements made to meet Beneficiary's special needs, and an accounting of all purchases by Trustee.

4. Upon request, Trustee shall provide the persons named in Section 3 of this article with copies of the trust's annual income tax returns.

Article 11. Termination of the Trust

At some point, the trustee will have to end the trust. This part of the trust document describes what circumstances justify ending the trust and what the trustee should do with any money left in the trust. (Wrapping up the trust is discussed in Chapter 1.)

What you need to do: Nothing.

ARTICLE 11. Termination of the Trust

1. Trustee shall terminate this trust if:

   • Trustee determines that the value of the trust property makes it impractical to administer the trust, or

   • Beneficiary doesn't qualify, or no longer qualifies, for SSI, Medicaid, or similar government benefits, or

   • Trustee determines that changes in Beneficiary's disability make a special needs trust unnecessary, or

   • Beneficiary dies.

2. If Trustee terminates the trust for any reason other than Beneficiary's death, upon termination of the trust, and after all debts and taxes legally owed by the trust have been paid, Trustee shall distribute the trust property and accumulated income to Beneficiary or Beneficiary's legal guardian, conservator, representative payee, or agent, if any, unless such distribution would deprive Beneficiary of needed government benefits. In that event, Trustee shall distribute as much of the property as possible to Beneficiary consistent with maintaining the benefits and distribute the rest of the property to the remainder beneficiaries named in Article 12.

3. If Trustee terminates the trust because of Beneficiary's death, the trust property and accumulated income shall be distributed to the remainder beneficiaries as set out in Article 12.

Article 12. Remainder Beneficiaries

Here, you name someone to inherit any property left in the trust after it's terminated. This "remainder" beneficiary can be one or more people or organizations. You can also name alternate (contingent) remainder beneficiaries.

Usually, the trust ends when the beneficiary dies. But the remainder beneficiary could also inherit if the trust ends for another reason but some trust property can't be given to the beneficiary because it would interfere with eligibility for SSI or Medicaid.

If the remainder beneficiary is under 18 when he or she inherits trust property, an adult must manage the property. It's the trustee's job to act as "custodian" under the Uniform Transfers to Minors Act or pick someone else to do it. A custodian, like a trustee, must manage, invest, and spend the money on behalf of the young beneficiary. Generally, the custodianship ends when the remainder beneficiary reaches age 21. (See Chapter 5 for more on this.)

Finally, this article restates that the trustee must act in the beneficiary's best interest and always put that interest ahead of the remainder beneficiary's interest. Because every disbursement from the trust for the beneficiary's benefit means there is less money left over for the remainder beneficiaries, a natural conflict of interest exists. This conflict is most evident if the trustee is also the remainder beneficiary, which is common but best avoided. (See Chapter 6.) Regardless of any such conflict, the trustee is duty-bound to always put the interests of the primary beneficiary first.

What you need to do: Fill in the names of the remainder beneficiaries and alternates you've chosen. If there's a chance that any of these people could inherit trust property before they're adults, fill in the state in which you (or the beneficiary) lives. If not, you can delete Section 4.

⚠ SPECIAL RULES FOR SOUTH CAROLINA AND VERMONT RESIDENTS. These two states have not adopted the Uniform Transfers to Minors Act, so you cannot direct your trustee to serve as a custodian for a young remainder beneficiary. You'll need to omit section 4 of Article 12.

ARTICLE 12. Remainder Beneficiaries

1. If Trustee terminates this special needs trust, and there are trust assets that Trustee does not distribute to Beneficiary under the terms of Article 11, Trustee shall distribute the remaining trust principal and accumulated income, after all debts and taxes legally owed by the trust have been paid, to ___*[name of remainder beneficiary[ies]].*___

2. If the remainder beneficiary or beneficiaries named in Section 1 of this article fails or fail to survive Beneficiary by 48 hours, Trustee shall distribute the property to *[name of alternate remainder beneficiary[ies]].*

3. While administering this special needs trust, Trustee shall in all cases exercise discretion in accordance with Article 9 and without regard to the interests of any remainder beneficiary named in this article.

4. If, when a remainder beneficiary inherits property under this article, he or she is not yet 18 years old, or, in the opinion of Trustee, is unable to prudently manage the property to be distributed and is under the age of 21, Trustee shall either a) retain that beneficiary's share as a custodian under the Uniform Transfers to Minors Act of ___*[state]*___, or b) name another person to serve as custodian for the property under that Act and distribute the property to that custodian. The custodianship shall end when the remainder beneficiary turns 21 unless the law requires it to end at age 18. When the custodianship ends, the custodian shall distribute any remaining custodial property to the beneficiary.

Article 13. Trustee Powers

This long clause spells out the powers that your trustee will have while administering the trust. The idea here is to give the trustee maximum authority to deal with trust property in a way that will provide the most benefit for the beneficiary, consistent with Article 2 (which states the purpose of the trust, to benefit your loved one and preserve eligibility for SSI and Medicaid) and Article 9 (which gives the trustee unfettered discretion over how trust funds are spent).

What you need to do: Enter the beneficiary's state in the first paragraph.

ARTICLE 13. Trustee Powers

Trustee shall, in addition to the powers given by law, and pursuant to the Prudent Investor Act, if any, enacted by the State of _____ [state] _____, have the following powers applicable to all property held in trust, whether principal or income, and exercisable without order of any court that has jurisdiction over Beneficiary:

1. To retain any property transferred to this trust, and to make such investments and reinvestments and in such proportions as Trustee considers beneficial and prudent in light of the trust purposes set out in Article 2.

2. To (1) participate in any merger or reorganization affecting securities held hereunder at any time; (2) deposit stock under voting agreements; (3) exercise any option to subscribe for stocks, bonds, or debentures; and (4) grant proxies, discretionary or otherwise, to vote shares of stock.

3. To manage, operate, or repair real estate or other property and to lease real estate and other property upon such terms and for such period as Trustee deems advisable.

4. To buy or sell (and to grant options for the sale of) any real or personal property at public or private sale for such prices and upon such terms as Trustee thinks proper.

5. To purchase, maintain, improve, or replace a residence, or any interest in it, where Beneficiary may reside, including any portion of the residence that may be owned by a family member.

6. To permit any person to reside at any real property held in this trust at which Beneficiary is residing, on such terms as Trustee deems proper, for the purpose of providing care, supervision, or simple companionship to Beneficiary.

7. To seek court permission to amend the trust only if necessary to fulfill the trust purposes set out in Article 2.

8. To make loans, but not gifts, for Beneficiary's benefit, provided the loans do not interfere with the trust purposes set out in Article 2.

9. To pay premiums to provide supplementary health insurance for Beneficiary or life insurance policies that may be owned or acquired by the trust. If Trustee is also the insured of any life insurance policy owned by the trust, then Trustee may exercise all rights and incidents of ownership with respect to such policy only in a fiduciary capacity, including the power to change the beneficiary, to surrender or cancel the policy, to assign the policy, to revoke any assignment, to pledge a policy for a loan, or to obtain a loan against the surrender value of the policy from the insurer.

ARTICLE 13. Trustee Powers, continued

10. To start or defend such litigation with respect to the trust or any property of the trust as Trustee deems advisable, at the expense of the trust.

11. To carry, at the expense of the trust, insurance of such kinds and in such amounts as Trustee deems advisable both to protect the trust property against any damage or loss and to protect Trustee against liability with respect to third persons.

12. To prepare and file returns and arrange for payment with respect to all local, state, federal, and foreign taxes incident to this trust, to prepare all necessary fiduciary income tax returns, and to make all necessary and appropriate elections.

13. To prepare and, if necessary, file all reports required of providers of government benefits received by Beneficiary, and to prepare and distribute annual reports of trust activity to Beneficiary and any named remainder beneficiaries.

14. Upon termination of the trust, to pay all debts and taxes determined by the trustee to be legally owed by the trust.

15. To hire attorneys, accountants, investment advisers, financial advisers, tax preparation services, and any other experts should Trustee, in Trustee's unfettered discretion, determine such expertise to be necessary for proper management of the trust.

Article 14. Compensation of Trustee

The issue of compensation is most problematic when you choose a friend or relative to handle the trustee chores.

Although your choice for trustee may initially turn down your offer of compensation, this may change down the road; serving as a trustee can be a time-consuming job. So this trust document entitles the trustee to reimbursement for out-of-pocket costs and reasonable payment for services rendered. The trustee determines what is "reasonable."

There is no easy way to define reasonable fees. You just need to trust your trustee—and given that you are asking him or her to take on such an important job, you surely do.

IF YOU'D RATHER SET OUT A DEFINITE FEE, SEE A LAWYER. If you have concerns about this arrangement, consult an attorney about customizing your trust document to address the issue of the trustee's compensation.

If you choose a corporate or professional trustee, you will be told about the trustee's fee. Most charge a flat rate—usually a percent of the property in the trust. (See Chapter 6.) Some add extra fees for particular actions, such as $50 per disbursement or $25 per phone conversation with the beneficiary. If you're paying a professional trustee, you can add this to the end of the last sentence of the clause: "unless the compensation has been set out in a written agreement between Grantor and Trustee."

What you need to do: Nothing. Unless you're using a professional trustee.

ARTICLE 14. Trustee Compensation

Trustee shall be entitled to reasonable compensation, from trust assets, commensurate with the services actually performed, and to reimbursement for expenses properly incurred. Trustee shall determine what compensation is reasonable.

Article 15. Spendthrift Provisions

Basically, this clause puts the trust property off-limits to everyone but the trustee, including the beneficiary. It prevents the beneficiary from transferring his or her interest in the trust to a third party, and protects trust assets from being grabbed by a creditor if the beneficiary files for bankruptcy. It also makes clear to SSI, Medicaid, and similar benefit programs that the trust property and income are unavailable to the beneficiary and that the trustee may use them only for the purposes stated in the trust document.

What you need to do: Nothing.

ARTICLE 15. Spendthrift Provisions

1. Beneficiary has no right or power, whether alone or in conjunction with others in whatever capacity, to amend, revoke, or terminate this special needs trust. No interest in the income or principal of this trust may be anticipated, assigned, encumbered, or subject to any creditor's claim or legal process.

2. Because trust funds will be conserved and maintained for Beneficiary's special needs, no part of the income or principal shall be construed as part of Beneficiary's "estate" or be subject to the claims of voluntary or involuntary creditors for the provision of care and services (including residential care) to or for Beneficiary by any city, county, or state government; the federal government; or any public or private agency except as otherwise provided in this trust instrument.

Article 16. Bond

This article states that the trustee does not need to obtain a bond. A bond, in the world of trusts, is a kind of insurance policy that would cover losses to the trust if the trustee embezzled trust funds or otherwise violated the duty of trust owed to the beneficiary.

With a special needs trust, there is rarely need for a bond. After all, you're choosing a trustee you trust. And if you did require a bond, the expense would be paid with trust money.

Also, it's possible that something in your trustee's background—a bankruptcy, perhaps, or an old criminal conviction—might make it difficult or even impossible to obtain a bond except at an exorbitant cost. This could prevent your choice from serving, a result you wouldn't want.

 IF YOU WANT A BOND. If you would gain peace of mind by requiring a bond and you're not concerned about the cost, see a lawyer.

What you need to do: Nothing.

ARTICLE 16. Bond

Unless required by a court of competent jurisdiction, Trustee is not required to post a bond.

Article 17. Trustee Not Liable for Good-Faith Actions

This clause states that a trustee who acts in good faith won't be personally liable for losses caused by his or her actions. (See Chapter 1 for more on the trustee's fiduciary duty.).

What you need to do: Nothing.

ARTICLE 17. Trustee Not Liable for Good-Faith Actions

Trustee shall be held harmless for all acts undertaken, or not undertaken, in good faith while Trustee is engaged in administering this special needs trust.

Making the Trust Legal and Effective

Congratulations! If you've worked your way through all those clauses, you should now have the special needs trust language you want. But this collection of clauses doesn't do anything on its own. You **must** make the special needs trust a part of your will or revocable living trust, so that it will take effect at your death.

How to proceed depends on the will or living trust you're starting with. Here are your options:

- If a lawyer drafted your will or revocable living trust, tell the lawyer you want to add this special needs trust to your will or living trust. (Chapter 9 explains in more detail how to have this conversation.)

- If you used a Nolo book or software to prepare your will or revocable living trust, Chapter 9 tells you, step-by-step, how to integrate this special needs trust into your will or trust.

- If you didn't use a lawyer or a Nolo product to create your will or trust, you'll need to amend your living trust, prepare a codicil to the will, or revoke the will and make a new one.

If you don't yet have a will or living trust, see Chapter 9 for some ideas about which document to use and how to get it written.

Keeping the Special Needs Trust Up to Date

Make it a point to review the special needs trust provisions of your will or living trust every few years. You can revise the trust at any time while you are alive—and you may need to if important changes occur in the law or your personal situation.

For example, if a new SSI rule makes the special needs trust obsolete, you would need to amend or revoke it. Or, if your choice for trustee becomes unable to handle the task, you can amend the trust to choose a new trustee.

The good news is that SSI and Medicaid rules regarding third-party special needs trusts (the kind covered in this book) have not changed significantly over the past 20 years. SSI and Medicaid rules regarding the treatment of income and resources have changed somewhat more frequently, but these changes have had little effect on third-party special needs trusts.

Of course, the fact that this area of the law has been stable in the past doesn't mean that a cash-strapped federal or state government won't change the rules in the future. Chapter 10 tells you how to stay current on the rules affecting third-party special needs trusts.

Hiring a Lawyer to Keep You Up to Speed

Most lawyers who specialize in drafting special needs trusts offer updating services as part of their overall package—which can easily cost more than $2,000. The lawyers periodically notify their clients to come in for a checkup—often for an additional fee. Clients are also notified if important changes in SSI and Medicaid rules occur. These update services are intended to give the clients peace of mind that comes with having a knowledgeable professional looking out for their interests. You'll have to decide whether or not this service is worth the price to you. See Chapter 10 for more information on finding lawyers who specialize in this area.

Sample Special Needs Trust Language

Here are the provisions of a special needs trust that will be included in your will or revocable living trust document. See Chapter 9 for an example of an entire estate planning document that includes this special needs trust language.

Special Needs Trust

Article 1. Creation of Trust

Gloria C. Escobar (Grantor) is creating this special needs trust for the sole benefit of Bessie Escobar (Beneficiary). At Grantor's death, this trust will become irrevocable.

Article 2. Purpose of Trust

Beneficiary has a disability and will likely require government assistance after Grantor's death. Grantor creates this special needs trust to enhance Beneficiary's quality of life while at the same time preserving Beneficiary's eligibility for government support and medical assistance programs, including SSI, Medicaid, or other similar programs. Grantor intends this Declaration of Trust to be interpreted in light of this purpose.

Article 3. Examples of Special Needs

1. Grantor intends this trust to provide Beneficiary with goods and services to fulfill special needs, which are needs that are not provided for by the support and medical assistance Beneficiary receives from government programs.

2. Special needs include but are not limited to: out-of-pocket medical and dental expenses; medical equipment not provided by Medicaid; eyeglasses; exercise equipment; annual independent checkups; transportation; vehicle maintenance; vehicle insurance premiums; life insurance premiums; physical rehabilitation services; essential dietary needs; materials for hobbies; tickets for recreational or cultural events; musical instruments; cosmetics; home furnishings; home improvements; computer or electronic equipment; cable television; telephones; televisions; radios; cameras; trips; vacations; visits to friends; entertainment; membership in book, health, record, video, or other clubs; newspaper and magazine subscriptions; athletic training or competitions; personal care attendant or escort; vocational rehabilitation or habilitation; professional services; costs of attending or participating in meetings, conferences, seminars, or training sessions; and tuition and expenses connected with all types of technical degree programs and higher education.

Article 4. Trustee

1. The following persons or entities shall serve, in the order listed, as trustee of this special needs trust:

    Trustee: Rafael M. Escobar
    First Successor Trustee: Jaime L. Sanchez
    Second Successor Trustee: Lola S. Sanchez

2. If at Grantor's death no trustee named here is available to serve, Grantor's executor may name a trustee to manage this special needs trust. If there is no executor, the successor trustee of Grantor's revocable living trust, if any, may name a trustee to manage this special needs trust.

Article 5. Powers of Successor Trustees

All authority and powers, including discretionary powers, conferred upon a trustee or cotrustee shall pass to all successor trustees.

Article 6. Contributions to the Trust

Trustee shall accept contributions to the trust only from third parties. No public assistance, Social Security benefits, or any other earned or unearned income received by Beneficiary shall be added to this trust for any reason.

Article 7. Use of Principal and Income

Income earned from trust property shall be retained in the trust to be used for trust purposes. When making disbursements for Beneficiary's benefit, Trustee shall keep adequate records to show that current and accumulated trust income is used first, and then trust principal.

Article 8. Trustee's Duty to Seek Government Benefits

Trustee shall seek support and maintenance of Beneficiary from all available public resources, including but not limited to the Supplemental Security Income program (SSI), the Social Security Disability Insurance program (SSDI), the In-Home Support Services Program, Medicare, Medicaid, or similar or successor programs.

Article 9. Trustee's Discretion Over Disbursements

1. Trustee shall have complete discretion in how the trust property is used, provided that the property is used only for the purpose of helping the Beneficiary, providing Beneficiary with goods and services that supplement those provided by the SSI and Medicaid programs, or similar programs, and never for a purpose that will impair Beneficiary's eligibility for those programs.

2. Trustee shall become and remain knowledgeable about the eligibility requirements for SSI and Medicaid, or similar programs, so that disbursements will not impair Beneficiary's eligibility for those programs. For example, under federal and state regulations in effect at the time Grantor executes this trust, Trustee may supplement Beneficiary's shelter cost without causing a loss of SSI and Medicaid eligibility, even though a portion of the SSI grant might be reduced. But if the laws change and supplementing rent would result in a loss of Medicaid eligibility, Trustee may not make a disbursement for that purpose.

3. Trustee's exercise of discretion under this Article may indirectly benefit another party, such as a relative, caretaker, or remainder beneficiary without violating this Article.

Article 10. Trustee's Duty to File Tax Returns and Make Reports

1. Trustee shall prepare and file all required trust tax returns.

2. Trustee shall provide to Beneficiary, or Beneficiary's legal guardian, conservator, representative payee, or agent, if any, all information necessary for the reports required by a government agency as a condition of the Beneficiary's continued eligibility for SSI, Medicaid, and other similar benefits.

3. Trustee shall annually provide Beneficiary, Beneficiary's legal guardian, conservator, representative payee, or agent, if any, and the remainder beneficiaries named in Article 12, with written information about trust activity, including an accounting of current trust assets, income earned by the trust, contributions from outside sources made to the trust, disbursements made to meet Beneficiary's special needs, and an accounting of all purchases by Trustee.

4. Upon request, Trustee shall provide the persons named in Section 3 of this article with copies of the trust's annual income tax returns.

Article 11. Termination of Trust

1. Trustee shall terminate this trust if:

   • Trustee determines that the value of the trust property makes it impractical to administer the trust, or

   • Beneficiary doesn't qualify, or no longer qualifies, for SSI, Medicaid, or similar government benefits, or

   • Trustee determines that changes in Beneficiary's disability make a special needs trust unnecessary, or

   • Beneficiary dies.

2. If Trustee terminates this trust for any reason other than Beneficiary's death, upon termination of the trust, and after all debts and taxes legally owed by the trust have been paid, Trustee shall distribute the trust property and accumulated income to Beneficiary or Beneficiary's legal guardian, conservator, representative payee, or agent, if any, unless such distribution would deprive Beneficiary of needed government benefits. In that event,

Trustee shall distribute as much of the property as possible to Beneficiary consistent with maintaining the benefits and distribute the rest of the property to the remainder beneficiaries named in Article 12.

3. If Trustee terminates the trust because of Beneficiary's death, the trust property and accumulated income shall be distributed to the remainder beneficiaries as set out in Article 12.

Article 12. Remainder Beneficiaries

1. If Trustee terminates this special needs trust and there are trust assets that Trustee does not distribute to Beneficiary under the terms of Article 11, Trustee shall distribute the remaining trust principal and accumulated income, after all debts and taxes legally owed by the trust have been paid, to Lola S. Sanchez.

2. If the remainder beneficiary or beneficiaries named in Section 1 of this article fails or fail to survive Beneficiary by 48 hours, Trustee shall distribute the property to Maria R. Sanchez.

3. While administering this special needs trust, Trustee shall in all cases exercise discretion in accordance with Article 9 and without regard to the interests of any remainder beneficiary named in this article.

4. If, when a remainder beneficiary inherits property under this article, he or she is not yet 18 years old, or, in the opinion of Trustee, is unable to prudently manage the property to be distributed and is under the age of 21, Trustee shall either a) retain that beneficiary's share as a custodian under the Uniform Transfers to Minors Act of Kentucky, or b) name another person to serve as custodian for the property under that Act and distribute the property to that custodian. The custodianship shall end when the remainder beneficiary turns 21 unless the law requires it to end at age 18. When the custodianship ends, the custodian shall distribute any remaining custodial property to the beneficiary.

Article 13. Trustee Powers

Trustee shall, in addition to the powers given by law, and pursuant to the Prudent Investor Act, if any, enacted by the State of Kentucky, have the following powers applicable to all property held in trust, whether principal or income, and exercisable without order of any court that has jurisdiction over Beneficiary:

1. To retain any property transferred to this trust, and to make such investments and reinvestments and in such proportions as Trustee considers beneficial and prudent in light of the trust purposes set out in Article 2.

2. To (1) participate in any merger or reorganization affecting securities held hereunder at any time; (2) deposit stock under voting agreements; (3) exercise any option to subscribe for stocks, bonds, or debentures; and (4) grant proxies, discretionary or otherwise, to vote shares of stock.

3. To manage, operate, or repair real estate or other property and to lease real estate and other property upon such terms and for such period as Trustee deems advisable.

4. To buy or sell (and to grant options for the sale of) any real or personal property at public or private sale for such prices and upon such terms as Trustee thinks proper.

5. To purchase, maintain, improve, or replace a residence, or any interest in it, where Beneficiary may reside, including any portion of the residence that may be owned by a family member.

6. To permit any person to reside at any real property held in this trust at which Beneficiary is residing, on such terms as Trustee deems proper, for the purpose of providing care, supervision, or simple companionship to Beneficiary.

7. To seek court permission to amend the trust only if necessary to fulfill the trust purposes set out in Article 2.

8. To make loans, but not gifts, for Beneficiary's benefit, provided the loans do not interfere with the trust purposes set out in Article 2.

9. To pay premiums to provide supplementary health insurance for Beneficiary or life insurance policies that may be owned or acquired by the trust. If Trustee is also the insured of any life insurance policy owned by the trust, then Trustee may exercise all rights and incidents of ownership with respect to such policy only in a fiduciary capacity, including the power to change the beneficiary, to surrender or cancel the policy, to assign the policy, to revoke any assignment, to pledge a policy for a loan, or to obtain a loan against the surrender value of the policy from the insurer.

10. To start or defend such litigation with respect to the trust or any property of the trust as Trustee deems advisable, at the expense of the trust.

11. To carry, at the expense of the trust, insurance of such kinds and in such amounts as Trustee deems advisable both to protect the trust property against any damage or loss and to protect Trustee against liability with respect to third persons.

12. To prepare and file returns and arrange for payment with respect to all local, state, federal, and foreign taxes incident to this trust, to prepare all necessary fiduciary income tax returns, and to make all necessary and appropriate elections.

13. To prepare and, if necessary, file all reports required of providers of government benefits received by Beneficiary, and to prepare and distribute annual reports of trust activity to Beneficiary and any named remainder beneficiaries.

14. Upon termination of the trust, to pay all debts and taxes determined by the trustee to be legally owed by the trust.

15. To hire attorneys, accountants, investment advisers, financial advisers, tax preparation services, and any other experts should Trustee, in Trustee's unfettered discretion, determine such expertise to be necessary for proper management of the trust.

Article 14. Trustee Compensation

Trustee shall be entitled to reasonable compensation, from trust assets, commensurate with the services actually performed, and to reimbursement for expenses properly incurred. Trustee shall determine what compensation is reasonable.

Article 15. Spendthrift Provisions

1. Beneficiary has no right or power, whether alone or in conjunction with others in whatever capacity, to amend, revoke, or terminate this special needs trust. No interest in the income or principal of this trust may be anticipated, assigned, encumbered, or subject to any creditor's claim or legal process.

2. Because trust funds will be conserved and maintained for Beneficiary's special needs, no part of the income or principal shall be construed as part of Beneficiary's "estate" or be subject to the claims of voluntary or involuntary creditors for the provision of care and services (including residential care) to or for Beneficiary by any city, county, or state government; the federal government; or any public or private agency except as otherwise provided in this trust instrument.

Article 16. Bond

Unless required by a court of competent jurisdiction, Trustee is not required to post a bond.

Article 17. Trustee's Liability for Good-Faith Actions

Trustee shall be held harmless for all acts undertaken, or not undertaken, in good faith while Trustee is engaged in administering this special needs trust.

by signing and recording a new deed to your house, putting it in the trust. And you must do the same any time you add new property to the trust.

Advantages of a Living Trust

A trust may sound unfamiliar and complicated, but for most people, a simple revocable living trust is no more difficult to prepare than the average will. It will be more expensive only if your wishes are complex and you need a lawyer's advice and drafting skills. For instance, if you want to use a trust to leave certain property to someone for life and then have it pass to others upon that person's death, you'll probably need a lawyer's help.

Here are some reasons why a revocable living trust is, for most people, probably the better document to use if you are including a special needs trust.

No probate. The big advantage of a living trust is that after your death, probate court proceedings are not required. Probate, which is usually necessary for property left through a will, can be a long and expensive detour (because most people hire a lawyer to handle it). Property left in a revocable living trust, however, can go quickly and directly to the people who inherit it, without probate court involvement. The person you name to serve as successor trustee handles it.

Speedy funding and operation of the special needs trust. With a revocable living trust, the special needs trust can quickly be funded and put into effect after your death. This is, again, because living trusts don't need to go through probate. Most wills, however, have to go through probate before the special needs trust can become effective. This can mean a delay of several months to a year or even more, during which time your loved one won't enjoy the trust's benefits.

Easier funding of the special needs trust with life insurance proceeds. A revocable living trust is an ideal way to route life insurance proceeds to a special needs trust. You name the successor trustee of your revocable living trust as the beneficiary of the policy. When you die, your successor trustee distributes the proceeds as you direct in the living trust document.

If you already have a will, you may want to create a revocable living trust in addition, even if its only purpose is to create your special needs trust. You can, if you wish, put some of the property you left in your will into the living trust. The property will pass under the terms of the trust document, because a will controls only property that hasn't been passed in some other legally binding way.

If You Already Have a Will or Trust

If you already have a will or living trust, you can add a special needs trust to your existing document.

Modifying a Will

If you have a will and don't want to create a revocable living trust specifically for the purpose of funding the special needs trust (another possibility), there are two ways to add a special needs trust to the will.

 Do not, under any circumstances, physically alter a signed and witnessed will. Changes made this way are not legally valid.

Make a codicil. The only legal way to change an existing will is with a document called a codicil. A codicil describes your changes and must be signed in front of witnesses (three in Vermont, two in other states) just like an original will. The problem with codicils (especially when there is more than one) is that they can sometimes cause ambiguities in the will, making it difficult or even impossible for your executor to carry out your wishes.

Make a new will. Because making a codicil is just about as much trouble as making a new will, most people just revoke an old will (by tearing it up) and start over. That way you end up with just one document, which is simpler for your executor.

WHEN TO SEE A LAWYER. If a lawyer drafted your will, you may want to talk to the lawyer before destroying your will—especially if you have a continuing relationship with the lawyer or you don't fully understand the will.

Modifying a Revocable Living Trust

If you already have a revocable living trust and have transferred property into your name as trustee, you'll want to amend the trust rather than start over. Unlike with a will, it's usually easier to amend a living trust than tear it up and create a new one.

The reason has to do with keeping the paperwork neat and logical. If you've already executed title documents for property transferred to the trust—real estate, for example—the title documents probably refer to the date you created the trust. For example, a typical deed transferring real estate to a trust might read: "Harry A. Smith conveys XXX property to Harry A. Smith as Trustee of the Harry A. Smith Revocable Living Trust dated February 4, 20xx." Creating a new trust document— with a later date—would make it appear that the property had been added to a trust that didn't yet exist.

If the only property items you hold in trust do not have title documents—for example, household furnishings—and you didn't create any kind of transfer document, you can choose between amending the trust and creating a new one.

When you amend your trust document, be careful to do two things:

- make it very clear in your amendment that you are creating a special needs trust, and

- study the trust document to see whether any language in it needs to be changed to refer to the new special needs trust.

Below is a sample trust amendment that adds a special needs trust.

Amendment to Living Trust

This amendment to the James P. Hansen Revocable Living Trust dated July 6, 20xx is made this 30th day of November 20xx by James P. Hansen, Grantor. Under the power of amendment reserved to Grantor by Section XX, Paragraph XX, of the Declaration of Trust, Grantor amends the trust as follows:

The following is added to the Declaration of Trust:

After Part 20, the following language is added:

Part 21. Special Needs Trust

If Samantha M. Hansen becomes entitled to any trust property under Part YY, that trust property shall be placed in a separate special needs trust as described below.

ARTICLE 1. CREATION OF SPECIAL NEEDS TRUST

James P. Hansen (Grantor), is creating this Special Needs Trust for the sole benefit of Samantha M. Hansen (Beneficiary). At Grantor's death, this trust will become irrevocable.

[The rest of the special needs trust would appear here.]

In all other respects, the Declaration of Trust as executed on July 6, 20xx by Grantor is affirmed.

Executed at _____ on
                        City   State

_____
Date

_____
Grantor

[notarization]

WHEN TO SEE A LAWYER. If you have an ongoing relationship with the lawyer who drafted your original living trust, you should seek his or her professional opinion on the amendment suggested here, as well as the special needs trust in this book.

Adding a Special Needs Trust to a Revocable Living Trust

This section shows you how to add a special needs trust to a living trust you create with a Nolo book or software. Again, if a lawyer prepared your living trust, consult the lawyer again to discuss how to modify the trust to include a special needs trust.

Nolo offers two ways to help you prepare your own revocable living trust:

• **Quicken WillMaker Plus** is software that lets you prepare a living trust and other estate planning documents, including wills, powers of attorney, and more. The program uses a question-and-answer format to get your information and then assembles the documents for your review.

• **Make Your Own Living Trust,** by Denis Clifford, guides you, step-by-step, through the process of making a valid revocable living trust for an individual or a couple. The book comes with a CD-ROM that has all of the clauses you need to create your trust.

Both the book and the software provide extensive help as you go through the trust-making process.

Making a Living Trust: Checklist

❏ Draft a revocable living trust document, directing that trust property left to your disabled loved one be held in the special needs trust.
  • Use a Nolo book or software, or hire a lawyer.

❏ Make sure your choice for trustee of the special needs trust is on board.
  • No one can be forced to act as trustee, so make sure the person you want is willing and able to do the job.

❏ Draft your special needs trust.
  • Follow the instructions in Chapter 8 of this book.

❏ Add the special needs trust to the revocable living trust document.
  • Follow the instructions in this chapter.

❏ Sign the trust document in front of a notary public.
  • Unlike a will, you don't need witnesses—but your signature must be notarized.

❏ Transfer property to yourself as trustee.
  • This is crucial—only assets held in the trustee's name will pass under the terms of the trust document.

Using *Quicken WillMaker Plus*

You can make either an individual trust or a shared trust with *Quicken WillMaker Plus*.

Making the Trust Document

After you enter information about your beneficiaries and the property you wish to leave them, *WillMaker* will ask you whether you wish to impose controls over property you are leaving to a minor or young adult. Answer no. You don't want either of the program's options (child's trust or custodianship) because you'll be adding a different one: the special needs trust.

Exporting the Trust Document

After you have finished entering information, review your trust document to make sure it accurately reflects your personal information and your wishes about your beneficiaries and property. Once you're satisfied that it does, export the program to your word processor. (This should be quite easy, but if it's not obvious how to do it, consult the user's manual.) This will give you a file you can work with, so you can insert the special needs trust you prepare with this book.

Using *WillMaker*: Individual Trust

You'll need to modify a few of the boilerplate provisions of the trust document you create with *WillMaker*. Here's how.

Trustee's Responsibility

Find the "Trustee's Responsibility" section and add the underlined language below.

Trust provision reads:	Change it to read:
(C) Trustee's Responsibility The trustee in office shall serve as trustee of all trusts created under this Declaration of Trust, including all children's trusts.	(C) Trustee's Responsibility The trustee in office shall serve as trustee of all trusts created under this Declaration of Trust, including all children's trusts <u>but excluding any special needs trusts that provide for a different trustee.</u>

Waiver of Bond

The next language to change is in the bond section.

Trust provision reads:	Change it to read:
(H) Bond Waived No bond shall be required of any trustee.	(H) Bond Waived No bond shall be required of any trustee <u>unless a special needs trust created in this Declaration of Trust provides differently for the trustee of that trust</u>.

Compensation of Trustee

You'll also need to change the very next item, about payment of trustees.

Trust provision reads:	Change it to read:
(I) Compensation No trustee shall receive any compensation for serving as trustee, unless the trustee serves as a trustee of a child's trust created by this Declaration of Trust.	(I) Compensation No trustee shall receive any compensation for serving as trustee, unless the trustee serves as a trustee of a child's trust <u>or a special needs trust</u> created by this Declaration of Trust.

Beneficiaries

Find the part labeled "Beneficiaries" and make the change below.

Trust provision reads:	Change it to read:
Part ___. Beneficiaries At the death of the grantor, the trustee shall distribute the trust property as follows, subject to provisions in this Declaration of Trust that create children's subtrusts or create custodianships under the Uniform Transfers to Minors Act.	Part ___. Beneficiaries At the death of the grantor, the trustee shall distribute the trust property as follows, subject to provisions in this Declaration of Trust that create children's subtrusts, custodianships under the Uniform Transfers to Minors Act, <u>or special needs trusts</u>.

Severability of Clauses

Next, look for this section, near the end of the document.

> __. Severability of Clauses. If any provision of this Declaration of Trust is ruled unenforceable, the remaining provisions shall stay in effect.

Directly after that clause, you'll want to insert the entire special needs trust. Just call it "Part ___. Special Needs Trust" and give it the appropriate number.

> Part __. Special Needs Trust
>
> If [*name of your loved one*] becomes entitled to any trust property under Part 10, that trust property shall be placed in a separate special needs trust described below.
>
> ARTICLE 1: CREATION OF SPECIAL NEEDS TRUST
> _____ (Grantor), is creating this Special Needs Trust for the sole benefit of _____ _____ (Beneficiary). At Grantor's death, this trust will become irrevocable.
>
> [*The rest of the special needs trust language would appear here.*]

Using *WillMaker*: Shared Trust

If you and your spouse want to make a shared trust (the *WillMaker* manual discusses the pros and cons), then you'll need to make the changes outlined here.

Trustee's Responsibility

Find the "Trustee's Responsibility" part, and add the underlined language below.

Trust provision reads:	Change it to read:
(C) Trustee's Responsibility The trustee in office shall serve as trustee of all trusts created under this Declaration of Trust, including all children's trusts.	(C) Trustee's Responsibility The trustee in office shall serve as trustee of all trusts created under this Declaration of Trust, including all children's trusts <u>but excluding any special needs trusts that provide for a different trustee.</u>

Waiver of Bond

The next language to change is in the bond section.

Trust provision reads:	Change it to read:
(H) Bond Waived No bond shall be required of any trustee.	(H) Bond Waived No bond shall be required of any trustee <u>unless a special needs trust created in this Declaration of Trust provides differently for the trustee of that trust.</u>

Compensation of Trustee

You'll also need to change the very next item, about payment of trustees.

Trust provision reads:	Change it to read:
(I) Compensation No trustee shall receive any compensation for serving as trustee, unless the trustee serves as a trustee of a child's trust created by this Declaration of Trust.	(I) Compensation No trustee shall receive any compensation for serving as trustee, unless the trustee serves as a trustee of a child's trust <u>or a special needs trust</u> created by this Declaration of Trust.

Beneficiaries

Find the part labeled "Beneficiaries" and make the changes below.

Trust provision reads:	Change it to read:
Part ___. Beneficiaries	Part ___. Beneficiaries
A. Husband's Beneficiaries	A. Husband's Beneficiaries
At the death of [*husband*], the trustee shall distribute the trust property listed on Schedule C, plus accumulated interest; the share of the property on Schedule A owned by [*husband*] before it was transferred to the trustee, plus accumulated interest; and if [*husband*] is the second spouse to die, any property listed on Schedule B left to him by the deceased spouse, plus accumulated interest; as follows, subject to provisions in this Declaration of Trust that create children's subtrusts, or custodianships under the Uniform Transfers to Minors Act:	At the death of [*husband*], the trustee shall distribute the trust property listed on Schedule C, plus accumulated interest; the share of the property on Schedule A owned by [*husband*] before it was transferred to the trustee, plus accumulated interest; and if [*husband*] is the second spouse to die, any property listed on Schedule B left to him by the deceased spouse, plus accumulated interest; as follows, subject to provisions in this Declaration of Trust that create children's subtrusts, custodianships under the Uniform Transfers to Minors Act, <u>or special needs trusts:</u>
[*property dispositions*]	[*property dispositions*]
B. Wife's Beneficiaries	B. Wife's Beneficiaries
At the death of [*wife*], the trustee shall distribute the trust property listed on Schedule B, plus accumulated interest; the share of the property on Schedule A owned by [*wife*] before it was transferred to the trustee, plus accumulated interest; and if [*wife*] is the second spouse to die, any property listed on Schedule C left to her by the deceased spouse, plus accumulated interest; as follows, subject to provisions in this Declaration of Trust that create children's subtrusts or custodianships under the Uniform Transfers to Minors Act:	At the death of [*wife*], the trustee shall distribute the trust property listed on Schedule B, plus accumulated interest; the share of the property on Schedule A owned by [*wife*] before it was transferred to the trustee, plus accumulated interest; and if [*wife*] is the second spouse to die, any property listed on Schedule C left to her by the deceased spouse, plus accumulated interest; as follows, subject to provisions in this Declaration of Trust that create children's subtrusts, custodianships under the Uniform Transfers to Minors Act, <u>or special needs trusts:</u>
[*property dispositions*]	[*property dispositions*]

Severability of Clauses

Next, look for this section, near the end of the document.

___. Severability of Clauses. If any provision of this Declaration of Trust is ruled unenforceable, the remaining provisions shall stay in effect.

Directly after that clause, you'll want to insert the entire special needs trust. Just call it "Part ___. Special Needs Trust" and give it the appropriate number.

Part ___. Special Needs Trust

If [*insert name of your beloved loved one*] becomes entitled to any trust property under Part 10, that trust property shall be placed in a separate special needs trust described below.

ARTICLE 1: CREATION OF SPECIAL NEEDS TRUST
_____ (Grantor), is creating this Special Needs Trust for the sole benefit of ____ _____ (Beneficiary). At Grantor's death, this trust will become irrevocable.

[*The rest of the special needs trust would appear here.*]

Using *Make Your Own Living Trust*: Individual Trust

If you use *Make Your Own Living Trust* to create a single revocable living trust (not a shared trust with your spouse), you'll need to change a few of the boilerplate provisions. A sample trust made with that book, and modified to include a special needs trust from this book, is included at the end of this chapter, so you can get a general idea of what your document will look like.

Here are the provisions you must modify:

Trustee's Responsibility

Find the "Trustee's Responsibility" section, and add the underlined language below.

Trust provision reads:	Change it to read:
(C) Trustee's Responsibility The trustee in office shall serve as trustee of all trusts created under this Declaration of Trust, including all children's trusts.	(C) Trustee's Responsibility The trustee in office shall serve as trustee of all trusts created under this Declaration of Trust, including all children's trusts but excluding any special needs trusts that provide for a different trustee.

Waiver of Bond

Next, change the bond clause of the "Trustees" section.

Trust provision reads:	Change it to read:
(F) Bond Waived No bond shall be required of any trustee.	(F) Bond Waived No bond shall be required of any trustee unless a special needs trust created in this Declaration of Trust provides differently for the trustee of that trust.

Trustee Compensation Provision

Also in the "Trustees" section, find the paragraph that discusses compensation and make the following change:

Trust provision reads:	Change it to read:
(G) Compensation No trustee shall receive any compensation for serving as trustee, unless the trustee serves as a trustee of a child's trust created by this Declaration of Trust.	(G) Compensation No trustee shall receive any compensation for serving as trustee, unless a special needs trust created by this Declaration of Trust provides differently, or the trustee serves as a trustee of a child's trust created by this Declaration of Trust.

Distribution of Trust Property Upon Death of Grantor

Find the part that's headed "Distribution of Trust Property Upon Death of Grantor," and make the change shown below.

Trust provision reads:	Change it to read:
__. Distribution of Trust Property Upon Death of Grantor Upon the death of the grantor, the trustee shall distribute the trust property outright to the beneficiaries named in Section V, Paragraphs (A) and (B), subject to any provision in this Declaration of Trust that creates children's subtrusts or creates custodianships under the Uniform Transfers to Minors Act.	__. Distribution of Trust Property Upon Death of Grantor Upon the death of the grantor, the trustee shall distribute the trust property outright to the beneficiaries named in Section V, Paragraphs (A) and (B), subject to any provision in this Declaration of Trust that creates a special needs trust, children's subtrusts, or creates custodianships under the Uniform Transfers to Minors Act.

Children's Subtrusts

Next, skip down to "Children's Subtrusts" and "Custodianships." The changes you make depend on whether or not you need the subtrust provisions of the document for a young beneficiary. (You don't need the subtrust provisions for your disabled beneficiary—the special needs trust provisions will be enough.)

If you are not creating a child's subtrust for another beneficiary, delete the text under "Children's Subtrusts" part and substitute the following—including the entire special needs trust—in its place. Number the new part accordingly.

Trust provision reads:	Change it to read:
Part __: Children's Subtrusts All trust property left to	Part __: Special Needs Trust All trust property left to [*name of special needs beneficiary*] shall be placed in the special needs trust set out below and managed according to its terms. ARTICLE 1. CREATION OF SPECIAL NEEDS TRUST [*your name*] (Grantor), creates this Special Needs Trust for the sole benefit of [*name of beneficiary*] (Beneficiary). Upon the death of Grantor, this trust will become irrevocable. [*The rest of the special needs trust would appear here.*]

If you are creating a child's subtrust for another beneficiary but not a custodianship under the Uniform Transfers to Minors Act, keep the subtrusts part but delete the entire "Custodianships" part and substitute the language set out above.

If you are creating both a child's subtrust and a custodianship for other beneficiaries, keep the subtrusts and custodianships parts. Also create a new part for the special needs trust and insert the language set out above in it. Then renumber the rest of the parts in the document.

Using *Make Your Own Living Trust*: Shared Trust

If you and your spouse use *Make Your Own Living Trust* to create a shared revocable living trust, you'll need to modify a few of the boilerplate provisions. (Generally, only married couples create shared trusts; *Make Your Own Living Trust* explains how to decide whether you and your spouse should make separate trusts or one shared trust.)

Here are the modifications you'll need to use a basic shared living trust made with *Make Your Own Living Trust.*

AB *Trusts*

For married couples whose net worth is expected to exceed $1.5 million when they die, one common estate planning technique is to create what's known as an AB or bypass trust. This trust lets the couple minimize or eliminate federal estate taxes at the second spouse's death. You can make an AB trust with Nolo products, but combining it with a special needs trust gets complicated. If you have that kind of wealth, see an estate planning specialist to make a plan and create the necessary documents.

Trustee's Responsibility

Find the "Trustee's Responsibility" section, and add the underlined language below.

Trust provision reads:	Change it to read:
(C) Trustee's Responsibility The trustee in office shall serve as trustee of all trusts created under this Declaration of Trust, including all children's trusts.	(C) Trustee's Responsibility The trustee in office shall serve as trustee of all trusts created under this Declaration of Trust, including all children's trusts <u>but excluding any special needs trusts that provide for a different trustee.</u>

Waiver of Bond

The next language to change is in the bond section.

Trust provision reads:	Change it to read:
(H) Bond Waived No bond shall be required of any trustee.	(H) Bond Waived No bond shall be required of any trustee <u>unless a special needs trust created in this Declaration of Trust provides differently for the trustee of that trust.</u>

Compensation of Trustee

You'll also need to change the very next item, about payment of trustees.

Trust provision reads:	Change it to read:
(I) Compensation No trustee shall receive any compensation for serving as trustee, unless the trustee serves as a trustee of a child's trust created by this Declaration of Trust.	(I) Compensation No trustee shall receive any compensation for serving as trustee, unless the trustee serves as a trustee of a child's trust <u>or a special needs trust</u> created by this Declaration of Trust.

Administration of Trust Property

Keep going until you get to the part that covers the administration of trust property. Then add a few words, as shown below.

Trust provision reads:	Change it to read:
V. Administration of Trust Property .... (B) Division and Distribution of Trust Property on Death of Grantor ..... 2. Trust I shall contain all the property of The [*your names*] Living Trust owned by the deceased spouse at the time it was transferred to the trust, plus accumulated income, appreciation in value, and the like attributable to the ownership interest of the deceased spouse and his or her share of any property acquired in the trust's name, EXCEPT trust property left by the terms of this trust to the surviving spouse. Trust I becomes irrevocable at the death of the deceased spouse. The trustee shall distribute the property in Trust I to the beneficiaries named by the deceased spouse in Section IV of this Declaration of Trust, subject to any provision of this Declaration of Trust that creates children's trusts or creates custodianships under the Uniform Transfers to Minors Act.	V. Administration of Trust Property .... (B) Division and Distribution of Trust Property on Death of Grantor .... 2. Trust I shall contain all the property of The [*your names*] Living Trust owned by the deceased spouse at the time it was transferred to the trust, plus accumulated income, appreciation in value, and the like attributable to the ownership interest of the deceased spouse and his or her share of any property acquired in the trust's name, EXCEPT trust property left by the terms of this trust to the surviving spouse. Trust I becomes irrevocable at the death of the deceased spouse. The trustee shall distribute the property in Trust I to the beneficiaries named by the deceased spouse in Section IV of this Declaration of Trust, subject to any provision of this Declaration of Trust that creates children's trusts <u>or special needs trusts,</u> or creates custodianships under the Uniform Transfers to Minors Act.

Distribution of Property in Trust 2

Further down in the "Administration of Trust Property" part is material on the distribution of property in Trust 2 (when the first spouse dies, a shared trust is split into Trust 1 and Trust 2, as is explained thoroughly in *Make Your Own Living Trust*). Make the minor change shown below.

Trust provision reads:	Change it to read:
V. Administration of Trust Property …. (D) _____ …. 3. Distribution of Property in Trust 2 Upon the death of the surviving spouse, Trust 2 becomes irrevocable, and the property in Trust 2 shall be distributed to the beneficiaries listed in Section IV, subject to any provision of this Declaration of Trust that creates children's trusts, or creates custodianships under the Uniform Transfers to Minors Act.	V. Administration of Trust Property …. (D) _____ …. 3. Distribution of Property in Trust 2 Upon the death of the surviving spouse, Trust 2 becomes irrevocable, and the property in Trust 2 shall be distributed to the beneficiaries listed in Section IV, subject to any provision of this Declaration of Trust that creates children's trusts, <u>special needs trusts,</u> or creates custodianships under the Uniform Transfers to Minors Act.

Children's Subtrusts and Custodianships

Next, skip down to the parts that cover children's subtrusts and custodianships.

If you are <u>not</u> creating a child's subtrust for another beneficiary, delete the "Children's Subtrusts" part and substitute the following—including the entire special needs trust—in its place.

Trust provision reads:	Change it to read:
Part ___: Children's Subtrusts All property left to ….	Part ___: Special Needs Trust All trust property left to [*name of special needs beneficiary*] shall be placed in the special needs trust set out below and managed according to its terms. ARTICLE 1. CREATION OF SPECIAL NEEDS TRUST [*your name*] (Grantor), creates this Special Needs Trust for the sole benefit of [*name of beneficiary*] (Beneficiary). At Grantor's death, this trust will become irrevocable. [*The rest of the special needs trust goes here.*]

If you are creating a child's subtrust for another beneficiary but not a custodianship under the Uniform Transfers to Minors Act, keep the subtrusts part but delete the "Custodianships" part. Insert a new part ("Special Needs Trust") in its place.

If you are creating both a child's subtrust and a custodianship for other beneficiaries, keep both those parts and create a new one ("Special Needs Trusts") and insert the language set out above in it. Then renumber the rest of the parts in the document.

Adding a Special Needs Trust to a Will

As mentioned earlier, it's usually better to use a revocable living trust as the basis for a special needs trust. But it's also possible (and required, if you're making a special needs trust for your spouse) to use a will.

To make your will, you can use either of these Nolo products:

• **Quicken WillMaker Plus,** software that lets you prepare a will and other estate planning documents, including a living trust, powers of attorney, and more. The program uses a question-and-answer format to get your information and then assembles documents for your review.

  • **Nolo's Simple Will Book,** by Denis Clifford, lets you make a will tailored to your situation by using tear-out forms or a CD-ROM.

Once you've made your will, you'll need to make some minor changes to it in order to add a special needs trust.

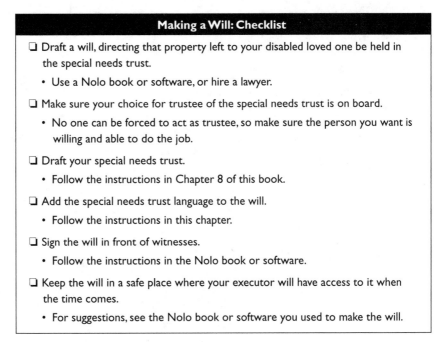

Making a Will: Checklist

❏ Draft a will, directing that property left to your disabled loved one be held in the special needs trust.

• Use a Nolo book or software, or hire a lawyer.

❏ Make sure your choice for trustee of the special needs trust is on board.

• No one can be forced to act as trustee, so make sure the person you want is willing and able to do the job.

❏ Draft your special needs trust.

• Follow the instructions in Chapter 8 of this book.

❏ Add the special needs trust language to the will.

• Follow the instructions in this chapter.

❏ Sign the will in front of witnesses.

• Follow the instructions in the Nolo book or software.

❏ Keep the will in a safe place where your executor will have access to it when the time comes.

• For suggestions, see the Nolo book or software you used to make the will.

Using *Nolo's Simple Will Book*

Nolo's Simple Will Book contains basic will forms as well as a collection of clauses that you can assemble into a custom will. You'll want to build a custom will and add your special needs trust to it.

When you've assembled your will, look for the clauses near the end of the will that provide for management of property left to minors or young adults. These clauses cover the gifts left under the Uniform Transfers to Minors Act (custodianships) and trusts for children. If the only controls you are placing on property are those that are part of your special needs trust, you can delete all of those clauses and substitute the language shown below.

If you do wish, in addition, to place controls on property left to one or more minor or young adult beneficiaries who are not disabled, use the appropriate clause and then add the special needs trust language set out below.

Delete:	Replace with:
Whichever of the property management clauses you're not using	Part __. Special Needs Trust All property left to [*name of special needs beneficiary*] in this will shall be placed in the special needs trust as set out below and managed according to its terms. ARTICLE I. CREATION OF SPECIAL NEEDS TRUST This special needs trust shall be managed for the sole benefit of [*name of beneficiary*] (Beneficiary). Upon my death, this trust shall become irrevocable. [*the rest of the special needs trust goes here*]

Using *Quicken WillMaker Plus*

If you use Nolo's *Quicken WillMaker Plus* to create a will, you'll need to review your will and export it into an editable text file. (Follow the program's instructions for exporting the file and saving it in a folder where you can keep track of it.)

Open the exported will file and scroll down until you see the part labeled "Severability." After that part, create a new part and insert this text:

> Part __: All property left to [*name of special needs beneficiary*] in this will shall be placed in the special needs trust set out below and managed according to its terms.
>
> ARTICLE I: CREATION OF SPECIAL NEEDS TRUST
>
> This special needs trust shall be managed for the sole benefit of [*name of beneficiary*] (Beneficiary). Upon my death this trust shall become irrevocable.
>
> [*The rest of the special needs trust language would appear here.*]

Using a Will or Trust to Leave Property to a Pooled Trust

If you decide you want to join a pooled trust (discussed in Chapter 7). you'll need to use your will or living trust to route your loved one's inheritance to the pooled trust.

Fortunately, every pooled trust either has its own instructions you can use for this purpose, or will be able to hook you up with a lawyer for the language that particular pooled trust prefers you to use. This section provides some general instructions to give you an idea of the process.

If You Sign Up With a Pooled Trust Now

If you sign up with a pooled trust during your life and want to fund it with property you leave at your death, then in your revocable living trust or will, name the trustee of the pooled trust to receive any property you want to go to your disabled loved one. This will authorize the successor trustee of your revocable living trust or the executor of your will to distribute the property to the pooled trust. For this to work, you'll need to know the identity of the trustee—usually either a bank or an individual who coordinates with a bank.

EXAMPLE: Michael has a developmentally disabled daughter, Annie, who receives SSI benefits. Michael signs a joinder agreement with a local pooled trust operated by The Arc. He plans to fund the trust when he dies by leaving money through his revocable living trust.

Michael finds out that the trustee of the pooled trust is Bank of America (under contract with the pooled trust), but that the pooled trust wants him to use the name of an individual cotrustee instead of the bank. So he names John C. Parcival, trustee of the Arc Pooled Trust of Iowa, to receive property left by Michael to Annie in his living trust. In the living trust, Annie is named as beneficiary of five CDs worth about $10,000 each.

Here is how this would appear in a revocable living trust document:

V. Beneficiaries

Upon grantor's death, the property listed on Schedule A shall be distributed to the beneficiaries named in this section.

(A) Primary and Alternate Beneficiaries

1. Anne L. Casey shall be given five CDs numbered 0004546, 0004547, 0004548, 0004549, and 00045410, issued by Charles Schwab.

2. ………..

Part IX: Special Needs Trust

All trust property left to Anne L. Casey shall be given to John C. Parcival, Trustee of the Arc of Ohio Pooled Trust, to be used for Anne L. Casey's benefit under the joinder agreement signed by Grantor on January 3, 20xx.

If You Don't Sign Up Now

What if you're interested in using a pooled trust, but can't find a suitable one that's available to you? In that event, you can still include a special needs trust in your will or revocable living trust, but direct the executor of your will or the successor trustee of your living trust to try to find a suitable pooled trust after your death. (See Chapter 7.) With luck, a suitable pooled trust will have come into existence by then.

Below is language you can insert at the very beginning of the clause where you introduce the special needs trust.

Part ___. Special Needs Trust

Grantor has created a special needs trust as set out below. However, Grantor directs the trustee, before placing property in that trust, to explore the possibility of joining a pooled trust for the purpose of managing all property left to Anne L. Casey. If after such exploration, no suitable pooled trust is located and joined, all trust property [or "property left through this will"] left to Anne L. Casey shall be placed in the special needs trust as set out below and managed according to its terms.

Sample Revocable Living Trust With Special Needs Trust

Basic Living Trust for One Person
Declaration of Trust

I. Trust Name

This trust shall be known as The Gloria C. Escobar Revocable Living Trust.

II. Trust Property

(A) Property Placed in Trust

Gloria C. Escobar, called the grantor or trustee, declares that she has set aside and holds in The Gloria C. Escobar Revocable Living Trust all her interest in that property described in the attached Schedule A.

The trust property shall be used for the benefit of the trust beneficiaries and shall be administered and distributed by the trustee in accordance with this Declaration of Trust.

(B) Additional or After-Acquired Property

The grantor may add property to the trust at any time.

III. Reserved Powers of Grantor

(A) Amendment or Revocation

The grantor reserves the power to amend or revoke this trust at any time during his/her lifetime, without notifying any beneficiary.

(B) Rights to Trust Property

Until the death of the grantor, all rights to all income, profits, and control of the trust property shall be retained by the grantor.

(C) Homestead Rights

If the Grantor's principal residence is transferred to the trust, Grantor has the right to possess and occupy it for life, rent-free and without charge, except for taxes, insurance, maintenance, and related costs and expenses. This right is intended to give Grantor a beneficial interest in the property and to ensure that Grantor does not lose eligibility for a state homestead tax exemption for which Grantor otherwise qualifies.

(D) Incapacity of Grantor

If the grantor has become physically or mentally incapacitated, as certified in writing by a licensed physician, the successor trustee shall manage this trust. The successor trustee shall pay trust income at least annually to, or for the benefit of, the grantor and may also spend any amount of trust principal necessary in the trustee's discretion for the needs of the grantor, until a licensed physician certifies that the grantor is no longer incapacitated or until the grantor's death.

(E) Grantor's Death

After the death of the grantor, this trust becomes irrevocable. It may not be altered or amended in any respect, and may not be terminated except through distributions permitted by this Declaration of Trust.

IV. Trustees

(A) Original Trustee

The trustee of The Gloria C. Escobar Revocable Living Trust and all children's trusts created under this Declaration of Trust shall be Gloria C. Escobar.

(B) Successor Trustee

Upon the death of the trustee, or his/her incapacity as certified in writing by a licensed physician, the successor trustee shall be Rafael Escobar. If he/she/all of them is/are unable to serve or continue serving as successor trustee, the successor trustee shall be Jamie Sanchez.

(C) Trustee's Responsibility

The trustee in office shall serve as trustee of all trusts created under this Declaration of Trust, including all children's trusts but excluding any special needs trusts that provide for a different trustee.

(D) Resignation of Trustee

Any trustee in office may resign at any time by signing a notice of resignation. The resignation must be delivered to the person or institution who is either named in this Declaration of Trust, or appointed by the trustee under Section IV, Paragraph (E), to next serve as trustee.

(E) Power to Appoint Successor Trustee

If all the successor trustees named in this Declaration of Trust cease to, or are unable to, serve as trustee, any trustee may appoint an additional successor trustee or trustees to serve in the order nominated. The appointment must be made in writing, signed by the trustee, and notarized.

(F) Terminology

In this Declaration of Trust, the term "trustee" includes any successor trustee or successor trustees.

(G) Bond Waived

No bond shall be required of any trustee.

(H) Compensation

No trustee shall receive any compensation for serving as trustee, unless a special needs trust created by this Declaration of Trust provides differently, or the trustee serves as a trustee of a child's trust created by this Declaration of Trust.

(I) Liability of Trustee

With respect to the exercise or nonexercise of discretionary powers granted by this Declaration of Trust, the trustee shall not be liable for actions taken in good faith.

V. Beneficiaries

Upon the death of the grantor, the property listed on Schedule A shall be distributed to the beneficiaries named in this section.

(A) Primary and Alternate Beneficiaries

1. Dora Escobar shall be given the house at 3456 First St., Lakeport, Ky., and its contents. If Dora Escobar does not survive the grantor, that property shall be given to Phil Sanchez.

2. Rosa Escobar shall be given Certificate of Deposit #2342424 with WestAmerica Bank. If Rosa Escobar does not survive the grantor, that property shall be given to Dora Escobar

3. Bessie Escobar shall be given the proceeds of Tex Life Insurance policy #2345675 on grantor's life, payable in the amount of $200,000 to the trustee of this trust. If Bessie Escobar does not survive the grantor, that property shall be given to Dora Escobar

(B) Residuary Beneficiary

The residuary beneficiary of the trust shall be Rosa Escobar, who shall be given all trust property not specifically and validly disposed of by Section V, Paragraph (A). If Rosa Escobar does not survive the grantor, that property shall be given to Dora Escobar

VI. Distribution of Trust Property Upon Death of Grantor

Upon the death of the grantor, the trustee shall distribute the trust property outright to the beneficiaries named in Section V, Paragraphs (A) and (B), subject to any provision in this Declaration of Trust that creates children's trusts or special needs trusts, or creates custodianships under the Uniform Transfers to Minors Act.

VII. Trustee's Powers and Duties

(A) Powers Under State Law

To carry out the provisions of The Gloria C. Escobar Revocable Living Trust, and any children's trusts created under this Declaration of Trust, the trustee shall have all authority and powers allowed or conferred on a trustee under Kentucky law, subject to the trustee's fiduciary duty to the grantor and the beneficiaries.

(B) Specified Powers

The trustee's powers include, but are not limited to:

1. The power to sell trust property, and to borrow money and to encumber that property, specifically including trust real estate, by mortgage, deed of trust, or other method.

2. The power to manage trust real estate as if the trustee were the absolute owner of it, including the power to lease (even if the lease term may extend beyond the period of any trust) or grant options to lease the property, to make repairs or alterations, and to insure against loss.

3. The power to sell or grant options for the sale or exchange of any trust property, including stocks, bonds, debentures, and any other form of security or security account, at public or private sale for cash or on credit.

4. The power to invest trust property in property of any kind, including but not limited to bonds, debentures, notes, mortgages, and stocks.

5. The power to receive additional property from any source and add to any trust created by this Declaration of Trust.

6. The power to employ and pay reasonable fees to accountants, lawyers, or investment experts for information or advice relating to the trust.

7. The power to deposit and hold trust funds in both interest-bearing and non–interest-bearing accounts.

8. The power to deposit funds in bank or other accounts uninsured by FDIC coverage.

9. The power to enter into electronic fund transfer or safe deposit arrangements with financial institutions.

10. The power to continue any business of the grantor.

11. The power to institute or defend legal actions concerning the trust or grantor's affairs.

12. The power to execute any document necessary to administer any child's trust created in this Declaration of Trust.

13. The power to diversify investments, including authority to decide that some or all of the trust property need not produce income.

(C) Payment by Trustee of the Grantor's Debts and Taxes

The grantor's debts and death taxes shall be paid by the trustee. The trustee shall pay these from the following trust property: The Certificate of Deposit #2222222 at Bank of America, payable to the trustee of this trust.

If the property specified above is insufficient to pay all the grantor's debts and death taxes, the trustee shall determine how such debts and death taxes shall be paid from trust property.

VIII. General Administrative Provisions

(A) Controlling Law

The validity of The Gloria C. Escobar Revocable Living Trust shall be governed by the laws of Kentucky.

(B) Severability

If any provision of this Declaration of Trust is ruled unenforceable, the remaining provisions shall nevertheless remain in effect.

(C) Amendments

The term "Declaration of Trust" includes any provisions added by amendments.

(D) Accountings

No accountings or reports shall be required of the trustee.

IX. Special Needs Trust

Special Needs Trust

Article 1. Creation of Trust

Gloria C. Escobar (Grantor) is creating this special needs trust for the sole benefit of Bessie Escobar (Beneficiary). At Grantor's death, this trust will become irrevocable.

Article 2. Purpose of Trust

Beneficiary has a disability and will likely require government assistance after Grantor's death. Grantor creates this special needs trust to enhance Beneficiary's quality of life while at the same time preserving Beneficiary's eligibility for government support and medical assistance programs, including SSI, Medicaid, or other similar programs. Grantor intends this Declaration of Trust to be interpreted in light of this purpose.

Article 3. Examples of Special Needs

1. Grantor intends this trust to provide Beneficiary with goods and services to fulfill special needs, which are needs that are not provided for by the support and medical assistance Beneficiary receives from government programs.

2. Special needs include but are not limited to: out-of-pocket medical and dental expenses; medical equipment not provided by Medicaid; eyeglasses; exercise equipment; annual independent checkups; transportation; vehicle maintenance; vehicle insurance premiums; life insurance premiums; physical rehabilitation services; essential dietary needs; materials for hobbies; tickets for recreational or cultural events; musical instruments; cosmetics; home furnishings; home improvements; computer or electronic equipment; cable television; telephones; televisions; radios; cameras; trips; vacations; visits to friends; entertainment; membership in book, health, record, video, or other clubs; newspaper and magazine subscriptions; athletic training or competitions; personal care attendant or escort; vocational rehabilitation or habilitation; professional services; costs of attending or participating in meetings, conferences, seminars, or training sessions; and tuition and expenses connected with all types of technical degree programs and higher education.

Article 4. Trustee

1. The following persons or entities shall serve, in the order listed, as trustee of this special needs trust:

Trustee: Rafael M. Escobar

First Successor Trustee: Jaime L. Sanchez

Second Successor Trustee: Lola S. Sanchez

2. If at Grantor's death no trustee named here is available to serve, Grantor's executor may name a trustee to manage this special needs trust. If there is no executor, the successor trustee of Grantor's revocable living trust, if any, may name a trustee to manage this special needs trust.

Article 5. Powers of Successor Trustees

All authority and powers, including discretionary powers, conferred upon a trustee or cotrustee shall pass to all successor trustees.

Article 6. Contributions to the Trust

Trustee shall accept contributions to the trust only from third parties. No public assistance, Social Security benefits, or any other earned or unearned income received by Beneficiary shall be added to this trust for any reason.

Article 7. Use of Principal and Income

Income earned from trust property shall be retained in the trust to be used for trust purposes. When making disbursements for Beneficiary's benefit, Trustee shall keep adequate records to show that current and accumulated trust income is used first, and then trust principal.

Article 8. Trustee's Duty to Seek Government Benefits

Trustee shall seek support and maintenance of Beneficiary from all available public resources, including but not limited to the Supplemental Security Income program (SSI), the Social Security Disability Insurance program (SSDI), the In-Home Support Services Program, Medicare, Medicaid, or similar or successor programs.

Article 9. Trustee's Discretion Over Disbursements

1. Trustee shall have complete discretion in how the trust property is used, provided that the property is used only for the purpose of helping the Beneficiary, providing Beneficiary with goods and services that supplement those provided by the SSI and Medicaid programs, or similar programs, and never for a purpose that will impair Beneficiary's eligibility for those programs.

2. Trustee shall become and remain knowledgeable about the eligibility requirements for SSI and Medicaid, or similar programs, so that disbursements will not impair Beneficiary's eligibility for those programs. For example, under federal and state regulations in effect at the time Grantor executes this trust, Trustee may supplement Beneficiary's shelter cost without causing a loss of SSI and Medicaid eligibility, even though a portion of the SSI grant might be reduced. But if the laws change and supplementing rent would result in a loss of Medicaid eligibility, Trustee may not make a disbursement for that purpose.

3. Trustee's exercise of discretion under this Article may indirectly benefit another party, such as a relative, caretaker, or remainder beneficiary without violating this Article.

Article 10. Trustee's Duty to File Tax Returns and Make Reports

1 Trustee shall prepare and file all required trust tax returns.

2. Trustee shall provide to Beneficiary, or Beneficiary's legal guardian, conservator, representative payee, or agent, if any, all information necessary for the reports required by a government agency as a condition of the Beneficiary's continued eligibility for SSI, Medicaid, and other similar benefits.

3. Trustee shall annually provide Beneficiary, Beneficiary's legal guardian, conservator, representative payee, or agent, if any, and the remainder beneficiaries named in Article 12, with written information about trust activity, including an accounting of current trust assets, income earned by the trust, contributions from outside sources made to the trust, disbursements made to meet Beneficiary's special needs, and an accounting of all purchases by Trustee.

4. Upon request, Trustee shall provide the persons named in Section 3 of this article with copies of the trust's annual income tax returns.

Article 11. Termination of Trust

1. Trustee shall terminate this trust if:

   - Trustee determines that the value of the trust property makes it impractical to administer the trust, or

   - Beneficiary doesn't qualify, or no longer qualifies, for SSI, Medicaid, or similar government benefits, or

   - Trustee determines that changes in Beneficiary's disability make a special needs trust unnecessary, or

   - Beneficiary dies.

2. If Trustee terminates this trust for any reason other than Beneficiary's death, upon termination of the trust, and after all debts and taxes legally owed by the trust have been paid, Trustee shall distribute the trust property and accumulated income to Beneficiary or Beneficiary's legal guardian, conservator, representative payee, or agent, if any, unless such distribution would deprive Beneficiary of needed government benefits. In that event,

Trustee shall distribute as much of the property as possible to Beneficiary consistent with maintaining the benefits and distribute the rest of the property to the remainder beneficiaries named in Article 12.

3. If Trustee terminates the trust because of Beneficiary's death, the trust property and accumulated income shall be distributed to the remainder beneficiaries as set out in Article 12.

Article 12. Remainder Beneficiaries

1. If Trustee terminates this special needs trust and there are trust assets that Trustee does not distribute to Beneficiary under the terms of Article 11, Trustee shall distribute the remaining trust principal and accumulated income, after all debts and taxes legally owed by the trust have been paid, to Lola S. Sanchez.

2. If the remainder beneficiary or beneficiaries named in Section 1 of this article fails or fail to survive Beneficiary by 48 hours, Trustee shall distribute the property to Maria R. Sanchez.

3. While administering this special needs trust, Trustee shall in all cases exercise discretion in accordance with Article 9 and without regard to the interests of any remainder beneficiary named in this article.

4. If, when a remainder beneficiary inherits property under this article, he or she is not yet 18 years old, or, in the opinion of Trustee, is unable to prudently manage the property to be distributed and is under the age of 21, Trustee shall either a) retain that beneficiary's share as a custodian under the Uniform Transfers to Minors Act of Kentucky, or b) name another person to serve as custodian for the property under that Act and distribute the property to that custodian. The custodianship shall end when the remainder beneficiary turns 21 unless the law requires it to end at age 18. When the custodianship ends, the custodian shall distribute any remaining custodial property to the beneficiary.

Article 13. Trustee Powers

Trustee shall, in addition to the powers given by law, and pursuant to the Prudent Investor Act, if any, enacted by the State of Kentucky, have the following powers applicable to all property held in trust, whether principal or income, and exercisable without order of any court that has jurisdiction over Beneficiary:

1. To retain any property transferred to this trust, and to make such investments and reinvestments and in such proportions as Trustee considers beneficial and prudent in light of the trust purposes set out in Article 2.

2. To (1) participate in any merger or reorganization affecting securities held hereunder at any time; (2) deposit stock under voting agreements; (3) exercise any option to subscribe for stocks, bonds, or debentures; and (4) grant proxies, discretionary or otherwise, to vote shares of stock.

3. To manage, operate, or repair real estate or other property and to lease real estate and other property upon such terms and for such period as Trustee deems advisable.

4. To buy or sell (and to grant options for the sale of) any real or personal property at public or private sale for such prices and upon such terms as Trustee thinks proper.

5. To purchase, maintain, improve, or replace a residence, or any interest in it, where Beneficiary may reside, including any portion of the residence that may be owned by a family member.

6. To permit any person to reside at any real property held in this trust at which Beneficiary is residing, on such terms as Trustee deems proper, for the purpose of providing care, supervision, or simple companionship to Beneficiary.

7. To seek court permission to amend the trust only if necessary to fulfill the trust purposes set out in Article 2.

8. To make loans, but not gifts, for Beneficiary's benefit, provided the loans do not interfere with the trust purposes set out in Article 2.

9. To pay premiums to provide supplementary health insurance for Beneficiary or life insurance policies that may be owned or acquired by the trust. If Trustee is also the insured of any life insurance policy owned by the trust, then Trustee may exercise all rights and incidents of ownership with respect to such policy only in a fiduciary capacity, including the power to change the beneficiary, to surrender or cancel the policy, to assign the policy, to revoke any assignment, to pledge a policy for a loan, or to obtain a loan against the surrender value of the policy from the insurer.

10. To start or defend such litigation with respect to the trust or any property of the trust as Trustee deems advisable, at the expense of the trust.

11. To carry, at the expense of the trust, insurance of such kinds and in such amounts as Trustee deems advisable both to protect the trust property against any damage or loss and to protect Trustee against liability with respect to third persons.

12. To prepare and file returns and arrange for payment with respect to all local, state, federal, and foreign taxes incident to this trust, to prepare all necessary fiduciary income tax returns, and to make all necessary and appropriate elections.

13. To prepare and, if necessary, file all reports required of providers of government benefits received by Beneficiary, and to prepare and distribute annual reports of trust activity to Beneficiary and any named remainder beneficiaries.

14. Upon termination of the trust, to pay all debts and taxes determined by the trustee to be legally owed by the trust.

15. To hire attorneys, accountants, investment advisers, financial advisers, tax preparation services, and any other experts should Trustee, in Trustee's unfettered discretion, determine such expertise to be necessary for proper management of the trust.

Article 14. Trustee Compensation

Trustee shall be entitled to reasonable compensation, from trust assets, commensurate with the services actually performed, and to reimbursement for expenses properly incurred. Trustee shall determine what compensation is reasonable.

Article 15. Spendthrift Provisions

1. Beneficiary has no right or power, whether alone or in conjunction with others in whatever capacity, to amend, revoke, or terminate this special needs trust. No interest in the income or principal of this trust may be anticipated, assigned, encumbered, or subject to any creditor's claim or legal process.

2. Because trust funds will be conserved and maintained for Beneficiary's special needs, no part of the income or principal shall be construed as part of Beneficiary's "estate" or be subject to the claims of voluntary or involuntary creditors for the provision of care and services (including residential care) to or for Beneficiary by any city, county, or state government; the federal government; or any public or private agency except as otherwise provided in this trust instrument.

Article 16. Bond

Unless required by a court of competent jurisdiction, Trustee is not required to post a bond.

Article 17. Trustee's Liability for Good-Faith Actions

Trustee shall be held harmless for all acts undertaken, or not undertaken, in good faith while Trustee is engaged in administering this special needs trust.

Chapter Ten

Where to Get More Help

In the course of using this book, you may find yourself in need of some expert advice, or at least some additional information. This chapter steers you to resources available online or in the library and offers some tips on working with professionals.

> 💡 **SEARCH ENGINES ARE GREAT RESOURCES.** Getting answers can be as simple as entering "special needs trust" and other words that describe your questions, such as "Illinois," "cotrustees," "pooled trust," or "SSI eligibility standards," into your favorite search engine. (Google works great in his situation.) You'll quickly get a lot of hits. Be patient and you likely will find what you need.

Robert Berring, a well-known law professor, always advises that the first step in all research is: Talk to a human being who knows something about the subject. The humans you will want to talk to about your special needs trust are:

- lawyers who specialize in elder law and Medicaid issues and who can give you individualized advice
- financial planners, who can help you figure out how much property you'll need to put in the trust and how to set up a sensible budget, and
- high-level employees in your local SSA office, who can help with questions about how property you are leaving in your special needs trust will affect your loved one's benefits.

Lawyers

You can't beat lawyers for good legal advice. In fact, they are the only people permitted to give it. Other professionals such as financial planners, insurance agents, Social Security Administration (SSA) personnel, and paralegals may incidentally dole out information related to special needs trusts as part of their overall services. Lawyers, however, are the only people you can go to for legal advice tailored to your individual situation.

When to See a Lawyer

First and foremost, you'll want to talk to a lawyer if you feel discomfort about doing this important task yourself. Many lawyers who specialize in this sort of work believe that drafting special needs trusts is a job for a lawyer, plain and simple. Nolo disagrees, but you'll have to decide for yourself what you feel comfortable doing yourself.

Even if you are comfortable with drafting your own trust, it's important to keep in mind that special needs trusts are intended to last for many years. Questions are sure to arise that weren't anticipated in this book, such as big changes in the SSI and Medicaid rules. Having a lawyer on tap whose job it is to keep track of new legislation might save you a lot of grief down the line.

Finally, this book tries to cover the situations that most people encounter, but it doesn't contain details that might be important to you if your situation is unusual. If you have questions that aren't answered between these covers, a lawyer can help.

Why You May Have Difficulty Getting Help From a Lawyer

If you want to draft your own special needs trust but just need some additional information, ideally you should be able to have a short consultation with a special needs trust lawyer, pay a reasonable fee, and get all your questions answered. Even better, for an additional fee, the lawyer would review your trust, make helpful suggestions, and give you the peace of mind that comes from having a knowledgeable professional looking over your shoulder. Unfortunately, this scenario is unlikely, for two reasons:

- Almost without exception, special needs trust lawyers think people shouldn't create special needs trusts themselves.

- Lawyers are concerned that if they give you piecemeal advice or services, and down the road something goes wrong, you'll blame them even if it wasn't their fault.

Why Lawyers Think Special Needs Trusts Are Too Complex for Nonlawyers

Many estate planning lawyers refer clients who want special needs trusts to other lawyers who specialize in SSI and Medicaid issues. This is because most estate planning lawyers are unfamiliar with SSI and Medicaid, which are programs designed for the poor. And if a regular estate planning lawyer isn't competent to handle special needs trusts, a nonlawyer certainly isn't—or so the thinking goes.

This attitude toward self-help law has been around for years. Nolo's first book— *How to Do Your Own California Divorce*—was attacked by a local bar association, which warned people that doing your own divorce was like doing your own brain surgery. Now, more than 30 years later, more than half of the divorces in many states are handled without a lawyer—both because many people can't afford lawyers and many others realize they aren't necessary in many cases. And hundreds of thousands of people have drafted their own living trusts and wills (as well as patents, trademarks, and partnership agreements) with the help of good materials written for nonlawyers.

With a little time, lawyers will also get used to the idea of nonlawyers creating special needs trusts. But for now, if you approach a special needs trust lawyer for help, you risk being scolded or cajoled into hiring the lawyer to do it all, for a hefty fee.

In fact, the special needs trust in this book isn't as complicated as most lawyers think. There are two types of special needs trusts: third-party trusts and self-settled trusts. (Chapter 1 explains this.) Self-settled trusts can be problematic because they involve the beneficiary's own money—money that Medicaid would dearly love to get its hands on. But third-party trusts involve property that never belonged to the beneficiary in the first place, and Medicaid has little or no interest in it. For that reason, the law of third-party special needs trusts has been remarkably stable; while the law regarding self-settled trusts has been subject to more frequent changes.

Why Lawyers Try to Avoid Giving Piecemeal Services

Even a lawyer who is comfortable with the idea of you using this book may be reluctant to get involved on a piecemeal basis. Lawyers learn early that the only way to make sure something is done right is to do it all themselves. They are worried that if you end up doing something that messes up your trust, they will be held responsible.

It's also difficult for a lawyer to analyze someone else's trust document—even one created by another lawyer. They much prefer to simply use the one they're familiar with. The trust document in this book is a product of research, thought, and experience. It's also written in plain English, at least compared to typical trusts drafted by other lawyers. Lawyers who are used to their own wordy trusts may not know quite what to make of it.

How to Find Special Needs Trust Lawyers

The world is full of lawyers—but finding one who has the expertise you need and a manner you like can take some shopping around.

General Estate Planning Lawyers

If you are already working with an estate planning lawyer—perhaps for your will or revocable living trust—that lawyer will most likely be able to help you or refer you to a special needs trust specialist.

An estate planning lawyer might send you to a special needs trust lawyer for all your estate planning. Or you might work with both. For example, your estate planning lawyer might charge you $500 to draft your will, and the specialist might charge you another $1,000 to add the special needs trust to it.

Elder Law Attorneys

Most lawyers who handle special needs trusts call themselves "elder law" attorneys. The reason is that many of them got their start helping elderly people obtain federal support and medical benefits. Because special needs trusts also require knowledge of SSI and Medicaid rules, special needs trusts have become a second specialty for these lawyers.

You may well be able to get a recommendation from someone in your own informal network of friends and acquaintances. You undoubtedly know people with a family member who has the same or similar disability as your loved one—they may have already found a lawyer who could also help you.

You can also check in with any local or national group that concerns itself with a particular disabled population. The two most widely known organizations are The Arc (primarily serving people with developmental or cognitive disabilities) and the National Alliance for the Mentally Ill (NAMI). However, hundreds of other groups focus on specific disabilities such as spina bifida, paraplegia, cystic fibrosis, and autism. Chances are these groups work with lawyers who not only are adept at special needs trusts but who also may cut you a break on the fees. Often, these lawyers have a child or relative of their own with a disability, and have both practical and legal insights to offer.

Organizations that create pooled trusts (discussed in Chapter 7) can be an excellent place to obtain a referral. Appendix A contains contact information for pooled trusts.

Two other places to find elder law attorneys are:

- The National Academy of Elder Law Attorneys website, www.naela.org, which lets you search for member lawyers by zip code or city.

- The Special Needs Alliance (a national network of disability attorneys), at www.specialneedsalliance.com.

What to Look for in a Lawyer

First and foremost, you want a lawyer who has experience in drafting special needs trusts. But you'll also want a lawyer you feel comfortable with.

In many parts of the country, you may have little choice of special needs trust lawyers. If so, as the old song goes, "Love the one you're with." But if you have several lawyers to pick from, here are a few questions to consider after an initial meeting:

- Does the lawyer seem interested in helping you resolve your specific questions and issues?

- Is the lawyer respectful of your self-help efforts even if he or she believes you would be better off using a lawyer?

- Does the lawyer seem confident (but not overconfident) of having the skills and knowledge to do the job well?

- Is the lawyer willing to charge a reasonable fee based on the services you are requesting, taking into account that you won't need as much counseling or handholding as someone who hasn't learned about special needs trusts?

- Are you willing and able to pay the lawyer's fee?

- Perhaps most important, is the chemistry right? Do you feel reassured that you'll get exactly the services you need, no more and no less?

Paralegals

Social Security regulations explicitly authorize nonlawyer paralegals to represent clients in administrative proceedings dealing with benefit disputes. So if you have questions about your state's SSI and Medicaid income and resource rules, a paralegal may be just the ticket.

You can find paralegals in your area by using the Yellow Pages. Look under the paralegal heading. Look for a paralegal who specializes in SSI and Medicaid matters, and compare fees.

Paralegals who work in the Social Security area are unregulated. If you want recourse in case you get bum advice, hire a paralegal who carries "errors and omissions" insurance—many do. Of course you may have to pay more if your paralegal is insured, but it may well be worth it.

If you need information about customizing your special needs trust or your options for a different type of trust—for instance, one that takes effect during your life—you'll need to see a lawyer. Paralegals are limited to advice and information about Social Security matters.

Certified Financial Planners

Special needs trusts often involve financial planning over a long period of time. Financial planners are people with accounting, investment, and insurance knowledge who can help you compute how much money you will need to accomplish your general estate planning goals and adequately fund your special needs trust.

Financial planners are not licensed professionals, but a central board certifies them. (For information about the certification process, visit www.cfp.net.)

Financial planners can provide a wealth of information on:

- how much money the special needs trust will need to accomplish your goals for your loved one

- a budget for the trustee who will manage the trust, and

- the best sources of funding for the trust, including advice on insurance options.

To find a local certified financial planner, visit these websites (or enter "certified financial planner" and your city's name into your favorite search engine):

- www.fpanet.org

- www.paladininvestors.com

- www.wiseradvisor.com.

FINANCIAL PLANNERS AREN'T ALWAYS DISINTERESTED ADVISERS. Many financial planners are affiliated with one or more insurance companies. Their advice may be sound, but they also have an interest in selling insurance at rates that might not be in your best interest. Especially when you are exploring insurance options, make sure you ask the right questions. As mentioned earlier, term life insurance is often the cheapest and best way to go.

SSA and Medicaid Personnel

A special needs trust is designed to preserve your loved one's SSI and Medicaid benefits. If you need more information about those benefits than this book provides, ask someone at your local SSA office. Most likely you'll get your question answered.

If there is a program near where you live that delivers legal services to the poor, you might visit it and see what materials it has. You may find written resources explaining various aspects of the SSI and Medicaid programs, and the staff may be able to answer your questions.

Keeping Up to Date

Many years may pass between the time you draft a special needs trust and when the trust actually goes into effect. For example, if you are in your 40s or 50s when you create a special needs trust, at least 30 or 40 years will probably go by before you die and the trust goes into effect. Anything could happen, including:

- SSI and Medicaid rules change in ways that require you to amend the trust
- SSI and Medicaid rules change and make your loved one ineligible for benefits—which would eliminate the need for a special needs trust
- your loved one develops additional needs that you want to specifically provide for in the trust
- your loved one is no longer disabled and can inherit the property outright, or
- a single-payer health care system is implemented (don't hold your breath), making a special needs trust unnecessary in many cases.

Obviously, you need to stay on top of such developments.

Disability Groups' Newsletters and Websites

One excellent way to keep up to date on changes is to hook up with a group that cares about disabilities and check its newsletters and website. These organizations will pick up on any changes in government regulations. Some groups are listed below. You can also get information from groups that focus on a specific condition, such as autism or Down syndrome.

Some Sources of Information About Disability Benefits and Laws
National Academy of Elder Law Attorneys, www.naela.org
National Senior Citizens Law Center, www.nsclc.org
Special Needs Alliance (a lawyer group), www.specialneedsalliance.org
Exceptional Parent magazine, www.eparent.com/lifeplanning/default.htm
Metropolitan Life Insurance division for special needs, www.metlife.com/desk 877-MetDESK (638-3375)
The Arc, www.thearc.org

Federal Statutes and Regulations

If you want to be connected directly to the source of SSI and Medicaid regulation changes, you can read the government regulations themselves. Some of the language is dense, but the regs can be helpful if you are willing to take some time to read and digest them. Most of them are in Volume 20 of the Code of Federal Regulations (C.F.R.), Section 416. Online sources are listed below.

Topic of Regulation or Statute	Citation	Website
Regulations issued by the Social Security Administration	20 C.F.R. §§ 101-416.2227	www.gpoaccess.gov/cfr/index.html
SSI resource rules	20 C.F.R. §§ 416.1210-416.1238	www.gpoaccess.gov/cfr/index.html
SSI in general	20 C.F.R. §§ 416.101-416.2227	www.gpoaccess.gov/cfr/index.html
Medicaid	42 C.F.R. §§ 430-456.657	www.gpoaccess.gov/cfr/index.html
Medicaid eligibility	42 C.F.R. §§ 435.700-435.740	www.gpoaccess.gov/cfr/index.html
Guidelines relied on by workers at the Social Security and local district offices	POMS (*Program Operations Manual System*)	http://policy.ssa.gov/poms.nsf/aboutpoms
State rules for Medicaid		www.cms.hhs.gov/medicaid/consumer.asp
How local SSI and Medicaid offices must treat special needs trusts	42 U.S.C. § 1396r-5 (Medicare Catastrophic Coverage Act of 1998), 42 U.S.C. §1396p(d)(4) (A-C)(a-e)	www.ssa.gov
Medicaid. Especially useful: Transmittal 64 (treatment of special needs trusts by SSI and Medicaid) and Transmittal 75 (estate recoveries)		www.cms.hhs.gov

The particular areas of interest to you at all these sites are:

- how the SSI and Medicaid programs view special needs trusts funded by third parties

- what property the SSI and Medicaid programs consider the recipient's countable resources for eligibility purposes

- what the SSI and Medicaid programs consider to be income, and

- what the SSI and Medicaid programs consider to be income in kind, including in-kind support and maintenance (ISM).

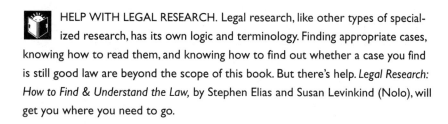 HELP WITH LEGAL RESEARCH. Legal research, like other types of specialized research, has its own logic and terminology. Finding appropriate cases, knowing how to read them, and knowing how to find out whether a case you find is still good law are beyond the scope of this book. But there's help. *Legal Research: How to Find & Understand the Law,* by Stephen Elias and Susan Levinkind (Nolo), will get you where you need to go.

Books

Needless to say, a fair number of books discuss special needs trusts. Most deal with raising children with special needs and address the entire subject, from cradle to grave. Special needs trusts are but one subject of many.

To find these books, simply go to a good bookstore and look in the special needs or parenting sections. Or try an online bookstore and search for "special needs." You may be surprised at how many titles appear.

A few books provide a more detailed discussion of special needs trusts, both self-settled and third-party trusts. Many of them were written for lawyers, and you're mostly likely to find them in a law library. Law libraries accessible to the general public typically are located in courthouses, civic center buildings, or public law schools.

All law libraries have reference librarians, who are generally most helpful and willing to get you started. Just ask for materials on special needs trusts and you'll probably be given more than you can comfortably deal with.

Antitransfer laws. Laws that penalize people who, in order to become eligible for means-tested benefits such as SSI and Medicaid, have transferred their assets to others for less than fair market value.

Asset. Anything of value, including cash, promissory notes, tangible and intangible personal property, and real estate.

Beneficial interest. A type of property ownership held by people who are expected to benefit from trust assets in some way but who currently have no legal claim to them. The beneficiary of a special needs trust has a beneficial interest in the trust assets.

Beneficiary. Any person or entity entitled to inherit or receive property under a will or trust. The person for whom a special needs trust is created and whose needs will be paid for under the terms of the trust is the trust beneficiary.

Beneficiary designation. A document in which the owner of a deposit, retirement, or brokerage account names a beneficiary to receive any funds left in the account at the owner's death.

Burial policy. An insurance policy that covers the cost of disposing of a person's remains.

Code of Federal Regulations (C.F.R.). A set of publications containing regulations issued by federal agencies and organized by subject. Regulations for the SSI program are found in 20 C.F.R. §§ 416.101 and following.

Community trust. See Pooled trust.

Conditional SSI payments. Temporary SSI payments made on the condition that the recipient get rid of certain assets in an appropriate manner. They are made if an applicant for SSI has too many assets to qualify for that program.

Conservator. A person appointed by a court to make personal and/or financial decisions for another person (the conservatee) who is not able to make them.

Conservatorship. The relationship between a conservator and conservatee.

Corporate trustee. A bank or other financial institution that provides trustee services for various types of trusts. Many special needs trusts expected to be funded with $250,000 or more have a corporate trustee, instead of a family member, manage trust assets.

Corpus. A Latin term for the assets held in a trust.

Cotrustee. One of two or more persons or institutions named to manage trust assets together.

Countable resource. Property that the SSI and Medicaid programs consider available to an applicant or recipient when determining that person's eligibility for benefits. Assets held in a properly drafted third-party special needs trust are not countable assets.

Custodianship. An arrangement created under a state law called the Uniform Transfers to Minors Act, under which a person may name an adult (the custodian) to manage property left to a minor until the minor turns an age between 18 and 25, depending on the state.

Direct inheritance. Property left outright to someone. SSI and Medicaid benefits may be reduced or eliminated if a recipient receives a direct inheritance, since the inheritance will be counted as income in the month received and as a resource in the following months. Property left to a special needs trust is not counted as a direct inheritance.

Disability. In general, a physical, sensory, psychiatric, learning, or intellectual impairment that affects daily living activities. Disabilities may be either temporary or permanent; they may arise from illness or injury or be present from birth. For the purpose of obtaining SSI and Medicaid, a disability is a mental or physical condition that leaves someone permanently unable to "do any substantial gainful activity."

Disabled. Having a disability. Many people with disabling conditions prefer to be identified according to their specific disability, such as "a person with paraplegia" or "a person with cerebral palsy."

Disbursements. Payments of trust funds by the trustee. In a special needs trust, the trustee typically makes disbursements to pay for the beneficiary's needs that aren't covered by SSI or Medicaid, such as a companion, school tuition, books, or hobby equipment.

Earned income. Wages paid by an employer or income from self-employment. Earned income can result in a reduced SSI payment.

Elder law. Legal issues typically faced by the elderly, including government benefits, nursing home care, and elder abuse.

Estate planning. Creating documents necessary to carry out your wishes for what should happen to your property and children after your death. Often, estate planning involves strategies designed to minimize probate fees so that more is left for inheritors.

Estate tax. Federal and state taxes imposed on the value of a person's net worth at death. Federal estate taxes currently apply to estates with a net worth exceeding $1.5 million, but some states tax smaller estates.

Executor. The person named in a will to carry out the will's provisions, including filing the will in the proper court, inventorying the deceased person's property, paying debts and taxes, and distributing the remaining property to the beneficiaries named in the will. Called personal representative in some states.

Exempt asset. See Noncountable asset.

Federal benefit rate. The share of the SSI grant paid by the federal government. Many states add a supplementary grant to the federal benefit rate.

Fiduciary. A person who owes a special duty of trust to another person or entity. In a special needs trust, the trustee owes a fiduciary duty to the beneficiary of the trust to strictly comply with the trust's terms and to manage the trust solely for the beneficiary's benefit.

Financial planner. A person skilled in assessing people's financial needs and the various options for meeting them, including various types of insurance and investments. Many financial planners are certified by a central trade organization, but governments don't license them.

Food. Ordinary food—that is, food that isn't necessary because of special medical needs—is supposed to be paid for by SSI. If the trustee of a special needs trust pays for the beneficiary's food, the amount paid is considered income to the beneficiary and deducted from the grant, up to a certain amount.

Funding a trust. Putting property in trust by assigning the property to the trust or changing title documents to reflect the trust's ownership. Technically, the trustee owns the trust property, subject to the trust's terms and the trustee's fiduciary duty.

Furniture and personal effects. As defined by the SSA, just about any property typically used in a home. Furniture and personal effects are not counted as resources for the purpose of determining a person's eligibility for SSI and Medicaid.

Gift. Property permanently transferred to someone without receiving anything in return. Property transferred to an irrevocable living trust while the giver is alive is considered a gift because the property can't be taken back. However, property transferred to a revocable living trust is not a gift, because the giver does not give up control over it and can revoke the trust at any time. Finally, property left at death under a will or living trust is commonly called a gift.

Gift tax. A federal tax imposed on gifts to any one person that exceed $11,000 in one calendar year. The tax is not payable when the gift is made but rather when the person giving the gift dies. Every person can make up to $1 million in taxable gifts before gift tax is owed.

Good faith. The honest belief that one's actions are correct and appropriate. Most special needs trusts provide that trustees are not liable for losses caused by actions taken in good faith.

Grantor. Someone who creates a trust. Also called settlor or trustor.

Group home. For purposes of the Medicaid program, a home in which two or more SSI recipients live and receive food and shelter for one overall price.

Guardian. A person appointed by a court to handle the personal and financial affairs of a child, or of an adult who has been judged to be unable to handle these matters alone. In many states, the term conservator is used when the incompetent person is an adult.

Independent trustee. A trustee who is not related to the beneficiary of the trust and does not stand to inherit any property under the trust. Independent trustees are preferred when family members are likely to disagree over management of the trust. However, independent trustees' fees are usually higher than those charged by a family member.

Inheritance. Property received as a result of another person's death. Typically, a person receives an inheritance under the terms of a will, revocable living trust, or state law (termed the law of intestate succession).

In-kind income. See In-kind support and maintenance.

In-kind support and maintenance (ISM). Shelter or food provided to an SSI recipient. The value of ISM is considered income. An SSI recipient's monthly grant is reduced dollar for dollar by the total value of the ISM received in a month, up to a certain amount. Also called in-kind income.

Inter vivos trust. A trust created by a person during his or her lifetime (inter vivos is Latin for "between the living"). The most popular form of inter vivos trust is the revocable living trust. However, an inter vivos trust may also be irrevocable—for example, a special needs trust that is created and immediately put into effect by a living grantor.

Joinder agreement. The written contract between a person who contributes funds to a pooled trust on behalf of a disabled loved one and the nonprofit organization operating the pooled trust. The joinder agreement "joins" the beneficiary's funds with the other funds in the pooled trust.

Letter of intent. A term commonly used to describe a letter in which the creator of a special needs trust provides personal details about the trust beneficiary for the guidance of future trustees of the trust.

Living trust. A trust created during the grantor's lifetime, usually to avoid probate and sometimes to also avoid federal estate tax. The grantor is usually the trustee during his or her life; then the successor trustee takes over and distributes the trust property to beneficiaries named in the trust document. Sometimes called inter vivos trust or revocable living trust.

Long-term care. Nursing home care that lasts more than two months. Nursing home care typically is paid for by long-term care insurance, or by Medicaid if the patient meets strict income and resource limitations.

Master trust. A special needs trust under which a nonprofit organization operates a pooled trust on behalf of many individual beneficiaries.

Medicaid. A health care delivery program intended to serve people with limited income and resources. Medicaid is paid for with state and federal funds. It is administered by the states, which, under federal rules, determine who is eligible for benefits.

Medically needy. People whose income is too high for regular Medicaid eligibility but who are eligible for benefits if they contribute part of their income (called their share of cost) towards their medical care.

Medicare. A health care delivery system available to people who qualify because of age or disability and work history. Medicare eligibility does not depend on a person's income or resources. People who qualify for Medicare may still need Medicaid to pay for prescriptions and long-term care, and many people with limited income and resources receive benefits under both programs.

Negligence. Failure to act in a way that a reasonable and prudent person would act under similar circumstances.

Noncountable resource. Property that is not considered as a resource by the SSI and Medicaid programs for purposes of determining program eligibility.

OBRA. The federal Omnibus Budget Reconciliation Act, a law that, among other things, describes the circumstances under which property in a special needs trust may be considered the trust beneficiary's resource for the purpose of determining eligibility for SSI and Medicaid. (42 U.S.C. §§ 1395 and following.)

Payback provision. A provision in a special needs trust requiring that, after the beneficiary dies, the trustee must use any property left in the trust to reimburse Medicaid for benefits the beneficiary received. Special needs trusts containing property originally belonging to the beneficiary (self-settled trusts) must have a payback provision to avoid having the property considered the beneficiary's resource for program eligibility purposes. Third-party trusts, like the one in this book, do not have a payback provision.

Personal representative. See Executor.

Plan for Achieving Self-Support (PASS). A plan (approved by SSI) that allows an SSI recipient to own otherwise countable resources as part of an effort to become self-supporting.

POMS. *Program Operations Manual Systems*, a set of guidelines issued by the Social Security Administration to help lower-level employees interpret the federal statutes and regulations that govern the SSI and Medicaid programs.

Pooled trust. A special needs trust operated by a nonprofit organization for the benefit of several beneficiaries. Assets are jointly managed and invested. SSI does not consider pooled trust funds donated by a third party for a beneficiary to be a resource available to the beneficiary.

Presumed maximum value (PMV). The presumed value of food or shelter provided to an SSI recipient by a third party. The PMV is the amount of the federal portion of the SSI grant plus $20. In 2005, this amount is $213. The recipient can prove that the value is in fact less.

Principal. Property held in trust. Income generated by the trust principal is considered income in the year received and principal if retained in the trust after that time. Also called trust corpus.

Principal residence. A person's home and the land on which it is situated. SSI does not consider a person's principal residence a resource, regardless of its value.

Probate. A court proceeding in which 1) the authenticity of a will (if any) is established, 2) the person whose responsibility it is to handle the person's estate (executor or administrator) is appointed, 3) the deceased person's debts and taxes are paid, 4) the people who inherit are identified, and 5) the property is distributed to them. Probate happens only if someone petitions the court to open a probate proceeding, and only affects property that hasn't been disposed of in some other way—for example, through a trust.

Prudent Investor Act. A law containing investment principles articulated by a group of nationally respected judges and law professors. Most states apply these principles to trustees in the absence of contrary investment instructions in the trust document. As a whole, the law requires trustees to make commonsense investment decisions that will best serve the purposes of the trust.

Remainder beneficiary. A person or institution named in a special needs trust to receive trust property that remains in the trust at the death of the disabled beneficiary.

Representative payee. Typically, a person authorized by a government agency such as the Social Security Administration to receive benefits such as SSI payments on behalf of a recipient who is not competent to handle his or her own money.

Resource. For purposes of determining SSI eligibility, any property that the SSI program considers available to the applicant. See Countable resource and Noncountable resource.

Revocable living trust. See Living trust. The term revocable refers to the fact that the person who sets up the trust can amend or revoke it.

Section 8 housing. A federal rent subsidy program under which landlords accept low-income tenants. Tenants pay a portion of their income, and the agency pays the rest.

Self-settled trust. A special needs trust funded with property belonging to the beneficiary, such as a direct inheritance, recovery in a personal injury lawsuit, or gift.

Settlor. Another term for grantor.

Shelter. For SSI purposes, any item commonly associated with housing such as rent, heat, utilities, and mortgage payments. Disbursements from special needs trusts for shelter are considered in-kind support and maintenance (ISM) and are deducted from the SSI grant up to a certain amount.

Sheltered workshop. A place of employment designed and managed to accommodate the needs of people with disabilities.

Social Security Act. A collection of federal statutes that govern a variety of federal programs, including Social Security retirement and disability benefits, Medicare, SSI, and Medicaid.

Social Security Administration (SSA). The agency charged with administering the programs created under the Social Security Act, including SSI and Medicaid.

Special needs. All needs of a disabled person for goods and services other than food and shelter, which SSI deems to be provided in the SSI grant itself.

Special needs trust. A trust designed to hold and disburse property for the benefit of an SSI recipient without the SSI and Medicaid programs considering the trust property or disbursements to be a resource or income. To accomplish this purpose, the trust typically gives the trustee sole discretion over trust disbursements and bars the trustee from making disbursements that would impair the beneficiary's eligibility for SSI and Medicaid. In addition, the trust must be for the beneficiary's sole benefit and bar creditors from going after trust assets. A special needs trust funded with the beneficiary's own property (a self-settled trust) is subject to additional restrictions.

Spend down. To spend resources on medical needs when an applicant for certain Medicaid benefits has resources over the resource limit. When the applicant's resources are sufficiently reduced, he or she will qualify for Medicaid.

Spendthrift provisions. Clauses in a trust aimed at protecting the trust property from the beneficiary's creditors, or allowing the beneficiary to use the trust property as collateral for a loan. All special needs trusts contain spendthrift provisions.

SSDI. Social Security Disability Insurance. This federal program provides monthly cash payments to disabled persons who qualify because they have paid enough Social Security taxes. There are no resource or income ceilings.

SSI. Supplemental Security Income, a federal program that provides cash payments to persons of limited income and resources who are disabled (according to federal standards), over age 65, or blind. SSI is the main form of government support for people who aren't eligible for Social Security retirement or disability benefits and who meet the program's income and resources requirements.

Successor trustee. A person named in a trust to take over as trustee when the first trustee dies or is otherwise unable to serve. In a revocable living trust, the first trustee is the person who sets up the trust (the grantor). The successor trustee is the person who carries out the provisions of the trust after the grantor's death.

Supplemental needs trust. Another name for a special needs trust.

Support trust. A type of trust that allows the trustee to make disbursements for the beneficiary's general support as well as other needs. A support trust does not qualify as a special needs trust for the purpose of sheltering trust property from consideration as a resource by SSI and Medicaid.

Term life insurance. A type of life insurance that pays out the face value of the policy at the policy owner's death but that does not have an investment or savings feature. Term life insurance is often used to fund a special needs trust.

Testamentary trust. A trust created as part of a will that goes into effect at the willmaker's death.

Testator. Someone who makes a will.

Third-party trust. A special needs trust funded exclusively with property given by people other than the beneficiary. The trust in this book is a third-party trust. Compare self-settled trust, which contains property originally belonging to the beneficiary.

Transfer of assets. The act of getting rid of property for less than its fair market value in order to become eligible for SSI or long-term care benefits under Medicaid.

Trust. An arrangement under which a person called a trustee has a duty to manage certain property in a way that benefits a beneficiary. Trusts are created for many different purposes. See Special needs trust and Living trust.

Trust administration. A trustee's management of trust property according to the trust's terms and for the benefit of the beneficiaries.

Trustee. A person named in a trust instrument, or chosen by an existing trustee, to manage the trust under the terms of the trust document. The trustee must be loyal to the trust and avoid conflicts of interest with the trust beneficiaries. In a special needs trust, the trustee owes a duty to manage the trust so that the beneficiary's special needs may be met without jeopardizing the beneficiary's eligibility for SSI and Medicaid.

Trustee powers. Specific grants of authority given to a trustee by the trust document in addition to, or in place of, authority granted by state law.

Unearned income. For SSI purposes, all income that does not result from employment.

Uniform Transfers to Minors Act. A law adopted by all but two states (Vermont and South Carolina) that provides a method for transferring property to minors and arranging for an adult, called a custodian, to manage the property until the child is older.

Whole life insurance. A type of life insurance that builds up equity in the policy owner's name and pays out a predetermined amount—when the insured person dies—to beneficiaries designated by the policy owner. Compare Term life insurance.

Will. A legal document in which someone leaves property and names a guardian to raise any surviving minor children after death.

Pooled Trusts

We've tried to make this list of pooled trusts in the United States as complete and up-to-date as we could, but you should always check with a local disability advocacy group, too. If a pooled trust exists in your locale or state, they will know about it.

Alaska

Foundation of The Arc of Anchorage
2211 Arca Dr.
Anchorage, AK 99508
907-277-6677
www.arc-anchorage.org

California

Special Needs Trust Foundation
9575 Aero Drive
San Diego, CA 92123
858-715-3780

PLAN of California
1336 Wilshire Blvd., 2nd Floor (LA MHA)
Los Angeles, CA 90017
or
17602 17th St., #102-240
Tustin, CA 92780
213-413-1130
714-997-3310
888-574-1258
www.planofcalifornia
(website under construction)

Colorado

The Colorado Fund for People with Disabilities
One Broadway, Suite A-330
Denver, CO 80203
303-733-2867
www.codisabilitytrust.org

Delaware

Delaware CarePlan, Inc.
1016 Center Road, Suite One
Wilmington, DE 19805-1234
302-633-4000
decareplan@aol.com
(Website has limited access; call to receive
information in the mail.)

Florida

Advocate Trust, Inc.
1501 N. Belcher Rd., Suite 219
Clearwater, FL 33765
727-791-3972
www.atrustinc.org

The Florida Pooled Trust
2600 First Avenue North
St. Petersburg, FL 33713
877-766-5331
www.firstpooledtrust.org

PLAN of Florida
4605 Community Drive
West Palm Beach, FL 33417
561-684-1991
www.jfcspb.org

Illinois

Life Plan, Inc.
2801 Finley Road
Downers Grove, IL 60515
630-628-7168
www.lifesplaninc.com
www.lifesplaninc.org

Indiana

The Arc of Indiana Master Trust
P.O. Box 80033
Indianapolis, IN 46280-0033
317-259-7603
877-589-8848
www.arcind.org

Kansas

ARCare - Master Trust I & II and Guardianship
8001 Conser
Overland Park, KS 66204
913-648-0233
www.arcare.org

Massachusetts

Berkshire County Arc Pooled Trust
395 South Street
Pittsfield, MA 01201
413-499-4241
www.bcarc.org

Jewish Family & Children's Service
of Greater Boston
174 Portland Street
Boston, MA 02114
617-227-6641
www.jfcsboston.org

MARC Trust, Inc.
1301 Centre Street
Newton Centre, MA 02459
617-244-5552
info@marctrust.org (URL not yet available)

The Arc of Massachusetts
217 South St.
Waltham, MA 02453
781-891-6270
www.arcmass.org

Michigan

The Arc of Midland
220 West Main Street, Suite #101
Midland, MI 48640
989-631-4439
www.thearcofmidland.org

New Hampshire

Enhanced Life Options Group
15 Constitution Drive, Suite 169
Bedford, NH 03110
603-472-2543
603-524-4189
www.elonh.org

New Jersey

PLAN of New Jersey
P.O. Box 547
Somerville, NJ 08876-0547
908-575-8300
(Website under construction—no URL available yet)

Sussex Arc
SCARC Guardianship Services, Inc.
11 U.S. Route 206, Suite 100
Augusta, NJ 07822 973-383-7442
www.scarc.org

New Mexico

The Arc of New Mexico
Master Trust One and Two Program
3655 Carlisle, NE
Albuquerque, NM 87110-5564
505-883-4630
www.arcnm.com

New York

NYSARC, Inc., New York State Guardianship
Services
393 Delaware Ave.
Delmar, NY 12054
518-439-8311
www.nysarc.org

F·E·G·S
Community Trust and PLAN
(in cooperation with UJA-Federation of New York,
Inc.)
315 Hudson Street
New York, NY 10013
212-366-8008
www.fegs.org

UJA-Federation of New York, Inc.
Community Trusts (in cooperation with F·E·G·S
Community Trust and PLAN)
130 East 59th Street, Suite 1504
New York, NY 10022
212-836-1339
www.ujafedny.org

Life Services Third-Party-Funded Trust for People
with Disabilities, Disabled and Alone/Life Services
for the Handicapped, Inc.
352 Park Avenue South, 11th Floor
NY, New York 10010
212-532-6740
800-995-0066
www.disabledandalone.org

North Carolina

The Arc of North Carolina
Life Plan Trust
122 Salem Towne Court
Apex, NC 27502
919-589-0017
www.arcnc.org

Ohio

Community Fund Management Foundation
1275 Lakeside Avenue East
Cleveland, OH 44114-1132
216-736-4540
www.cfmf.org

The Disability Foundation, Inc.,
c/o The Dayton Foundation
The Ohio Community Pooled Trust
2300 Kettering Tower
Dayton, OH 45423
937-225-9939
www.daytonfoundation.org

Oregon

The Arc of Oregon
The Oregon Special Needs Trust
1745 State St.
Salem, OR 97301
503-581-2726
877-581-2726
www.arcoregon.org/index.htm

Pennsylvania

The Arc of Berks County
Berks Community Trust
1829 New Holland Rd., Suite 9
Reading, PA 19607-2228
610-603-0227
www.Berksiu.org/arc

Achieva
The Family Trust
711 Bingham St.
Pittsburgh, PA 15203-1007
412-995-5000
www.achieva.info

Rhode Island

Self-Sufficiency Trust of Rhode Island
1255 North Main Street
Providence, RI 02904
401-331-3060
www.namiri.org

Texas

The Arc of Texas Master Pooled Trust
8001 Centre Park Drive, Suite 100
Austin, TX 78754
512-454-6694
www.thearcoftexas.org

Virginia

Commonwealth Community Trust
P.O. Box 29408
Richmond, VA 23233
804-740-6930
www.commonwealthcommunitytrust.org

Norfolk Community Services Board
Norfolk Community Trust
248 West Bute Street
Norfolk, VA 23510-1404
757-441-5300
www.norfolk.gov/norfolkcsb

The Arc of Northern Virginia
The Personal Support Trusts
100 North Washington Street, Suite 234
Falls Church, VA 22046
703-532-3214
www.thearcofnova.org

Community Services Board
Virginia Beach Department of Human Services
Virginia Beach Community Trust (MR and MR/SA)
Pembroke Six, Suite 218
Virginia Beach, VA 23462
757-437-6100
www.vbgov.com/dept/hs/mhmrsa/contact
www.vbgov.com/dept/hs/mhmrsa/services

Washington

Lifetime Advocacy Plus
11000 Lake City Way NE, Suite 401
Seattle, WA 98125-6748
206-367-8055
www.laplus.org

The Arc of King County
10550 Lake City Way NE, Suite A
Seattle, WA 98125-7752
206-364-6337
www.arcofkingcounty.org

Appendix B

Letter to Trustee/Trustee's Duties

Letter to Trustee

Dear _____:

Thank you for agreeing to be the trustee of a special needs trust for [name of beneficiary]. Here you will find some basic information about how that special needs trust works and what your job as trustee will entail.

You won't have to handle the trustee's job alone; [name of cotrustee(s)] is also being named as a trustee of the trust. The trust document will tell you whether you can act independently or whether you must all agree to any actions taken behalf of the trust. You should do your best to cooperate with the other cotrustees to fulfill the purposes of the trust.

If you have questions that aren't answered here, the terms of the actual trust document are the final authority. The trust document was created using *Special Needs Trusts: Protect Your Child's Financial Future*, by Stephen Elias (Nolo). You may want to look at that book for explanations of the various trust provisions. (If your trust document was drafted by an attorney, contact that attorney for specific instructions; don't rely on these instructions.)

Again, sincere thanks for taking on this responsibility.

Managing a Special Needs Trust

This trust was created because the beneficiary is receiving—or will receive—benefits under the Supplemental Security Income (SSI) and Medicaid programs because of a disability or age. Both programs are available only to people with limited income and resources. The trust is designed to enhance the beneficiary's quality of life without interfering with SSI and Medicaid benefits.

As trustee, you have complete discretion over disbursements. The beneficiary has no legal control over trust property. As a result, the SSI and Medicaid programs don't consider trust assets to be a resource available to the beneficiary, and don't interfere with the beneficiary's eligibility for those programs.

An overview

You are responsible for:

- communicating with the beneficiary
- investing trust assets prudently
- spending trust money to meet the beneficiary's special needs in a way that minimally interferes with his or her SSI and Medicaid benefits
- keeping good records
- preparing reports and notices required by SSI, Medicaid, and other interested parties identified in the trust document, and
- filing trust tax returns.

Each of these duties has a learning curve. You can get expert help with all of them, as discussed below.

Communicating with the beneficiary

The core purpose of the special needs trust is to enhance the beneficiary's quality of life. This means you'll need to be sensitive to the beneficiary's special needs and have a basic understanding of how those needs can best be met. In some cases there will be another person in the beneficiary's life—an advocate, conservator, or guardian—whose job it is to look out for the beneficiary. But in other situations, you will be the primary person the beneficiary depends on for help. If the beneficiary is unable to act independently, you may be called on to function as a surrogate parent.

If you are already well acquainted with the beneficiary—perhaps you are a sibling or other close relative—you will know what to do. But if you do not have much of a prior acquaintance with the beneficiary, you will need a lot of information. Ideally the person creating the special needs trust—the grantor—will have prepared a beneficiary information letter that informs you about such things as the beneficiary's family and medical history, education, employment, living situation, social life, routines, and religion. If not, you should try to find these things out by talking to others who are familiar with the beneficiary.

Your fiduciary duty

As trustee, you are a "fiduciary"—someone who occupies a special position of trust. And because you have been entrusted with someone else's money, you have what is called a fiduciary duty to faithfully implement the trust's terms. This means you'll need to give the trust document a very close reading and make sure you understand what you can and cannot do. For example, no matter how much you want to make a particular disbursement, you can't if doing so would result in the beneficiary losing SSI and Medicaid.

You must administer the trust for the beneficiary's sole benefit. If a conflict of interest arises, your first duty is to the beneficiary. For example, if you are also the remainder beneficiary—the person who will receive any money left in the trust when the beneficiary dies—there is a conflict of interest between your duty to spend money to benefit the beneficiary and a natural desire to conserve the trust money in case you inherit it. This conflict doesn't legally prevent you from being trustee, but it does require that you put your own interests aside and administer the trust solely in the interests of the beneficiary.

Others can benefit indirectly from your acts as trustee, as long as your primary purpose is to benefit the beneficiary. For example, you could use trust funds to buy the beneficiary a car even if a friend or relative might use it on occasion. Similarly, you could buy a house for the beneficiary even if you also live there.

Spending trust money to meet the beneficiary's needs

All spending decisions are completely up to you. The beneficiary has no legal right to require any payments from the trust for any reason.

When you use trust property to benefit the beneficiary, you must make sure your disbursements don't cause the beneficiary to exceed the SSI income and resource limits. The trust prohibits you from making such disbursements, which would cause the beneficiary to lose SSI and Medicaid benefits.

SSI and Medicaid eligibility rules

SSI and Medicaid are available only to people who have limited resources and income. In most states, someone who qualifies for SSI also qualifies for Medicaid.

To avoid running afoul of SSI resource and income limits, follow these guidelines:

- **Never give the beneficiary cash or items that could easily be converted into cash.** A beneficiary who receives too much income will lose SSI benefits—and so Medicaid—at least temporarily. Except for the first $20 a month, all unearned income that is reported to SSI is deducted dollar-for-dollar from the SSI grant. And if you give too much income to the beneficiary, the SSI grant will be terminated for that month, along with Medicaid benefits.

- **Make payments from the trust directly to the provider of the goods or services for the benefit of the beneficiary.** The reason? Payments directly to the beneficiary count as income (regardless of what it's spent for), but payments to a third party for the beneficiary's benefit do not.

- **Don't use trust funds to pay for food or shelter unless you know it won't cause the beneficiary to lose SSI benefits.** (See below.)

- **Don't buy the beneficiary items that would put him or her over the SSI resource limit of $2,000 in assets.** (Many items, however, aren't counted toward the limit. See below.)

Exceptions to rule that SSI eligibility equals Medicaid eligibility. In 11 states, Medicaid eligibility is determined independently of SSI eligibility. These states are Connecticut, Hawaii, Illinois, Indiana, Minnesota, Missouri, New Hampshire, North Dakota, Ohio, Oklahoma, and Virginia. If the beneficiary lives in one of these states, you'll need to contact the state Medicaid office to get an exact fix on the effect of resources and income on Medicaid eligibility. Medicaid eligibility standards in these states are roughly similar to those in the other states but, where there are variances, the rules tend to be a tad stricter. In these states, you will want to find a good contact person in the Medicaid department, or a private Medicaid specialist, to answer your questions.

Some Things Special Needs Trusts Can Pay For

out-of-pocket medical and dental expenses

medical equipment not provided by Medicaid

eyeglasses

exercise equipment

annual independent checkups

transportation

motor vehicle

vehicle maintenance

vehicle insurance premiums

life insurance premiums

physical rehabilitation services

essential dietary needs

materials for hobbies

tickets for recreational or cultural events

musical instruments

cosmetics

home furnishings

home improvements

computer or electronic equipment

cable television

telephones, televisions, and radios

cameras

trips and vacations

visits to friends

entertainment

membership in book, health, record, video, or other clubs

newspaper and magazine subscriptions

athletic training or competitions

personal care attendant or escort

vocational rehabilitation or habilitation

professional services

costs of attending or participating in meetings, conferences, seminars, or training sessions

tuition and expenses connected with education

SSI and Medicaid resource rules: the $2,000 limit

The beneficiary may own the following assets and still be eligible for SSI:

- a home, regardless of its value

- one vehicle of any value

- furniture and personal effects (such things as clothing, jewelry, recreation equipment, games and crafts, books, magazines, videotapes, telephone and answering machine, TV, radio, VCR, DVD, computers, musical instruments, and stereo)

- a total of $2,000 worth of any other kind of asset, including a bank account

- any property necessary for a plan (approved by the SSI program) of self-support (such as office equipment), and

- a life insurance policy and/or burial policy worth less than $1,500.

Trust funds are not, for purposes of SSI eligibility, counted as a resource available to the beneficiary. The beneficiary's special needs trust is called a third-party trust because the trust money in it never belonged to the beneficiary. It's important to keep it that way. So never put any of the beneficiary's own property into the trust. Doing so could jeopardize the beneficiary's eligibility for SSI and Medicaid.

Payments for food and shelter

If you never give the beneficiary cash, you probably won't have a problem with the SSI income limits. But you can also jeopardize SSI benefits by providing the beneficiary with food or shelter.

That's because trust money used to pay for food or shelter is counted as income to the beneficiary. It has a special name: "in-kind income" or "in-kind support and maintenance" (ISM).

SSI is intended to pay for food and shelter. If you use trust funds to give the beneficiary these items, the SSI grant will be reduced. The value of the food and shelter the trust pays for in a given month will be deducted, dollar-for-dollar, from the SSI grant—up to a maximum deduction of one-third of the federal portion of the grant, plus $20. As of 2005, the maximum deduction is $213/month. This cap will increase slightly every year, so you'll want to keep up to date.

If the SSI grant is wiped out completely by this deduction, Medicaid benefits will be lost as well. So to avoid even a temporary loss of Medicaid eligibility, make sure that ISM doesn't exceed the SSI grant. In most states, the beneficiary's SSI grant is more than the $213 cap, so you don't have to worry.

For example, depending on where the beneficiary lives and the amount of money in the trust, you might reasonably pay $1,000 a month for the beneficiary's rent, causing a reduction of only $213 in the SSI grant. Not a bad deal. But if the SSI grant were less than $213, paying that rent would disqualify the beneficiary for SSI and therefore for Medicaid.

If you are a tad nervous by now, here are two comforting thoughts to keep in mind:

- ISM payments count as income only in the month they're received. So if you blow it and give the beneficiary too much income of whatever type, SSI and Medicaid will be restored the next month, provided the resource limit isn't violated.

- Even if the beneficiary is kicked off SSI because of too much income, there may be a way of reestablishing Medicaid eligibility if the trust pays the Medicaid program a certain amount every month as a share of cost.

What is "shelter"? Expenses related to the beneficiary's residence count as shelter expenditures and can cause a reduction in the SSI grant under the ISM rule.

Items that count as shelter and trigger an ISM reduction	Items that don't count as shelter
• mortgage payments	• telephone
• rent	• cable or satellite TV
• real estate taxe	• premiums for personal property insurance
• gas	• paper products
• electricity	• laundry and cleaning supplies
• water	• staff salaries
• sewer	• capital improvements to the home
• homeowner's insurance required by lender	• repairs to the home
• condo charges that include the above items	

(416 C.F.R. § 1130(b); POMS SI 00835.465D)

Setting and sticking to a budget

Once you know the ground rules for keeping the beneficiary eligible for SSI and Medicaid, you'll want to decide how much the trust can reasonably spend every year on the beneficiary's special needs without bankrupting the trust. A ballpark budget would be based on four variables:

- value of the trust property
- the beneficiary's life expectancy
- the beneficiary's likely special needs, and
- how the trust property is invested.

You know, roughly, the value of the trust property. You can also obtain a rough life expectancy from actuarial tables and, if necessary, the beneficiary's doctors.

The information about the beneficiary's likely special needs will come from your personal knowledge or conversations with the beneficiary's family and friends. Also read any written information about the beneficiary that accompanies the trust document.

If you have financial skills you may be able to sort this out yourself. But it would certainly be reasonable for you to hire a financial planner to help you arrive at a tentative initial budget.

One of the most difficult aspects of managing the trust may be sticking to your budget even if the beneficiary protests. For example, if the trust's annual budget is roughly $2,000 a year, and the beneficiary wants something that would cost the trust $10,000, should you honor the request or deny it? There is no easy answer. You'll have to use your best judgment. Whatever you decide, do your best to explain your decision to the beneficiary.

Investing trust assets

Your trust requires that you follow the investment guidelines set out in a law called the Prudent Investor Act. So when investing trust assets, you must:

- balance risk against return
- diversify investments
- consider the purpose of the trust, and
- evaluate the investment portfolio as a whole.

Because the purpose of the trust is to supplement an SSI grant, your investments will normally be conservative and favor liquidity over long-term growth. A mix of money market funds, index funds, equity funds, and bond funds would be a typical investment portfolio for a special needs trust.

A closer look at these rules follows. A financial planner or other investment expert will be well-versed in these requirements.

Balance risk against return. The Prudent Investor Act allows high-risk investments only if there is the reasonable possibility of a high return. Pretty reasonable.

For example, most investment advisers would tell you not to put trust money in a start-up business that you think will return about 13% on your investment. Given that you could expect close to 10% from much safer investments, the risk of the start-up failing is far greater than the extra return of 3%.

A high-risk investment can be justified, as part of a diversified portfolio, if, for example, the trust property has little value and the beneficiary has large projected special needs over a long period of time. In that case, you might want to invest as much as possible in a high-risk, high-return investment that will, if successful, have a much better chance of meeting the beneficiary's needs over time than conserving the small amount of trust property. On the other end of the spectrum, if you have a lot of money to work with, you might feel secure in investing part of it in a risky investment, given the potential return. The greater the value of the trust property, the more there is to spread around in different types of investments without serious risk that the trust will be depleted by a particularly bad investment.

Diversify investments. To reduce risk, the Act requires you to diversify investments. For example, if all of the trust property were invested in high-risk volatile stocks or in a low-risk savings account, the investment would not be diversified. Similarly, putting all the property in equity stocks, rather than part in stocks and part in bonds or other government securities, would fail the diversification test.

Consider the purpose of the trust. The purpose of the trust is to pay for the beneficiary's special needs for as long as possible without jeopardizing eligibility for SSI and Medicaid. The purpose is definitely not to build the value of the trust assets beyond what the beneficiary will need. Although all special needs trusts have essentially the same purpose, that doesn't mean that one investment strategy is right for all special needs trusts. You must take into account:

- the type of assets in the trust
- their value
- the beneficiary's life expectancy, and
- the projected cost of the beneficiary's special needs.

For example, a typical investment strategy might be to keep some cash in the bank to meet immediate needs and invest the rest in diversified mutual funds, keep a house that the beneficiary lives in, and sell trust assets that the beneficiary isn't interested in and that don't generate income—jewelry or a car, for example.

Evaluate the portfolio as a whole. Every investment decision is looked at as it relates to how all the other trust assets are being invested. And to plan a coherent investment strategy for all trust assets, you are allowed to look at all kinds of circumstances, including the economic climate, taxes, and unique nature of some assets.

Here are some of the factors the Prudent Investor Act allows you to consider:

General economic conditions. If economic conditions are good, it makes more sense to invest in a growth stock than if economic conditions are bad. Put differently, optimistic investing should be justified by marketplace conditions.

Possible inflation or deflation. In inflationary times, it makes more sense to invest in real estate than in bonds. Similarly, inflation renders the value of money in a bank account stagnant, but investing in securities gives the trust property a chance to grow with the rest of the economy.

Tax consequences. As tax laws change, so should the types of investment you make. For instance, if the tax laws someday removed the capital gains tax on appreciation in real estate, it might make a lot of sense to invest some trust funds in real estate, as opposed to an investment that is subject to capital gains tax.

The expected total return. When making investment decisions, you'll want to consider the income that the trust assets are likely to generate and the expected appreciation of the value of tangible assets such as real estate or art collections.

The beneficiary's other resources. If the beneficiary already owns a house (which is not considered a resource under SSI/Medicaid rules), investing trust funds in something other than real estate may make sense. But if the beneficiary needs adequate shelter, and the trust has enough cash for his or her special needs, it makes sense to buy a house.

Need for liquidity. A special needs trust always needs liquid assets that can be used to pay for expenses not covered by government benefits. So you must put a priority on investments that provide enough cash to pay for the beneficiary's special needs. It's not the trustee's goal to have trust property appreciate in value in a way that will benefit only the remainder beneficiary.

An asset's special value. If some of the trust property consists of family heirlooms, furnishings, or personal effects that are important to the disabled beneficiary, it may make sense to hold on to them, even if it would benefit the trust economically to sell them and invest the proceeds.

Handling taxes

You'll need to obtain a taxpayer ID for the trust from the IRS, and file annual federal and state tax returns. You can get the taxpayer ID online. Once you have it, you can open a deposit account for the trust. You'll use the taxpayer ID for all your transactions with trust funds.

Trust income is taxed at a much higher rate than personal income. If the trust income is kept in the trust, this higher rate will apply. But if you spend the income on behalf of the beneficiary (but don't give it directly to the beneficiary), the income may be taxed at the beneficiary's lower personal rate and still not be considered income to the beneficiary for the purpose of SSI and Medicaid eligibility. To accomplish this result, the trust's records should match the trust income against the trust expenditures.

If you are also the beneficiary's guardian, don't mix the beneficiary's income with trust property. For instance, if in addition to your role as trustee you are authorized by the Social Security Administration to receive the beneficiary's grant on his or her behalf (termed a representative payee), you'll want to maintain one bank account for the beneficiary's income and another for the trust assets. This separation is necessary to keep the special needs trust from interfering with the beneficiary's SSI and Medicaid benefits.

Unless you are a tax expert, you'll be wise to work with one to set up your record keeping system and in to prepare and file the trust tax returns.

Making reports

You'll need to keep careful records of all trust transactions so that you can make required reports.

Reports to SSI and Medicaid. SSI and Medicaid recipients are required to file monthly reports on any changes in their income, assets, or living arrangements and annual reports on trust activity. As long as you keep accurate books of trust activity, the beneficiary (or you, or the beneficiary's representative payee, guardian, or conservator) will have an easy time of meeting the beneficiary's reporting obligations.

Reports to other interested parties. There is no reason to keep trust activity private. The more you communicate trust activity to the beneficiary's family, guardian (if any), and beneficiaries who may eventually inherit trust property, the better. There may be some second-guessing about your decisions, but as long as they are reasonable, you shouldn't encounter any serious opposition to your trust management.

Keep yourself informed about SSI and Medicaid. The SSI and Medicaid laws governing resources and income are subject to change. Because you must avoid trust disbursements that jeopardize the beneficiary's eligibility, you'll want to become and stay familiar with some key rules. You can probably find them online. There are two sets of rules for SSI:

- Regulations issued by the Social Security Administration and published in volume 20 of the Code of Federal Regulations (C.F.R.), starting with Section 416.101 and ending with Section 2227. The income rules are found in Section 1100 and the resource rules in Section 1200. These regulations are available online at www.ssa.gov.
- Guidelines relied on by workers at the Social Security and local district offices are referred to as POMS (*Program Operations Manual System*), found at http://policy.ssa.gov/poms.nsf/aboutpoms.

Each state issues its own Medicaid rules. Find them at: www.cms.hhs.gov/medic-aid/consumer.asp.

Terminating the trust

Someday, you'll need to wrap up the trust. The trust document gives you the authority to terminate the trust when:

- the beneficiary dies
- the beneficiary is no longer disabled
- the funds in the trust are exhausted, or
- SSI or Medicaid regulations change to make the trust a liability.

If the beneficiary dies, you must distribute any remaining trust assets to the people named as "remainder beneficiaries" in the trust document (Article 12).

If the beneficiary is no longer disabled, then you will distribute the trust funds outright to the beneficiary. If the funds are about to run out, there is no reason to continue the trust. Simply close any existing accounts and file a tax return indicating that the trust has been terminated. Check with the IRS to see whether other forms are necessary.

If SSI or Medicaid regulations change so that maintaining the trust would knock the beneficiary off those programs, the trust requires you to give the beneficiary as much of the property as you can without making him or her ineligible for SSI and Medicaid. You would distribute the rest to the remainder beneficiaries.

If the regulations change so that there are no longer any resource limits for SSI or Medicaid, you would distribute the property to the beneficiary outright.

Before you terminate the trust, you are responsible for making sure that any debts and taxes owed by the trust are paid out of remaining trust assets. Specifically, you are required to:

- pay any legitimate debts that the trust still owes, such as legal or tax preparation fees
- file final federal and state income tax returns for the trust
- prepare what's known as a final account, showing a zero balance in the trust account
- pay any administrative expenses incurred in winding up the trust, such as attorney fees, and
- pay the beneficiary's funeral costs if there no other sources.

If there is not enough money in the trust to take care of all these expenses, get some legal advice on setting priorities.

Getting help

Most trustees need expert help from time to time. You can pay a reasonable amount, from trust funds, to hire such help. Here are some examples.

Kind of Help You Need	Where to Get It
Bookkeeping and tax preparation	• accountants, tax preparers
Investment advice	• on the Internet • brokers • financial planners • books
Help with SSI and Medicaid rules	• on the Internet • nonlawyer Medicaid experts • elder law lawyers

Here are a couple of books that may help you:

- **Special Needs Trust Administration Manual: A Guide for Trustees,** by Barbara D. Jackins, Richard S. Blank, Ken W. Shulman, Peter M. Macy, and Harriet H. Onello (iUniverse). This book is written by Massachusetts lawyers, but most of it applies to third-party special needs trusts in all states. The authors clearly state where the material (usually about Medicaid) is state-specific.

- *Loring Trustee's Handbook,* by Charles E. Rounds (Aspen), is a general book on trustee duties. You may want consult it in a library (the cover price is $175) or buy it to have on hand in case questions arise regarding such issues as the Prudent Investor Act or conflicts of interest.

Lawyers. You may find it necessary to get legal advice about your duties or the operation of the trust. Most lawyers who handle special needs trusts call themselves "elder law" attorneys. The reason is that many of them got their start helping elderly people obtain federal support and medical benefits. Because special needs trusts also require knowledge of SSI and Medicaid rules, special needs trusts have become a second specialty for these lawyers.

Two places to find elder law attorneys are:

The National Academy of Elder Law Attorneys website, www.naela.org, which lets you search for lawyers by zip code or city.

The Special Needs Alliance, a national network of lawyers specializing in disability law, at www.specialneedsalliance.com.

Paralegals. Social Security regulations authorize nonlawyer paralegals to represent clients in administrative proceedings dealing with benefit disputes. So if you have questions about your state's SSI and Medicaid income and resource rules, a paralegal may be just the ticket. Just look under "paralegals" in the Yellow Pages. Paralegals cannot advise you on other matters having to do with administering the trust.

Certified financial planners. Financial planners are people with accounting, investment, or insurance backgrounds who are adept with the numbers necessary to compute how much money you will need over time to accomplish a particular result. They are not licensed professionals, but a central board certifies them. They can provide a wealth of information on a feasible budget.

To find a certified financial planner in your area, visit these websites or enter "certified financial planner" and your city into your favorite search engine.

- www.fpanet.org
- www.paladininvestors.com
- www.wiseradvisor.com.

Sample Beneficiary Information Letter

Sample Beneficiary Information Letter

May 6, 20xx

To the Trustee of the Special Needs Trust for Paul Sanchez:

We appreciate your future efforts on behalf of our beloved Paul and hope that you delight in him and his uniqueness as we have. We hope the following information will be helpful.

Family History

Paul has three older siblings who have always been affectionately involved in his life. We feel it is significant that each brother and his sister approached us individually years ago to ask to be his guardian if anything were to happen to us.

David Sanchez, 41, (wife Rebecca Chang, daughter Tiena Mei Sanchez, 2), 3211 Bayview Ave., Alameda, CA 94501, 510-865-4567. Paul spends weekends with David and his family about once every six weeks, and has phone contacts between visits. David often helps Paul find special DVDs he wants.

Mark Sanchez, 40, (wife Sonja Sanchez, sons Benjamin, 3, and Thomas, 1, and a child expected in a few months), 2445 Oak Ave. South, Minneapolis, MN 55405, 612-308-3219. Paul visits Mark and his family perhaps twice a year and has occasional phone conversations with Mark. Because Mark is a physician, we feel it is wise to consult him about any medical problems that Paul may have before making final treatment decisions.

Juliet Sanchez, 35, (partner Juliana Sorenstram, daughter Annika, 2, son Marcus, nine months), 815 Marcos Ct., Santa Rosa, CA 95404, 707-545-9876. Juliet was a constant companion to Paul throughout his childhood, unbidden, a veritable "second mommy." Juliet and Paul share frequent phone calls. Paul spends the weekend with Juliet and her family about once per month. Among other helpful acts, Juliet is comfortable with Paul's personal needs, like helping him buy new shoes that accommodate his unusually small but wide feet, or even clipping toenails if she notices a need.

 (Uncle) Steve Sanchez, (wife Catherine Sanchez), P.O. Box 1750, Lakeport, CA 95453, 707-263-7895. Uncle Steve and Aunt Catherine have taken a warm and cheerful interest in Paul from his birth. One of Paul's first words was "Nunc" for "uncle." If Paul were ever to have any needs of a legal nature, we feel it would be wise to discuss them with Steve, who is an attorney.

(Cousin) Nicole Davis, 40, 1290 Eighth St., San Francisco, CA 94122, 415-665-4369. Nicole spends time with Paul, usually at family celebrations, several times per year.

Other relatives with whom he has cordial but less frequent dealings are **Anne Davis and Richard Ross** and **Carol and Mickey Forlani** (aunts and their spouses), **Ken Sanchez and Sara Sanchez** (uncle and his wife), **Rubin Sanchez** (cousin), **Megan Sanchez** (cousin), **Dionne Davis** (cousin), and **Walter and Olivia Forlani** (cousin and wife).

General Medical History

Paul was born on July 31, 1975; he has Down syndrome. As a young child, he enjoyed good health but needed consistent medical attention for frequent ear infections, sore throats, and colds that regularly morphed into sinus infections. Fortunately he had no cardiac problems, an issue for half the children with Down syndrome. He had pneumonia two times as a child. We find that yearly flu shots and pneumonia immunization as directed by his physician are important preventive measures.

His dentition was irregular and late. His skin is very fair and he sunburns easily. He continues to need to use sunscreen daily and to wear dark glasses outdoors. He has dry skin; flaking on his face or hair is treated with Aquanil HC, an over-the-counter preparation.

When he was about 12 he had a difficult episode lasting many days of fearfully thinking he was changing into an animal. The episode faded, but as the years passed, occasionally other fears dominated his waking hours, basically unpleasant thoughts that he could not banish from his mind. When he was 17, his father (a psychiatrist) realized that Paul had a form of obsessive-compulsive disorder. Treated with Zoloft, the uncomfortable symptoms disappeared at once. He continues to take Zoloft.

As a teenager he underwent a hernia operation.

At 22, he became very ill when he was thrown abruptly from a supportive school program (work experience for a couple of hours a day and a few more hours spent learning to make his way in the community), into an eight-hour work day with a brand-new 1½-hour bus ride on either end of the already exhausting regimen. Whatever sort of illness he had resulted in a painful mouth and gum infection. He already was having some problems with his gums, and the illness greatly exacerbated them. Then began serious dental work: gum grafts that were unsuccessful, rigorous training in dental hygiene and oral rinses with Periogard, and extractions of a number of teeth. He does not wear a prosthesis because it would have to be attached to teeth that are already loosening and would hasten their loss. He now alternates appointments for cleaning and checkups between his dentist and periodontist every two months. (Contact information below.)

In his mid-20s he developed low thyroid, and now takes Levoxyl to normalize his thyroid levels. Nevertheless, he tires easily and needs significantly more rest than average. He uses Beconase inhalant to prevent sinus infections. Paul has had a lifelong tendency toward constipation. He takes mineral oil nightly to control the problem.

Paul has a high pain tolerance. If he says something is painful, it is advisable to obtain medical assistance. He may have difficulty in localizing or explaining what is happening to him physically. For example, he might say, "My throat hurts," when he is nauseated. His internist is Kent Yasuda, M.D.

None of these health issues is particularly alarming, but like most people with Down syndrome, Paul benefits greatly from regular, consistent medical and dental care.

Paul has a tendency to put on weight. We try to advise him and monitor his eating habits, but with limited success. We worry that this tendency may cause health problems eventually.

Paul has severe obstructive sleep apnea and must always sleep—naps included—with his CPAP (continuous positive air pressure) mask in place.

Some additional caveats: people with Down syndrome have a severe hypersensitivity to atropine, a substance that may be used in eye examinations and sometimes following a surgery. Doctors treating Paul should be reminded of this. People with Down syndrome have more problems with anesthesia because of "sloppy airways" due to their low muscle tone; surgery should not be lightly undertaken. Some people with Down syndrome develop weakness in their spinal cord due to atlanto-axial subluxation; Paul did not have the condition when he had spinal X-rays as a child, but it can develop later in life.

Paul handles the regimen of health measures and medicines described above on his own. He benefits from regular reminders, lists, and discussion. Often when asked, for example, if he is remembering to take his Beconase, he will say, "Oh, that's right, I forgot."

Paul had therapy and counseling for several years after some traumatic events. He enjoyed the support and benefited greatly from therapy. If he seemed troubled, we would like him to have this opportunity again. It would be best to investigate which therapists are comfortable, experienced, and interested in working with Paul.

Current Medical/Dental Providers

We have always kept Paul on our medical insurance; at this time he uses Medicare and has a supplemental insurance plan from the County Health Plan. He has no dental insurance. We feel adequate medical and dental care are a priority and prefer to have Paul cared for by specialists who have treated other people with Down syndrome and are familiar with the medical needs that may accompany the syndrome.

Kent Yasuda, MD, internist, 4710 Yolanda Ave., Santa Rosa, CA 95403; 546-8764

Robert Jeffords, DDS, dentist, 40 North Main St., Santa Rosa, CA 95403; 545-4567

Richard Smithson, DDS, periodontist, 1416 Mountain View Lane, Santa Rosa, CA 95403; 578-6589

Education

Paul was "mainstreamed," as the practice of attending regular school classes was termed when he was a boy, until he was 17 years old. He was extremely well liked by other students, with many friendships extending to the present. He was usually supported academically by the Resource Room Specialist. He reads at about a fourth- or fifth-grade level, and writes perhaps like a third-grader. Paul can add a little and used to be able to subtract.

He developed a talent for writing unique poems. They are quite wonderful. If asked, he will write one for any occasion.

Paul's speech is often difficult to understand; his missing teeth compound the problem. Patience is sometimes required. His thought processes are much more advanced than one would expect listening to his articulation.

At 17 he began attending Special Education classes to prepare him for practical issues like work experience, bus riding, and money management. It was also an opportunity for him to have classmates who were true peers. He finished school at 22 years of age. During those years he enjoyed attending classes at Santa Rosa Junior College, and continues to talk of wishing for such an opportunity again. He lives in walking distance of SRJC, but the logistics of working during the day, doing chores with housemates when he returns home after a lengthy bus ride, and his fatigue have militated against taking more courses. He does delight in thinking of any meeting or class as a "graduate school class."

Employment

Paul has been in supported employment in the community since he was 22. He is with an enclave of several workers with a supervisor on site. We feel this situation is preferable to working alone since he takes a number of weeks of vacation, some without pay; this custom might be difficult if a business was depending only on Paul for certain services. During these approximately four weeks per year, spread out, he travels and celebrates family occasions, as when cousins visit from Sweden. We also feel it is beneficial for him to have peers who are work colleagues. It is possible that as he grows older, Paul may need a different work situation—less stressful perhaps, or perhaps with transportation provided. Time will tell.

Currently he is at Dynamat, a technology company in Rohnert Park. He does assembly work. He is accurate and quite slow compared to the average worker. His supervisor, Tom De Leon, is ideal for Paul. Paul has a tendency to become too easily offended by other people, especially authorities. Mr. De Leon is limitlessly pleasant and respectful with Paul.

The organization that currently supports Paul's employment is **North Coast Industries,** 585-9641. He takes part in the occasional social events such as The Human Race in May, and a dinner dance during the year. Generally speaking, Paul needs transportation to these and any social events. He is capable of riding the bus only on routes on which he has been trained. He rides the city and county buses to his workplace. North Coast Regional Center sends him his bus passes monthly.

At times there have been recurrent issues of Paul's not going to work when he was not ill. We feel it is important for him to be out in the world working during the week, like everyone else. We find that giving him an allowance of spending money contingent on his going to work daily is effective. He receives $30 per week in spending money if he goes to work every day. If he does not go one day, he receives only $5 per day. So if he stayed home one day, he would receive only $20 allowance that week. Naturally if he is ill or has a conflicting engagement like a medical appointment, his allowance is not docked.

It is common for Paul to ventilate frequently about mild negatives in his life, and not comment on the positives. Therefore, it is best to pay attention, evaluate, and not react too quickly when he complains about work, his supervisor or coworkers.

Lately he has been expressing a desire to work at Agilent Technologies, where his sister is employed, and which is near Arcangel House. Perhaps at some point he might try that, since there is a North Coast Industries work group located there which does assembly work.

In the past, Paul had jobs that involved too much heavy labor for him. For example, one job required him to lift many flats of soft drinks. He vastly prefers lighter work, more complex work too.

Current Living Situation

Our opinion is that Paul currently needs an arrangement between an overly protective group home, where he probably would not have his own room, and living in an apartment by himself with little oversight and companionship. In our county, a continuum of alternatives was not available. Personally, we were very happy living with Paul, but for many years he had been saying, "I want to move out. I want to be independent."

When he was 25, Jane Ford, a lifelong friend and advocate for Paul, called to say, "You know that project we are always talking about for Paul? I'm ready to do it." What a surprise! Jane bought a house, 4567 Arcangel Ave., in Santa Rosa, perfectly located near shops, markets, Santa Rosa Junior College, the Recreation Center, and buses. It is even across the street from a workshop for more involved people with special needs, so there are speed bumps in the street for safety. And wonderfully, the house is only two miles from our home and his sister Juliet's home. After living at Arcangel House for five weeks, Paul came home to celebrate Passover with all of us. He pointed to the place on the kitchen doorjamb where we have never painted over the dates and heights of our children. "Dad, you've got to measure me again. I'm tall now."

After a few years, Jane Ford wished to sell the house; we bought it so that the situation, which by then we knew worked so well for Paul and his housemates, could continue. The house has three bedrooms, two baths, and a modest garage apartment. Paul lives there with two other people his age who happen to have different special needs, but function roughly about like Paul. Paul has a voucher from HUD from the City of Santa Rosa which means that he pays up to one third of his income (including Social Security) for rent. The housing authority pays the difference. Right now, his rent is $500, of which he pays around $200.

He and his housemates are supported by a person, currently Cheryl Frost, who lives rent-free in the garage apartment. She earns money by being the three housemates' IHSS (In-Home Supportive Services) worker. She helps organize housekeeping chores among the housemates, cooks their evening meal, and generally stays in tune with how their lives are going. **Oaks of Hebron** (795-5927) is an organization that supports the housemates too, by assigning a Community Support Facilitator (CSF) who is available to Paul, and who visits him weekly, helps him pay bills or straighten out problems with the buses—generally is available to help solve problem as they arise. The CSF also may take him to medical or dental appointments. It has been our practice to be at such appointments also, and we usually drive Paul home afterwards.

In Paul's situation, the caregivers can purchase food at the Food Bank, so Paul pays only $150 per month for food. We like to supplement this weekly by buying him melon (cut into chunks), cottage cheese, eight cans of tomato juice, and a bag of romaine lettuce. We do so because he needs low-calorie alternatives to help him control his weight, and because he needs fruit and vegetables in some quantity to help with his chronic constipation.

As is his wont, Paul often complains about aspects of his living situation. We find it best to listen and let him express his feelings, even though we usually judge that his living situation, or job situation, or relationship situation is probably optimal. Paul is not apt to tell us about the positive aspects of his life, for some idiosyncratic reason. He may say he "wants to live in the apartments in Rohnert Park." These are individual apartments for people with special needs with no one permanently on site if a need arises. We do not feel that this situation is safe for Paul over the long haul. We feel he needs more support, especially since he has always had and continues to have difficulty saying "no" to any suggestions by others, which could lead obviously to dangerous situations.

It is possible that Paul may need a more supportive environment, probably a group home, as he grows older. If he were to develop a condition such as diabetes, we would definitely want him to live in a group home where his increased medical needs could be met.

Day-to-Day Routines

Paul is quite self-sufficient. He rises and prepares himself for his workday independently. He fixes his own breakfast, packs a lunch, and walks to the bus stop by 7:30 a.m. He takes the bus to work and begins work at 8:30 or so. He wears a fanny pack with identification, bus passes, cell phone, and dark glasses. He has a backpack with his lunch and other necessaries like his treasured Walkman and favorite Beatles tapes.

Because Paul fatigues more readily than the average person, we have had his workday shortened. He walks to the bus stop to catch a bus home around 2 p.m. He arrives home, walking from the bus stop around 3 p.m. He then does assigned household chores, like sweeping and mopping the floors. Whoever is living in the garage apartment prepares dinner for the household and the four of them share the meal.

Paul is accustomed to calling us each evening at around 7 p.m. This is his own idea, though I admit I find it pleasant. He likes to recount a little about his day and his thoughts. It is perhaps a ten-minute chat. We feel happy that his living "on his own" has not lessened the affectionate connection that we have with him.

In the evening, he listens to his music collection or looks at a video or DVD. He and his fiancee Annie share a phone call.

He does his own laundry weekly. Paul likes to wear all clean clothes daily.

He is well groomed. He needs occasional reminders about what to do about, say, flaking scalp.

On weekends, he often visits a family member or his fiancee. He may attend a movie or a party, perhaps with housemates. He doesn't mind being in his home (Arcangel House) on weekends; actually he likes it. On Sundays he likes to be there shortly after midday to make a transition to the upcoming workweek.

Paul has a longtime interest in and detailed knowledge of the Beatles, especially John Lennon. He likes to purchase tapes, books, videos, and DVDs, plus the occasional T-shirt about the Beatles or other topics. He likes to pore over books about the Beatles. He used to write poetry, and will do so now if encouraged.

He needs to exercise, but tires quickly on long walks or lap swimming. Something is better than nothing, we feel. He does better if the exercise is incorporated in his day—for example, walking to and from the bus stops.

Paul enjoys most foods. He always has, even as a small child.

Social Environment

Paul has always been a well-liked person. He dated frequently as a teenager. He and Princess (called "Annie") Priest (Eddington Hall Apartments, Rohnert Park; 585-7693) began dating in about 1995, and became engaged in 1997. The relationship continues. We strongly feel that their relationship should be celebrated, but we do not believe that the couple should live together or marry. Paul and Annie seem to get along best when they spend most of a weekend together. Longer contact results in quarreling. Paul spends part of a weekend with Annie about two times per month. We regard Annie as a daughter-in-law; she attends most family celebrations.

As stated above, Paul has frequent and loving contacts with his brothers and sister and their families. He has developed skills in relating to his young nephews and nieces.

Lejf Jensen is a few years younger than Paul; they have been lifelong friends. They continue to see each other socially several times per year. Usually they do an activity together and share a meal somewhere. Lejf is currently a disc jockey at "Four More," a trendy radio station in San Francisco; he also works as a substitute special education teacher.

Matt Conrack is a friend since elementary school. Paul visited him in New York last year, where he was in graduate school. Again, they have cordial social contacts several times per year—usually an outing and a meal together.

Pat and Cassie Garcia, brother and sister, were neighborhood playmates when they were all toddlers together. They remain interested in Paul and sometimes contact and visit him.

Any of these friends would probably need help in setting up a social contact with Paul. If Paul received a phone message, he would not be able to call the person back on his own (although he can do so with family members who are in the speed dial of his phone).

Currently, it seems difficult for Paul to mix socializing and working. Activities that take place during the workweek are too much for him. He thinks of social activities as taking place on the weekend.

Paul usually says "no" if asked if he wants to do something, especially something social. This is a knee-jerk first reaction to most suggestions of any kind, and should not be taken too seriously. We try to help him keep his social life going by encouraging, sometimes almost insisting, that he take part in a social activity. Maybe one or two per weekend. He is often tired after two or three hours at a social event, and it is reasonable for him to return home then if he wishes to.

We believe it is important for him to interact with friends who also have special needs. He and Annie often double-date with Brent North and Julia South, who live in the same apartments as Annie. Her apartment is located near many restaurants and a cineplex, allowing them to choose independently.

In recent years, Paul (and usually Annie) have been delightedly participating in wonderful, low-cost travels arranged by Jane Ford, an old friend, and her organization. This year he is traveling to the Grand Canyon next month, and will cruise the Inside Passage of Alaska in the fall. Many of the same people are present on each trip. The group also went Christmas shopping in San Francisco this year. Paul considers it "his club." We hope this opportunity will continue.

There are others in the community who understand Paul and his needs from long years of contact and experience. They would be available to consult.

Sue Lake, MA, special education teacher, (4672 Alejandro Dr., Santa Rosa, CA 95404; 528-4691), was his infant teacher and has remained in close contact with us. A great deal of problem-solving around issues that have arisen for Paul has included Sue's views.

Nancy Fernandez (9420 Glencannon Dr., Santa Rosa, CA 95405; 539-9321), is a longtime friend as well as the mother of Lejf Jensen. She is a Special Education Teacher too. Again, problem-solving for Paul usually includes her suggestions.

Nancy Barlotti, RN, (679 Purrington Rd., Petaluma, CA 94952; 778-0368), is a fellow parent of a person with special needs very different from Paul's and a former coworker in Early Intervention. Her perspective on Paul is wise.

Jane Ford, MSW, who originally bought Arcangel House where Paul lives so that he would have the opportunity, and who runs the trips for him and others, has known Paul all his life. Her views on any issues would be helpful.

Travel

Sometimes Paul flies to visit friends or relatives. He travels with a family member or on his own. When he flies alone, we buy what the airlines call their "unaccompanied minor program." This means that a staff person on board is assigned to be available to Paul if he needs help, or if the plane must change its itinerary due to weather or other exigency. Paul will be released only to the person whose name is given before Paul boards the plane. Under the program, whoever takes him to the airport or comes to pick him up is allowed through security to the gate. When he flies with a family member, we pay the family member the same amount of money for any supervision that may be helpful to Paul.

Religious Proclivities

As an interfaith family, we have always observed and celebrated both Jewish and Christian holidays. Very occasionally Paul attends First Methodist Church with me. He also participates with Oaks of Hebron personnel in occasional religious activities.

Preferences for Funeral Arrangements: We find it difficult to address this topic for one of our children, but here goes: We would like Paul to participate in organ donation, but are not sure if that is possible if a person has a different number of chromosomes from the average, as is the case with Paul's form of Down syndrome.

Arrangements should be whatever the surviving family deems appropriate. Perhaps a memorial service in a Methodist church or Jewish temple with spoken tributes from those of us who have loved him so, as well as thoughts from a clergyman. Certainly any service should include lots of Beatles music. We would very much like to have him laid to rest near us, his parents; we fervently hope he will never be far from us. Probably cremation is suitable. An informal family celebration of his life, with Beatles music and a buffet, might follow the service.

Other Relevant Information

Paul has a talent for choosing gifts for family and friends, as well as for planning parties.

Paul loves to have the opportunity to "be in charge" or be given a responsibility. For example, he was happy when he could volunteer at the Recreation Center, serving soft drinks. Sometimes when he travels with a small group, he is in charge of keeping track of the suitcases, or of calling everyone for dinner.

Paul is unfailingly punctual (far better than his mother); he organizes his belongings neatly; he remembers all appointments and engagements, and keeps an accurate calendar. He has an excellent memory for people, and for details about them like their birthdays (or even "half-birthdays").

He understands which amounts are more or less as far as money, but needs significant guidance in managing finances. Paul does not have a conservator, so it is necessary to obtain his cooperation through explanation and discussion regarding both medical treatment and financial management.

Paul cannot say something that is untrue, for example to manipulate a person or situation; he doesn't understand the concept. It may be important to know, however, that if he is asked a direct question, such as "Why did you do that?" he will probably interpret it as a demand for an answer. His response then will be his best guess, but he does not use niceties of expression like, "Well, it may have been because..." His answer will sound like a statement, because that is the syntax he understands how to use. This statement may not be accurate, but simply his effort at pleasing with a required response. Also, if he is worried about something, he may state it as a fact. He might say, "My supervisor said I have to get a new job," when what he really means is, "My supervisor reprimanded me today and I am worried that if he is mad at me maybe he won't want me to work here."

Paul is a lifelong client of **North Coast Regional Center**. A specific Client Program Coordinator, currently Dorothy Merriwhether, is assigned to him and available to discuss and help solve issues that arise.

If Paul disapproves of a comment or opinion we express, he may hang up the phone or storm off angrily. After about ten minutes, he will return to discuss the matter calmly and without anger. He is reasonable and ultimately open to support in the form of suggestions presented in a friendly manner.

We hope you find this account helpful. Paul's welfare has been a priority for our family all his life. We are now entrusting his welfare to you.

Sincerely,

Lois and Bob Sanchez

Appendix D

How to Use the CD-ROM

Letters and forms discussed in this book are included on a CD-ROM in the back of the book. This CD-ROM, which can be used with Windows computers, installs files that can be opened, printed, and edited using a word processor or other software. It is *not* a stand-alone software program. Please read this appendix and the README.TXT file included on the CD-ROM for instructions on using the Forms CD.

Note to Mac users: This CD-ROM and its files should also work on Macintosh computers. Please note, however, that Nolo cannot provide technical support for non-Windows users.

How to View the README File

If you do not know how to view the file README.TXT, insert the Forms CD-ROM into your computer's CD-ROM drive and follow these instructions:

- **Windows 9x, 2000, Me, and XP:** (1) On your PC's desktop, double click the My Computer icon; (2) double click the icon for the CD-ROM drive into which the Forms CD-ROM was inserted; (3) double click the file README.TXT.
- **Macintosh:** (1) On your Mac desktop, double click the icon for the CD-ROM that you inserted; (2) double click on the file README.TXT.

While the README file is open, print it out by using the Print command in the File menu.

A. Installing the Form Files Onto Your Computer

Word processing forms that you can open, complete, print, and save with your word processing program (see Section B, below) are contained on the CD-ROM. Before you can do anything with the files on the CD-ROM, you need to install them onto your hard disk. In accordance with U.S. copyright laws, remember that copies of the CD-ROM and its files are for your personal use only.

Insert the Forms CD and do the following:

1. Windows 9x, 2000, Me, and XP Users

Follow the instructions that appear on the screen. (If nothing happens when you insert the Forms CD-ROM, then (1) double click the My Computer icon; (2) double click the icon for the CD-ROM drive into which the Forms CD-ROM was inserted; and (3) double click the file WELCOME.EXE.)

By default, all the files are installed to the \Special Needs Trust Forms folder in the \Program Files folder of your computer. A folder called "Special Needs Trust Forms" is added to the "Programs" folder of the Start menu.

2. Macintosh Users

Step 1: If the "Special Needs Trust CD" window is not open, open it by double clicking the "Special Needs Trust CD" icon.

Step 2: Select the "Special Needs Trust Forms" folder icon.

Step 3: Drag and drop the folder icon onto the icon of your hard disk.

B. Using the Word Processing Files to Create Documents

This section concerns the files for forms that can be opened and edited with your word processing program.

All word processing forms come in rich text format. These files have the extension ".RTF." For example, the form for the Special Needs Trust discussed in Chapter 8 is on the file Trust.rtf. All forms and their filenames are listed in Section C, below.

RTF files can be read by most recent word processing programs including all versions of MS Word for Windows and Macintosh, WordPad for Windows, and recent versions of WordPerfect for Windows and Macintosh.

To use a form from the CD to create your documents you must: (1) open a file in your word processor or text editor; (2) edit the form by filling in the required information; (3) print it out; (4) rename and save your revised file.

The following are general instructions. However, each word processor uses different commands to open, format, save, and print documents. Please read your word processor's manual for specific instructions on performing these tasks.

Do not call Nolo's technical support if you have questions on how to use your word processor.

Step 1: Opening a File

There are three ways to open the word processing files included on the CD-ROM after you have installed them onto your computer.

- Windows users can open a file by selecting its "shortcut" as follows: (1) Click the Windows "Start" button; (2) open the "Programs" folder; (3) open the "Special Needs Trust Forms" subfolder; and (4) click on the shortcut to the form you want to work with.

- Both Windows and Macintosh users can open a file directly by double clicking on it. Use My Computer or Windows Explorer (Windows 9x, 2000, Me, or XP) or the Finder (Macintosh) to go to the folder you installed or copied the CD-ROM's files to. Then, double click on the specific file you want to open.

- You can also open a file from within your word processor. To do this, you must first start your word processor. Then, go to the File menu and choose the Open command. This opens a dialog box where you will tell the program (1) the type of file you want to open (*.RTF); and (2) the location and name of the file (you will need to navigate through the directory tree to get to the folder on your hard disk where the CD's files have been installed). If these directions are unclear you will need to look through the manual for your word processing program—Nolo's technical support department will not be able to help you with the use of your word processing program.

Where Are the Files Installed?

Windows Users

- RTF files are installed by default to a folder named \Special Needs Trust Forms in the \Program Files folder of your computer.

Macintosh Users

- RTF files are located in the "Special Needs Trust Forms" folder.

Step 2: Editing Your Document

Fill in the appropriate information according to the instructions and sample agreements in the book. Underlines are used to indicate where you need to enter your information, frequently followed by instructions in brackets. Be sure to delete the underlines and instructions from your edited document. You will also want to make sure that any signature lines in your completed documents appear on a page with at least some text from the document itself. If you do not know how to use your word processor to edit a document, you will need to look through the manual for your word processing program—Nolo's technical support department will *not* be able to help you with the use of your word processing program.

Editing Forms That Have Optional or Alternative Text

Some of the forms have optional or alternate text:

- With optional text, you choose whether to include or exclude the given text.
- With alternative text, you select one alternative to include and exclude the other alternatives.

When editing these forms, we suggest you do the following:

Optional text

If you *don't want* to include optional text, just delete it from your document.

If you *do want* to include optional text, just leave it in your document.

In either case, delete the italicized instructions.

NOTE: if you choose not to include an optional numbered clause, be sure to renumber all the subsequent clauses after you delete it.

Alternative text

First delete all the alternatives that you do not want to include, then delete the italicized instructions.

Step 3: Printing Out the Document

Use your word processor's or text editor's "Print" command to print out your document. If you do not know how to use your word processor to print a document, you will need to look through the manual for your word processing program—Nolo's technical support department will *not* be able to help you with the use of your word processing program.

Step 4: Saving Your Document

After filling in the form, use the "Save As" command to save and rename the file. Because all the files are "read-only," you will not be able to use the "Save" command. This is for your protection. *If you save the file without renaming it, the underlines that indicate where you need to enter your information will be lost, and you will not be able to create a new document with this file without recopying the original file from the CD-ROM.*

If you do not know how to use your word processor to save a document, you will need to look through the manual for your word processing program—Nolo's technical support department will *not* be able to help you with the use of your word processing program.

C. List of Forms Included on the Forms CD-ROM

The following files are in rich text format (RTF):

File Name	Form Name
Trust.rtf	Special Needs Trust
PooledTrustList.rtf	Pooled Trust List
SampleInfoLetter.rtf	Sample Beneficiary Information Letter
DutiesLetter.rtf	Trustee's Duties Letter

Index

CATALOG

...more from nolo

	PRICE	CODE
BUSINESS		
Becoming a Mediator: Your Guide to Career Opportunities	$29.99	BECM
Business Buyout Agreements (Book w/CD-ROM)	$49.99	BSAG
The CA Nonprofit Corporation Kit (Binder w/CD-ROM)	$59.99	CNP
Consultant & Independent Contractor Agreements (Book w/CD-ROM)	$29.99	CICA
The Corporate Minutes Book (Book w/CD-ROM)	$69.99	CORMI
Create Your Own Employee Handbook (Book w/CD-ROM)	$49.99	EMHA
Dealing With Problem Employees	$44.99	PROBM
Deduct It! Lower Your Small Business Taxes	$34.99	DEDU
The Employer's Legal Handbook	$39.99	EMPL
Everyday Employment Law	$29.99	ELBA
Federal Employment Laws	$49.99	FELW
Form Your Own Limited Liability Company (Book w/CD-ROM)	$44.99	LIAB
Hiring Independent Contractors: The Employer's Legal Guide (Book w/CD-ROM)	$34.99	HICI
Home Business Deductions: Keep What You Earn	$34.99	DEHB
How to Run a Thriving Business: Strategies for Success & Satisfaction	$19.99	THRV
How to Create a Noncompete Agreement (Book w/CD-ROM)	$44.95	NOCMP
How to Form a California Professional Corporation (Book w/CD-ROM)	$59.99	PROF
How to Form a Nonprofit Corporation (Book w/CD-ROM)—National Edition	$44.99	NNP
How to Form a Nonprofit Corporation in California (Book w/CD-ROM)	$44.99	NON
How to Form Your Own California Corporation (Binder w/CD-ROM)	$59.99	CACI
How to Form Your Own California Corporation (Book w/CD-ROM)	$34.99	CCOR
How to Get Your Business on the Web	$29.99	WEBS
How to Write a Business Plan	$34.99	SBS
Incorporate Your Business	$49.99	NIBS

Prices subject to change.

	PRICE	CODE
The Independent Paralegal's Handbook	$34.99	PARA
Leasing Space for Your Small Business	$34.95	LESP
Legal Guide for Starting & Running a Small Business	$34.99	RUNS
Legal Forms for Starting & Running a Small Business (Book w/CD-ROM)	$29.99	RUNSF
Marketing Without Advertising	$24.00	MWAD
Mediate, Don't Litigate	$24.99	MEDL
Music Law (Book w/CD-ROM)	$39.99	ML
Nolo's Guide to Social Security Disability	$29.99	QSS
Nolo's Quick LLC	$29.99	LLCQ
Nondisclosure Agreements (Book w/CD-ROM)	$39.95	NAG
The Small Business Start-up Kit (Book w/CD-ROM)	$24.99	SMBU
The Small Business Start-up Kit for California (Book w/CD-ROM)	$24.99	OPEN
The Partnership Book: How to Write a Partnership Agreement (Book w/CD-ROM)	$39.99	PART
Sell Your Business: A Step by Step Legal Guide (Book w/CD-ROM)	$44.99	SELBU
Sexual Harassment on the Job	$24.95	HARS
Starting & Running a Successful Newsletter or Magazine	$29.99	MAG
California Workers' Comp: How to Take Charge When You're Injured on the Job	$34.99	WORK
Tax Savvy for Small Business	$36.99	SAVVY
Workplace Investigations: A Step by Step Legal Guide	$39.99	CMPLN
Working for Yourself: Law & Taxes for the Self-Employed	$39.99	WAGE
Your Crafts Business: A Legal Guide (Book w/CD-ROM)	$26.99	VART
Your Limited Liability Company: An Operating Manual (Book w/CD-ROM)	$49.99	LOP
Your Rights in the Workplace	$29.99	YRW

CONSUMER

How to Win Your Personal Injury Claim	$29.99	PICL
Nolo's Encyclopedia of Everyday Law	$29.99	EVL
Nolo's Guide to California Law	$24.99	CLAW
Trouble-Free Travel...And What to Do When Things Go Wrong	$14.95	TRAV

	PRICE	CODE

ESTATE PLANNING & PROBATE

8 Ways to Avoid Probate	$19.99	PRAV
9 Ways to Avoid Estate Taxes	$29.95	ESTX
Estate Planning Basics	$21.99	ESPN
The Executor's Guide: Settling a Loved One's Estae or Trust	$34.99	EXEC
How to Probate an Estate in California	$49.99	PAE
Make Your Own Living Trust (Book w/CD-ROM)	$39.99	LITR
Nolo's Simple Will Book (Book w/CD-ROM)	$36.99	SWIL
Plan Your Estate	$44.99	NEST
Quick & Legal Will Book	$16.99	QUIC
Quicken Willmaker: Estate Planning Essentials	$49.99	QWMB

FAMILY MATTERS

Child Custody: Building Parenting Agreements That Work	$29.99	CUST
The Complete IEP Guide	$24.99	IEP
Divorce & Money: How to Make the Best Financial Decisions During Divorce	$34.99	DIMO
Do Your Own California Adoption: Nolo's Guide for Stepparents and Domestic Partners (Book w/CD-ROM)	$34.99	ADOP
Get a Life: You Don't Need a Million to Retire Well	$24.99	LIFE
The Guardianship Book for California	$34.99	GB
A Legal Guide for Lesbian and Gay Couples	$29.99	LG
Living Together: A Legal Guide (Book w/CD-ROM)	$34.99	LTK
Medical Directives and Powers of Attorney in California (Book w/CD-ROM)	$21.99	CPOA
Prenuptial Agreements: How to Write a Fair & Lasting Contract (Book w/CD-ROM)	$34.99	PNUP
Using Divorce Mediation: Save Your Money & Your Sanity	$29.99	UDMD

GOING TO COURT

Beat Your Ticket: Go To Court & Win! (National Edition)	$21.99	BEYT
The Criminal Law Handbook: Know Your Rights, Survive the System	$34.99	KYR
Everybody's Guide to Small Claims Court (National Edition)	$26.99	NSCC

	PRICE	CODE
Everybody's Guide to Small Claims Court in California	$29.99	CSCC
Fight Your Ticket & Win in California	$29.99	FYT
How to Change Your Name in California	$34.99	NAME
How to Collect When You Win a Lawsuit (California Edition)	$29.99	JUDG
How to Seal Your Juvenile & Criminal Records (California Edition)	$34.95	CRIM
The Lawsuit Survival Gide	$29.99	UNCL
Nolo's Deposition Handbook	$29.99	DEP
Represent Yourself in Court: How to Prepare & Try a Winning Case	$34.99	RYC
Sue in California Without a Lawyer	$34.99	SLWY

HOMEOWNERS, LANDLORDS & TENANTS

	PRICE	CODE
California Tenants' Rights	$27.99	CTEN
Deeds for California Real Estate	$24.99	DEED
Dog Law	$21.95	DOG
Every Landlord's Legal Guide (National Edition, Book w/CD-ROM)	$44.99	ELLI
Every Tenant's Legal Guide	$29.99	EVTEN
For Sale by Owner in California	$29.99	FSBO
How to Buy a House in California	$34.99	BHCA
The California Landlord's Law Book: Rights & Responsibilities (Book w/CD-ROM)	$44.99	LBRT
The California Landlord's Law Book: Evictions (Book w/CD-ROM)	$44.99	LBEV
Leases & Rental Agreements	$29.99	LEAR
Neighbor Law: Fences, Trees, Boundaries & Noise	$26.99	NEI
The New York Landlord's Law Book (Book w/CD-ROM)	$44.99	NYLL
New York Tenants' Rights	$27.99	NYTEN
Renters' Rights (National Edition)	$24.99	RENT

HUMOR

	PRICE	CODE
Poetic Justice	$9.95	PJ

	PRICE	CODE

IMMIGRATION

Becoming a U.S. Citizen: A Guide to the Law, Exam and Interview	$24.99	USCIT
Fiancé & Marriage Visas (Book w/CD-ROM)	$44.95	IMAR
How to Get a Green Card	$29.99	GRN
Student & Tourist Visas	$29.95	ISTU
U.S. Immigration Made Easy	$29.99	IMEZ

MONEY MATTERS

101 Law Forms for Personal Use (Book w/CD-ROM)	$29.99	SPOT
Bankruptcy: Is It the Right Solution to Your Debt Problems?	$21.99	BRS
Chapter 13 Bankruptcy: Repay Your Debts	$36.99	CHB
Creating Your Own Retirement Plan	$29.95	YROP
Credit Repair (Book w/CD-ROM)	$24.99	CREP
Getting Paid: How to Collect from Bankrupt Debtors	$24.99	CRBNK
How to File for Chapter 7 Bankruptcy	$34.99	HFB
IRAs, 401(k)s & Other Retirement Plans: Taking Your Money Out	$34.99	RET
Money Troubles: Legal Strategies to Cope With Your Debts	$29.99	MT
Stand Up to the IRS	$24.99	SIRS
Surviving an IRS Tax Audit	$24.95	SAUD
Take Control of Your Student Loan Debt	$26.95	SLOAN

PATENTS AND COPYRIGHTS

The Copyright Handbook: How to Protect and Use Written Works (Book w/CD-ROM)	$39.99	COHA
Copyright Your Software	$34.95	CYS
Domain Names	$26.95	DOM
Getting Permission: How to License and Clear Copyrighted Materials Online and Off (Book w/CD-ROM)	$34.99	RIPER
How to Make Patent Drawings Yourself	$29.99	DRAW
Inventor's Guide to Law, Business and Taxes (Book w/CD-ROM)	$34.99	ILAX

	PRICE	CODE
The Inventor's Notebook	$24.99	INOT
Nolo's Patents for Beginners	$29.99	QPAT
License Your Invention (Book w/CD-ROM)	$39.99	LICE
Patenting Art & Entertainment: New Strategies for Protecting Creative Ideas	$39.99	PATAE
Patent, Copyright & Trademark	$39.99	PCTM
Patent It Yourself..	$49.99	PAT
Patent Pending in 24 Hours	$29.99	PEND
Patent Searching Made Easy	$29.95	PATSE
The Public Domain	$34.95	PUBL
Trademark: Legal Care for Your Business and Product Name	$39.95	TRD
Web and Software Development: A Legal Guide (Book w/ CD-ROM)	$44.95	SFT

RESEARCH & REFERENCE

Legal Research: How to Find & Understand the Law	$39.99	LRES

SENIORS

Long-Term Care: How to Plan & Pay for It	$19.99	ELD
The Conservatorship Book for California	$44.99	CNSV
Social Security, Medicare & Goverment Pensions	$29.99	SOA

SOFTWARE
Call or check our website at www.nolo.com
for special discounts on Software!

LLC Maker—Windows	$89.95	LLP1
PatentEase—Windows	$349.00	PEAS
Personal RecordKeeper 5.0 CD—Windows	$59.95	RKD5
Quicken Legal Business Pro 2005—Windows	$109.99	SBQB5
Quicken WillMaker Plus 2005—Windows	$79.99	WQP5

SPECIAL UPGRADE OFFER
Get 35% off the latest edition of your Nolo book

It's important to have the most current legal information. Because laws and legal procedures change often, we update our books regularly. To help keep you up-to-date we are extending this special upgrade offer. Cut out and mail the title portion of the cover of your old Nolo book and we'll give you 35% off the retail price of the NEW EDITION of that book when you purchase directly from us. For more information call us at 1-800-728-3555. This offer is to individuals only.

Order Form

Name

Address

City

State, Zip

Daytime Phone

E-mail

Our "No-Hassle" Guarantee

Return anything you buy directly from Nolo for any reason and we'll cheerfully refund your purchase price. No ifs, ands or buts.

☐ Check here if you do not wish to receive mailings from other companies

Item Code	Quantity	Item	Unit Price	Total Price

Method of payment

☐ Check   ☐ VISA   ☐ MasterCard
☐ Discover Card   ☐ American Express

Subtotal	
Add your local sales tax (California only)	
Shipping: RUSH $9, Basic $5 (See below)	
"I bought 3, ship it to me FREE!" (Ground shipping only)	
TOTAL	

Account Number

Expiration Date

Signature

Shipping and Handling

Rush Delivery—Only $9

We'll ship any order to any street address in the U.S. by UPS 2nd Day Air* for only $9!

* Order by noon Pacific Time and get your order in 2 business days. Orders placed after noon Pacific Time will arrive in 3 business days. P.O. boxes and S.F. Bay Area use basic shipping. Alaska and Hawaii use 2nd Day Air or Priority Mail.

Basic Shipping—$5

Use for P.O. Boxes, Northern California and Ground Service.

Allow 1-2 weeks for delivery. U.S. addresses only.

For faster service, use your credit card and our toll-free numbers

Call our customer service group
Monday thru Friday 7am to 7pm PST

Phone	1-800-728-3555
Fax	1-800-645-0895
Mail	Nolo
950 Parker St.
Berkeley, CA 94710

Order 24 hours a day @
www.nolo.com

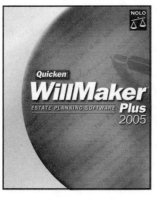

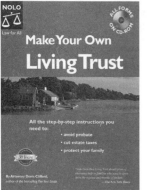

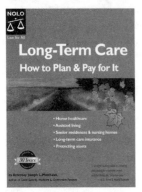
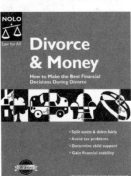

Remember:

Little publishers have big ears.
We really listen to you.

Take 2 Minutes & Give Us Your 2 cents

Your comments make a big difference in the development and revision of Nolo books and software. Please take a few minutes and register your Nolo product—and your comments—with us. Not only will your input make a difference, you'll receive special offers available only to registered owners of Nolo products on our newest books and software. Register now by:

PHONE
1-800-728-3555

FAX
1-800-645-0895

EMAIL
cs@nolo.com

or **MAIL** us
this registration card

- - - - - - - - - - - - - - fold here - - - - - - - - - - - - - - -

Registration Card

NAME		DATE	
ADDRESS			
CITY		STATE	ZIP
PHONE		EMAIL	

WHERE DID YOU HEAR ABOUT THIS PRODUCT?

WHERE DID YOU PURCHASE THIS PRODUCT?

DID YOU CONSULT A LAWYER? (PLEASE CIRCLE ONE)   YES   NO   NOT APPLICABLE

DID YOU FIND THIS BOOK HELPFUL?   (VERY)   5   4   3   2   1   (NOT AT ALL)

COMMENTS

WAS IT EASY TO USE?   (VERY EASY)   5   4   3   2   1   (VERY DIFFICULT)

We occasionally make our mailing list available to carefully selected companies whose products may be of interest to you.

☐ If you do not wish to receive mailings from these companies, please check this box.

☐ You can quote me in future Nolo promotional materials.
   Daytime phone number _____ .

SPNT 1.0

Nolo
in the
NEWS

"Nolo helps lay people perform legal tasks without the aid—or fees—of lawyers."
—USA TODAY

Nolo books are ..."written in plain language, free of legal mumbo jumbo, and spiced with witty personal observations."
—ASSOCIATED PRESS

"...Nolo publications...guide people simply through the how, when, where and why of law."
—WASHINGTON POST

"Increasingly, people who are not lawyers are performing tasks usually regarded as legal work... And consumers, using books like Nolo's, do routine legal work themselves."
—NEW YORK TIMES

"...All of [Nolo's] books are easy-to-understand, are updated regularly, provide pull-out forms...and are often quite moving in their sense of compassion for the struggles of the lay reader."
—SAN FRANCISCO CHRONICLE

fold here

- -

Place
stamp here

Nolo
950 Parker Street
Berkeley, CA 94710-9867

Attn: SPNT 1.0